Søren Larsen
HOMEWARD ROUND THE HORN

This is the lively story of a modern voyage under sail 'homeward round Cape Horn.'

'Søren Larsen', in company with another sailing ship 'Eye of the Wind', set off from Sydney and Auckland for the return voyage to Europe via the Horn, South America and the mid-Atlantic islands. In this combination of sailing adventure and travelogue, Captain Jim Cottier tells an entertaining tale of people and places along the way.

Described by the author as a 'Colchester Packet', the 'Søren Larsen' is famous for her starring role in television's *Onedin Line*. Now working out of Auckland, she is a familiar sight off the New Zealand coast during summer, while in winter she cruises among the Pacific Islands. 'Eye of the Wind' operates a similar schedule but is based in Australia.

On this voyage, both ships carry a crew of experienced sailors and volunteers (aged from the youthful to the elderly) who pay for the privilege of taking part in this adventure. Their voyage retraces the old route 'homeward' to Europe, the first British-registered sailing ships to 'double the Horn' for 50 years.

Cover and frontispiece photographs: TALLSHIP 'SØREN LARSEN'

Søren Larsen

HOMEWARD ROUND THE HORN

By Captain Jim Cottier

The Voyage of a Colchester Packet

For Ann,
Best wishes,
Capt. Jim Cottier.
Nov. 2006.

THE BUSH PRESS OF NEW ZEALAND

First published in 1997 by
THE BUSH PRESS OF NEW ZEALAND
Gordon Ell, Publisher
Reprinted 2005

Sales and distribution:
Captain Jim Cottier,
Roberton Island,
Private Bag, RUSSELL,
Bay of Islands, New Zealand.

Designed by Gordon Ell, and produced by
Bush Press Communications Ltd,
P.O.Box 33-029, Takapuna 1309, N.Z.

Printed in Hong Kong through
Bookprint International Ltd, Wellington, N.Z.

ISBN 0-908608-77-2

Acknowledgements

EVERYONE WHO TOOK PART in the 10-month voyage of 'Soren Larsen' is due acknowledgement as having supplied the basis of the book. I hope I have not been unfair to any of them. I thank them all for their large or small inputs, their companionship, their vital help towards the success of the voyage and for being shipmates. Many also deserve thanks for answering my demanding letters.

Particularly I wish to thank James for his fine drawings and Ian, Nigel, Brian, Chris Egan and Chris Roche for the use of their photographs.

I also gratefully acknowledge information promptly and freely given by the Falkland Islands Museum, the Administrator at Tristan da Cunha and the New Zealand Ministry of Foreign affairs and Trade.

I acknowledge also permission to use extracts from the following books:

White Sails and Spindrift by Capt. Frank H. Shaw, published by Stanley Paul, London.

The Brassbounder by David W. Bone, published by Duckworth, London.

Once is Enough by Miles Smeeton, published by Rupert Hart–Davis, London.

Of Ships and Men by Alan Villiers, published by Newnes, London.

Stand To Yer Ground by The Shanty Crew, published by Screw Productions, London.

Lastly I wish to thank three people vital to the whole enterprise. Firstly my original typist. I hope you enjoyed being my first reader, Barbara! Secondly Gordon Ell, editor and publisher, who lent a fair wind to my manuscript; and finally my most thorough and persistently encouraging critic, my proof reader and final typist, Terri, my most excellent wife.

Captain Jim Cottier, 1996

DEDICATION
To Tony, Fleur and the Old Lady herself

The Old Lady Herself

A NOTE ABOUT METRIC AND IMPERIAL MEASUREMENTS

Distances at sea are still measured in miles — *nautical* miles which are equal to 1.825 kilometres. In this international edition, the publishers have respected the author's preference for certain Imperial measurements which are no longer used in some territories. A foot is equivalent to 30.5 centimetres, a yard is .914 metre while a ton equivalates to 1.02 tonnes. The subject of traditional measures at sea is discussed in Chapter 7.

Contents

'Søren Larsen' (foreground)
with 'Eye of the Wind'
IAN HUTCHINSON

PREFACE

The Colchester Packet

IN 1987 THE BRIGANTINE 'Søren Larsen' sailed from London as flagship of a fleet of square rigged ships intent on re-enacting the voyage of the first convict transport fleet to Australia, 200 years before. At the successful conclusion of that voyage half way round the world, to Sydney via Rio de Janeiro, she settled to an adventure/ cruising life based in New Zealand. In the southern summer she plied the New Zealand coast. In winter she headed into the Pacific, usually to Tahiti, from where she began a series of island-hopping adventures making her way gradually westward as far as New Caledonia before returning to Auckland in October or November. She completed three years at this trade during which time many hundreds of adventurous folk of all ages, signed aboard and experienced 'Søren Larsen's' special ambience, and the magic of voyaging under sail. Her owner, Englishman Tony Davies and his wife Fleur had fallen in love with the South Pacific and determined to settle in New Zealand with their ship.

But they had a long-standing commitment to join in a large traditional-ship fleet exercise to commemorate the quincentennial of Columbus's first voyage and Tony had a boyhood dream to satisfy: to take his ship around Cape Horn and complete a circumnavigation of the world.

Thus was born the adventure to be known as 'Homeward Round the Horn'. It is that voyage with which this narrative is concerned, from Sydney to Liverpool.

'Homeward Round the Horn' was a joint venture. Tiger Timbs, the captain of another beautiful square rigger of similar size, had plans which closely matched Tony's, so it was natural that they should join forces. Two ships, sailing loosely in company, would add a spice, an extra dimension to the long voyage.

Both ships were extensively refitted for this arduous journey, both called upon the services of crew who had sailed on board their respective ships before, and both had full voyage crew berths when they left Sydney. These voyage crew are the lifeblood of the ships. It is their passage money that keeps these lovely ships in commission. It takes men like Tony and Tiger, with dreams and ability to realise them, it takes crew, mostly young men and women, to maintain and handle the ships with small remuneration, but the dreams and effort would be of no avail without the adventurous folk looking for seagoing experience and willing to pay for it.

Both permanent and voyage crew are of mixed gender: a happy circumstance. Seafaring language developed in days when those who went to sea were all male, however, (with rare exceptions) and it would be cumbersome and odd-sounding to change traditional terms, such as seaman, or man the pumps, so generally I have let such terms lie as they come off the tongue. To allow the story to flow without the interruption inevitably caused by footnotes I have included a glossary of sea terminology for those readers who may need definitions.

Sailor's songs, shanties, are male chauvinistic, and for that I make no excuse. They arose in that same all male world. There is no changing them and I feel sure no one on board 'Søren' would want to. Perhaps the sailors of old had a more profound understanding of the feminine essence than we might imagine, for his own ship, his home, his life-support, his inspiration, was always a 'she'!

Søren Larsen' has a special place in my heart. She was built in Denmark, as a working ship, in 1949 and named for her builder. Built in a very traditional manner entirely from that prince of salt water timbers — oak. She retains her working style and indeed she still works hard for her living. She is solid, heavy sparred and workmanlike; always shipshape. Handsome rather than pretty, smart rather than fancy. I've been on board at intervals since 1982, when she was specialising in taking physically handicapped people to sea, and at each rejoining I have been impressed with the quality of the crew Tony has recruited.... Quite exceptional young people;

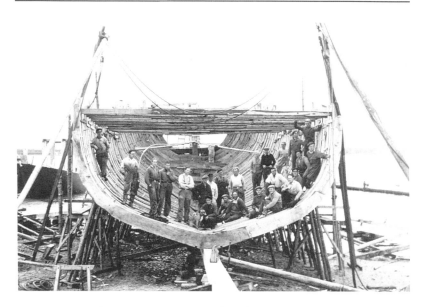

'Soren Larsen' under construction in Denmark, 1949.   TALLSHIP SØREN LARSEN

able, hard working, fun-loving, intelligent.... Crew willing and able to generate and foster a wonderful spirit on board. I have spent time on many ships but 'Søren ' is my favourite.

I was born a Manxman and as such the sea was at the front door. It was but a short step, at 15, to the half deck of a merchant ship. I remained happily in that service and obtained a Master's Certificate but it was not until I came to New Zealand in 1964 that the chance came to get involved with the traditional ships which had been a lifelong interest. Commercial shipping was declining, especially in its ability to give job satisfaction to anyone interested in seamanship and 'sailorising'. Square riggers were re-emerging in a new and adventurous role, offering endless opportunities for all seagoing skills. I jumped ship, you might say, and hove my kitbag aboard a windjammer. I never made a better decision.

Now I spend half my life on the most beautiful ships in the world and the other half on one of the world's most beautiful small islands. What more could a man want? Well, this man would want you to turn the page and begin your adventure!

But wait! A word about sea shanties, which are part of this narrative. 'Søren Larsen' is a singing ship and there are a thousand sea songs. Shanties are really working songs: rhythmic chants to help a bunch of sailors heave together at a job. We hoist our upper topsail to such a shanty still and furl our sails to another, but mostly we sing them now for pleasure, to conjure the ethos of the 'real' sailors and their ships. There were always ballads and folk songs of the sea too: 'forebitters'. The sailors sang them from the mooring posts, or bitts, right forward in the ship, which was the favourite place for whatever relaxation Jack could squeeze into his long working days. It was these 'forebitters' which rattled the windows and flooded from the open doors of dockside taverns too; never the shanties proper. They were strictly for shipwork. An important aspect of shanty singing was that the verses could, and often did, include a commentary on the hardships of the life and even the personal traits of the officers, (good or bad). Such comments were only countenanced in the shanties.

During the long voyage from Sydney to Liverpool I conjured up new words to an old capstan shanty, 'Liverpool Packet', especially to suit 'Søren'. I renamed it 'Colchester Packet'. Colchester is the old river port in East Anglia where 'Søren' is registered and a packet was a smart, fast, mail-carrying ship.

'Colchester Packet' is part of the ship now, embedded in her timbers I'm sure, by the frequent boisterous renditions. It is part of this narrative too and I hope its verses will help you, my reader, feel the lurch and swing of the ship, hear the people around her decks and smell the tang of salt air and Stockholm tar.

Read on!

CHAPTER ONE

Beginning at the End

We've crossed two great oceans, we've doubled the Horn,
We reckon we're shellbacks and steamships we scorn,
We're able and stable, aloft and alow,
She's a Colchester Packet, O Lord let her go!

I ALMOST STUMBLED on the little stone church huddled between Liverpool's sombre down-town tower blocks.

'Requiem service for Stan Hugill.'

I hadn't known that Stan had died. Not surprising perhaps, since I had just stepped ashore after a 10-month voyage from Australia by way of Cape Horn. My ship, the 142-foot, 300-ton brigantine 'Søren Larsen', lay in historic Canning Half Tide Dock not 400 yards away.

It was a splendid service, greatly enhanced by the presence of seafarers from more than 20 nations. Outside, the lofty spars of their ships bristle above the dockland warehouses as a sign that Stan's world of traditional seafaring has had a new lease of life.

A lone voice broke the heavy silence following the pastor's words of grief and condolence; a sailor's voice: rough edged, slightly nasal and pitched in a key evocative of wind and sea.

As I walked along on an ev'nin' so fair,
To see the still water and breath the salt air,
I heard an old sailorman singin' this song:
Oh, take me away boys, me time is not long.

The beautifully sung lament brought tears to many an eye and, hopefully, a catharsis of grief. The mighty chorus, from the congregation of several hundred, steadied us and must have gladdened Stan's heart.

Wrap me up in me oilskins and jumper,
No more on the docks I'll be seen,
Just tell me old shipmates I've taken a trip mates,
And I'll see them someday in Fiddler's Green.

The last time I'd heard it was off the Falkland Islands when we'd hove to and sung as we scattered the ashes of an islander to a raw gale.

The poignant singer again, and verses that, in typical sailor fashion, spiced melancholy with an irreverent line or two.

> *I don't need a harp or a halo, not me,*
> *Just give me a breeze and a fine rolling sea,*
> *Give me girls that are pretty and beer that is free,*
> *And bottles of rum growin' on ev'ry tree.*

And again the swelling chorus.

Stan will be seen on the docks no more but the shanties he sang and spent a lifetime recording and preserving were the cargo his ship brought home and his voyage was an inspiration to traditional seafarers the world over, not least to me.

It was through Merseyside's dockland that I had proudly and eagerly shouldered my kitbag as a 15-year-old heading for my first ship. Liverpool had been the gateway to a life at sea; and Stan an inspiring gatekeeper as a shanty-singing seamanship instructor at the Aberdovy Outward Bound Sea School which I had attended just prior to joining that first wonderful ship. Now I was back — full circle — with Stan an inspiration still.

The church crew turned out into the August sunshine and headed for their ships; a dozen big square riggers — tall ships — and scores of other traditionally rigged vessels all gathered at the end of a four month circumnavigation of the North Atlantic to commemorate the quincentennial of Columbus's voyage of discovery in 1492. They had converged first on Cadiz from Lisbon and Genoa, then raced to the Canary Islands and Puerto Rico from where they cruised to New York for the 4th July celebrations and on to Boston. The final race was to Liverpool. Four months of exciting sailing as a fleet; the greatest such fleet ever.

Two of the fleet, both flying the Red Duster, had come from the Antipodes: 'Søren Larsen' and 'Eye of the Wind'. They joined forces in Sydney in October 1991 for an epic adventure called 'Homeward Round the Horn' which saw them sail together across the wide Pacific, around the infamous Cape Horn and up the length of the

Atlantic to join the Columbus celebration in Lisbon.

They lie now in Canning Dock, berthed snugly alongside an ancient, grey, stone wall with their mooring lines over posts and bollards that have tethered a thousand such wind-driven ships. Ships redolent of tobacco, spices, wine and spirits and the most valuable cargoes from around the world, for here there were the bonded warehouses of the second most important port in Britain.

Surrounded by the ghosts of a thousand welcoming ships they lie snug but not peaceful or quiet. They are here at the end of a singular voyage: the first British square riggers to double the Horn for 55 years; 'Søren' the first wooden one for untold more years than that. So there is much revelry.

'Søren's' decks are continually full of people; crew, ex-crew, relatives, friends, well-wishers and reporters. I mean continually- day, night and early hours. The scuppers flow with champagne and other nameless drinks. The raucous hubbub is broken at intervals by somewhat wildly rendered, full volume versions of our favourite shanties and forebitters.

Radio Mersey even turns up to record some of our efforts. Live, on their Breakfast Show, accompanied by our two guitars, we sing the shanty I have rewritten especially for this voyage, 'The Colchester Packet'. One verse runs:

> *We've crossed two great oceans, we've doubled the Horn,*
> *We reckon we're shellbacks and steam ships we scorn,*
> *We're able and stable, aloft and alow,*
> *She's a Colchester Packet, O Lord let her go!*

But at 0730 we are not very able or stable, that's for sure!

There are 14 of us, among the 39 souls aboard for the Boston-Liverpool leg, who have sailed the long road from Australia, and six who have circumnavigated the world on 'Søren'. Two of these are remarkable ladies (one is uncertain about that title) of whom I shall have much more to tell later. Here sufficient to note their uniqueness in having completed a circumnavigation in a square rigger in 1992. The others are Captain Tony Davies, Second Mate John Gryska, Purser/deckhand Andy Riley and Tisha Cam, one of the cooks.

For Tony, captain and owner, arrival in Liverpool is overwhelming. The completion of a circumnavigation, including a 'doubling' of the Horn, in his own ship, is the crowning achievement of a life of endeavour to preserve, restore and sail traditional ships. His determination, vision and persistence in the face of a thousand practical difficulties, money problems and bureaucracy, is remarkable and truly commendable. Most ably assisted and bolstered by his equally remarkable wife Fleur, he is at once our good genius and irrascible governor, our thorough planner and careful purse-bearer, our loquacious teacher and deft ship-handler. Most importantly he is an inveterate romantic. A tough, small, sandy-haired man; practical, ambitious, determined but with a soft heart. A family man too, whose wife and two children have spent many years living at sea and sharing his love-affair with ships. How thankful we seafarers must be that there are such folk who can turn their dreams into reality.

My simple handshake with Tony, when 'Søren' was secure in Canning Dock, conveyed, I hope, my utmost respect for him as a seaman and my admiration at the fulfilment of a dream I knew he had held since he was a boy.

It was the end of a very special and eventful voyage for us all, and for me there could have been no better port at which to end — where for me it all began.

CHAPTER TWO

Sydney Town

At the Sydney docks at the break of the day
I saw this flash packet bound eastward away,
She was bound to the east, where the wild waters flow,
She's a Colchester Packet, O Lord let her go!

THE REAL BEGINNING of 'Søren Larsen's' voyage had been in Sydney in the shadow of the South Pacific's biggest city tower blocks. In Darling Harbour (it used to be Cockle Bay!) surely the glitziest waterside development east of the black stump as the Australians might say. An unlikely berth for a square rigger contemplating the long hard passage down to Cape Horn and up the length of the Atlantic to Europe.

Darling Harbour buzzes, jangles and jitterbugs its days away. At sunrise it is peaceful with the silky water reflecting one of the ugliest hotel blocks ever and transforming it, for half an hour, into a glowing golden Aztec palace. Then the Coca Cola trucks, the garbage collectors and toilet cleaners arrive followed, still before breakfast, by a bunch of girls intent on transforming our ship into a floral arrangement as part of Sydney's flower festival. Loops and cords of plastic blooms festoon the rigging and drape the hull. Before we have half finished arguing with the girls about the ignominy of this plastic art deco attack a sleek-haired festival organiser arrives to soothe us.

'This festival, boys, is the best Seednee's ever run an' you guys down here will be smack in the middle of it. Just imagine the free publicity,' his arms thrown wide, 'and the crowds. You guys could make a mint.' With a hideous wink he adds, 'and the girls; man you'll have them here in droves all day.' Then, realising that some of the crew he's placating are female he is momentarily taken aback. But only momentarily. 'The Seednee hunks'll all be down to see you girls too, scrambling round up there in the rigging,' Another loathsome wink.

'Piss off,' one of the crew stops him.

'Aw come on lady, this is a flower festival. Let's all be friendly.'

By 10 o'clock the fun fair just 100 yards down the dockside is cranking up. They are testing, testing, winding up the volume on their music machines, rigging balloon and candy floss stalls and giving the ferris wheel a trial spin. Sure enough, just like the man said, the crowds come.

By two in the afternoon it's all happening. The girls are screaming, stuck at the top of the ferris wheel, the kids are screaming on the big dipper and the octopus, candy floss is everywhere, balloons of every colour bounce and slither across the harbour, music assails from both sides of the dock and by golly the skimpily-clad girls are coming by in droves. The hunky guys are standing four-square on the dockside too, squinting up at our rigging. Perhaps he of the sleek hairdo has told them what to look for.

Amazingly, at two in the morning, the noise is only slightly less! As the fun fair fizzles so the disco across the water winds up and the girls and guys change into evening clothes and crowd the shops and bars and finally the disco. So you have to wait until after three to regain peace and quiet. Wow — Darling Harbour — Sydney.

It's not all bad of course. When you have a day off, or when the day's work is done, we can quaff a beer with the best in one of the quayside bars, laugh ourselves to tears over someone who falls into the harbour, or happily roam the shops and bazaars. We return with baubles and trinkets, bushranger hats and denims, certain of our bargains. Every night some return in a beer haze, to sit in the galley and put the world to rights. The disco is too expensive and upmarket for 'Jack' of course so much of our carousing is done in less salubrious places; pubs in old dockland or Irish taverns in slightly decrepit districts, where our forebitters are welcome and we feel at home.

One evening a large group from both 'Søren Larsen' and 'Eye of the Wind' make a wild taxi ride to a pub with a specially arranged Irish night, and what music we have with our Guinness. There are instruments I have never seen before played by such characters as belong in a Dickens' novel. But the prize goes to the raven-haired, twinkly eyed colleen with the fiddle who spins mighty magic from her lovely machine. From tear-jerking Gaelic ballads to furious jigs, fingers dancing and leaping, she has us enthralled.

James, 'Søren's' musician, not to be completely eclipsed, jumps into a brief gap in the proceedings, gets silence with a few sharp guitar chords and breaks into 'Molly Malone' complete with phoney Irish accent. It is not acceptable and one fervent Irish patriot, fierce of eye and Guinness livered, has to be restrained from attempting to demolish our James. He shoots withering glances across the room all night and makes as if to rise from his chair with fists clenched whenever James even looks at his guitar.

In all truth most of our three weeks in Sydney is spent alongside a crumbling wharf in Pyrmont, together with a fascinating selection of unusual craft. There are paddle wheelers, large yachts being converted to harbour tour boats, tourist launches, ugly in every variety of the word, abandoned barges, odd tugs and the totally anomalous 'Bounty', whose presence at the river end of our wharf each night lends an air of beauty and achievement to this dockful of nautical dross, (ourselves excluded of course). The form and tracery of her spars and rig soothes the heart and eye.

When a 40,000-ton container ship slides gigantically past her bowsprit, its slab sides towering far above her tapering masts, it heightens the awe I feel for the men who built and put to sea in 'Bounty' and her likes, and in the changes that have taken place in human conception to bring about the construction and operation of such behemoths.

It has happened in other fields too. Cottage to high rise tower block; bridle track to motorway; horse drawn buggy to trans-continental super-trucks. But one rarely sees the contrast at such close quarters or more dramatically displayed. These wall-sided leviathans are passing within 100 feet of 'Bounty's' delicate bowsprit. Here, the contrast sets the mind on edge and throws man's advancement into almost shocking perspective. This monster is manned by two dozen, the original 'Bounty' by a hundred. One hundred tons of fossil fuel daily instead of wind power. Steel from non-renewable resources against infinitely renewable timber. Highly technical remote technology rather than hands on skills. How far we have travelled this past 200 years, but to where?

Ah, but we are safer now, we live longer, we have more. But who would live some extra mediocre years, surrounded by, and worried about, his 'more', rather than know the sound and feel of a wild wind or a tropic breeze? Who would rather live with a pacemaker guiding his sluggish blood in an armchair than feel his heart pound and fret to urge some mighty effort when his ship is battling for life? Would we die in a car smash or on a wild, stormy coast? The death of the 'living' is no disaster, but what of a living death?

Enough of that. Back to work at Pyrmont! We are working long hours to ready our ship for the forthcoming voyage and nearby lies 'Eye of the Wind', a lovely English hermaphrodite brig which will acompany us the whole way. Her crew of ten, plus many Sydney helpers, are working longer and harder days than us because she is undergoing a major refit. 'Søren Larsen' went through that process some six months ago. 'Eye' is iron built and was launched in Germany in 1911 whereas 'Søren' is of Danish oak construction from 1949. They are similar in overall size but visually very different as 'Eye' has a black hull with tan sails whereas 'Søren' is white in both respects.

The old wharf lends itself ideally to our tasks. We can stretch coils of wire for constructing some extra 'Cape Horn' stays, we can spread sails for inspection and repair, we can weld and hammer, chip and paint, all without inconveniencing a soul. We can even kick a football around in our lunch break. There's a ghastly semi-abandoned washroom/toilet adjacent which serves us well enough after we take to it with a hose and scrubbing brushes.

The nearest shed is rented by a firm who audition actors. I occasionally gallop up the stairs to use their office telephone and feel decidedly odd in greasy dungarees amidst flowery, stagily dressed types with loud and over-enunciated voices.

'Oh, *do* come in my dear. No problem; don't mind us. Derek

(with an expansive gesture to the flamboyant gentleman checking himself before a big mirror) this is Jim from the *gorgeous* ship out there.'

Or perhaps a sleek young man will be readying himself for audition, or camera shots, with costume and make up girls fussing around. It is a bizarre place and seems totally at odds with the old disused wharf. The staff are very friendly and accommodating about the phone though.

The next section of the shed is even more weird. I am looking for sawdust to soak up some spilled oil and squeeze through a gap in a big cargo bay door to find myself in an Alice-like world peopled by gnomes, monster flowers, barrels and topsy-turvy furniture; hundreds of leering, laughing and squinting masks; trollies and pushchairs, a bus, bicycles and a thousand boxes holding everything from balloons to baseball caps. It is an immense store of film and theatre props. Perhaps the most amazing item is a sort of motorised caravan made from the fuselage of a D.C.3 aircraft.

Naturally they have bags of sawdust but more importantly they have about 20 pallets of cartons of beer which they darkly suggest are for sale at $10 a carton.

'Special for you guys. Left over from a big sponsored rally we organised.'

'A what — where? No never mind.' Inside an hour our beer store is bulging and the film prop. men are helping us down a few while they inspect our ship.

Little do they know that she has been a film prop. herself on many occasions; most notably as the major seagoing set for the British TV series 'The Onedin Line'. That was her first job after the Davies brothers had restored her in 1978, to be followed by a stint as 'Nimrod' and 'Endurance' in 'Shackleton', for which film she had spent a summer in Greenland amongst the sea ice and icebergs. Our ship's boat, slung in davits above the deckhouse, is still called the 'Dudley Docker', after one of Shackleton's famous boats onboard 'Endurance'.

For three weeks the weather remains gloriously fine as we spruce and straighten 'Søren' for her Southern Ocean venture. Paint and varnish are applied,rigging retensioned, shackles and bottlescrews overhauled, sails repaired, engine cleaned and stores checked. The heads are refurbished, cabins scrubbed, radios and safety equipment serviced, charts corrected and navigational equipment checked over. Extra steel supports are added to butress the deckhouse in case we should be inundated by the huge Cape Horn greybeards, and new securing devices are fitted to our fore and main hatches, which were to be well tested in the coming months. Everyone works with a will for this is to be the greatest adventure — a square rigger round the Horn. We expect it will be the ultimate test for our ship.

When we move to the dizzying Darling Harbour berth 'Eye' stays put and they work almost round the clock to get her ready for sea.

By October 5, 1991 we are ready and shipshape. The bridge into Darling Harbour swings open; a thousand balloons are released; Australia's latest America's Cup challenger slides through to the cheers of a multitude in holiday mood. The girls on the ferris wheel scream even louder than usual, water acrobats leap from our yardarms; he of the sleek hairdo, and others like him, smile and wave (and wink) and bands blare.

Accepting all this as our due we slip our lines and sneak through the bridge just before it swings shut. 'Australia' is in, 'Søren Larsen' is out. Our ten-month voyage has begun:

A wind's in the heart of me, a fire's in my heels,
I am tired of brick and stone and rumbling wagon wheels;
I hunger for the sea's edge, the limits of the land,
Where the wild old Pacific is shouting on the sand.

(With apologies to Masefield)

CHAPTER THREE

Four-letter Crew

The crew of the Søren have joined her today,
They'll be hazed and abused and for scant little pay,
But they sign with a smile for this hooker they know,
She's a Colchester Packet, O Lord let her go!

THE SHIP WAS READY but what of the crew? The captain has
been eulogised already and concerning myself, the Mate (the hazer,
the driver!), the reader will have to draw his, or her, own
conclusions as the yarn proceeds. I shall be a small mystery, as
perhaps I am still to some of the crew.

The second mate is a man of considerable proportions. A young
man, a true down-east Yankee and handsome with it. Clean cut,
white of tooth and with a hard, wide, curly-haired chest beloved
of many a young lady. John is an excellent seaman, not to be
forgotten. Stentorian voiced he can rouse us to a wild cheer for
'Boston and the U.S.A.' with a call as loud as the cheer itself. I
don't doubt for a moment that Boston remembers it! Rarely, John
gets drunk and you remember that too — loud and legless.

Then there's Andy, also of considerable proportions but
differently disposed. An Englishman with a penchant for good
whiskey, an eye for a good deal and a liking for ship's cooks,
(the female ones that is!). A man for all seasons and of unlimited
energy. An instigator, a social prime mover, full of fun and
shenanigans. 'Søren' is never quite the same when Andy is absent.
He is also a flamboyant and amazingly successful fixer of all
gadgetry, electrical, electronic or mechanical. He it is who repairs
our cameras, battery-chargers and typewriters, but rarely without
a flash and a bang and a side show. He is a competent seaman
too, aloft and on deck and can actually be serious although you
have to be onboard a while to discover that. He has been with
the ship for six years, partly as a deckhand and purser, partly as
a travelling public relations representative.

Now I am going to leap over everyone else to the cooks: Squizzy and Tisha. I once read that, after the compass, the cook is the most invaluable piece of equipment on board and have come to understand that it is true.

Life on board revolves around these two wonderful people. Good meals feed not only the body; they relax and soothe the heart and mind and even allow the soul to flourish. Or is that the wine which sometimes accompanies the food?

Good meals we surely have, fair weather and foul and with them come a banter and repartee that can stop the fork between plate and mouth of the hungriest.

The deckhouse/galley is the very centre of life on board because it is the main entrance and exit from the accommodation, the resting place for the idle members of the watch on deck, the venue for most lectures and talks, the watering hole for morning and afternoon tea breaks, a place for letter writing and the spot for an after-watch noggin or cuppa. Every night it is the scene of that almost magical, choreographed routine called 'making the bread'.

The social centre of the ship.   IAN HUTCHINSON

The procedure varies from a slow waltz-like routine on calm tropic nights, to a frenzied dervish-like dance with concurrent juggling acts in the wild Southern Ocean.

But to return to Tisha and Squizzy (I have reversed their names here to avoid any complaints about favouritism.) They do not bake the bread but they preside over the ingredients, they dictate the quantity to be produced and they expect results. Such is their power that the toughest of us quail at the thought of their censure. The hardy souls on the midnight to 4 am watch do the baking.

Both cooks love to dress up. I have memories of them labouring in their non-too-handy galley as fairies, leprechauns, street girls, punters at the races and even as pirates. Need I add that they always act their parts with zeal. A rare pair.

Irrespective of the weather, the meals come. Sometimes late but usually because the gas runs out, their fancy dress needs extra underpinning or someone gives them a rum at the wrong moment. Truly, theirs is a difficult task in a heaving galley, often awash and with up to 40 bellies to fill (some of them very large) at hours dictated by the changing watches.

Of course they have their weak points. Tisha is a problem to rouse at 0630 when it's her breakfast duty. She will sit up in her clothing festooned bunk and talk away, even ask about the weather, but the minute you've left she crashes back unconscious and swears you didn't call her. Squizzy's weakness is more disastrous. She plays either 'The Teddy Bears' Picnic' or 'Pomp and Circumstance' on the galley tape deck at breakfast with maddening regularity. She sometimes throws toast at people she doesn't like too.

Oh, and they are both lovely ladies. Good looking, good figures, wonderful sense of humour. I love them both!

Perhaps the only person the cooks fear is Marti, our shipwright. His appetite is stupendous. There are others aboard who run him close, but never surpass our Australian wastemaster. I will resist the temptation to describe his gastronomic feats. He is not fearsome in any other way, except perhaps the size of his mouth when he laughs. In fact Marti has a mild, sensitive disposition and voyage crew often turn to him when they need a sympathetic ear. Usually a quiet-spoken, attentive and observant young man, his humour and accompanying explosive and infectious laugh leap out readily. He is a monkey up aloft, working there as happily as if he had his feet firmly on the deck. He is an indefatigable worker (and player) with a useful ability to glean real rest and revitalisation from a 10-minute snooze on the deck. A good shipwright, a thoughtful officer (he sometimes takes charge of a watch) and a fit and sturdy body. But perhaps it's the eyes that attract the girls most. Certainly something does because he has lots of trouble with them everywhere!

Nigel too is a monkey in the rig. He delights in dangling from the most difficult places to get unusual camera angles: under the jiboom or at the end of the main boom. He is a smaller man, but well muscled and fit with a springy tread and plenty of stamina. An intelligent worker; thoughtful, observant and perhaps more mindful than most of the extra responsibilities carried by the certificated officers. Nigel is the unofficial bosun, looking after the deck stores and rigging materials as well as keeping a watch. I'll let him off without any further comment except to add that perhaps he's easily led astray in port!

This listing of the crew risks being boring and condescending. I'll let them climb the rig or stand a trick at the wheel or take a run ashore whenever they find a convenient page. Here you need only know they were fine young men and women, all 12 of them (I'm excluding the captain and myself as being no longer young) with adventure in their eyes and a capacity for helping others enjoy the adventure too. All are memorable people, none mediocre. All are fun loving and vital in their own ways.

For this voyage there were only two who have not sailed with 'Søren' previously; Grant the engineer and Joel the deckboy. Everyone else knows the ship and her master well.

The voyage crew, those that pay for the adventure, are the life blood of the ship and they are never mediocre either. To pay, and sign on, for an ocean voyage in a small square rigger, requires a determination and zest for adventure which precludes the

Garry checks out the middle staysail   IAN HUTCHINSON

'The beauty of squaresails'

AUTHOR

indifferent, the apathetic. So these good folk too will mostly appear as the pages turn and their mark will be left, fainter or stronger, but indelibly, just as their presence has left a memory, a story or an artifact on board the actual ship. Many of our voyage crew return again and again. This is a wonderful morale boost for the professional crew because it demonstrates that we are satisfying our customers, our efforts are worth while.

Two of the voyage crew are particularly notable. Both are female and both, in truth, must be described as elderly although the word does not describe their outlook or demeanour. As I mentioned earlier one of them, Margaret, will be happy to be described as a lady. Even more certainly she is one.

Her grandfather was a ship's captain in sail and as a teenager (read young lady) she had wished fervently to go to sea but it was out of the question. Widowed and living beside the English Channel with her sister, she heard on the radio, in 1987, about the First Fleet Re-enactment Voyage soon to commence from London. Eleven ships to re-enact the voyage of the first convict fleet to Australia in 1787. The B.B.C. commentator mentioned that some berths were still available for this exciting voyage. Within a month Margaret lay in one of those berths as the ship heaved and plunged over the Atlantic swell. Here was her dream come true in an incredibly vivid and real way. Not just a sea voyage but a passage to Australia in a square rigger, as part of a fleet, and with exciting stops at Rio, Cape Town and Mauritius to anticipate. Margaret was there still when the fleet entered Sydney harbour triumphantly on January 26, 1988 and now she was rejoining for the voyage home.

Here she is at the wheel, face alight, eyes blue and clear above a large English (Roman?) nose, red, white and blue silk scarf fluttering in the breeze and a mug of freshly made tea to hand. Margaret is happy.

'Jim, could I go on lookout next? It's so lovely on deck now. Then I'll be finished my deck duties and perhaps I might go below for a little before the end of the watch to dress for dinner?'

Amazing. This is a square rigger in the Southern Ocean.

It is Sunday and in any reasonable weather we make an effort to change into 'good' clothes, or at least something different, for the evening meal. For Margaret it is the highlight in each week. I must say she always looks good, belying her years, trim, hair 'done', eyes bright. She chooses to sit near Marti, one of her favourites, and well away from Chris R whom she finds rather rude. Chris is happy to be distant from Margaret too. He is irritated by her polished manner and naive views. Amusing, but with a potential for trouble and I make a mental note to keep them on different watches for a while longer.

Personality problems are very common on a long voyage but the sea is a great leveller too; a place where each and every person has to rely on each and every other at some time almost every day. You don't have to be nice to be reliable but being reliable does serve towards niceness.

Margaret put it another way, confiding: 'Jim, when I first joined this ship I had never heard a four letter word used in my presence but after a week I realised that the people were actually quite nice!'.

She never descends to using such words, of any number of letters, no matter what provocation. She is a valuable counterpoint to the rather rough and blasphemous language which many of us use when conditions get difficult or exciting.

Margaret may be somewhat naive but is a type of person seldom seen in sailing ships and the more interesting and valuable for that. Her enthusiasm for 'Søren' is only matched by Anne's.

Anne is a 'dinkum' Australian woman; tough, forthright and not one bit naive. She is a person of considerable intellect, an author and an art gallery owner but a woman who also knows about hard physical work, having spent years breaking in and maintaining a farm in the Australian bush. After a near fatal car smash in the early 80's Anne started life afresh and pursues it with a vigour that belies her age. She is unstoppable. Her main problem is to organise her days so as to miss as little as possible. Woe betide any watch officer if he omits to call Anne when there is any excitement or significant event such as a whale sighting or an exchange of signals with a passing ship. Anne is never short of a pungent or cogent phrase and at such times the officer will receive a broadside of them.

Anne made the First Fleet Re-enactment Voyage on 'Søren' and is loyal to 'her' ship almost to a fault. Her excellent book, *The Voyage Out,* may be followed by another concerning this passage and she makes copious notes on everything that happens, every day. Whether she is on lookout, at a lecture or even on the wheel, the notebook is there. She fills one after another and I shudder to think of some of the conversations she has recorded.

A fascinating, determined, even stubborn woman with a great flair for words and an incredible appetite for life. I regard it as an honour to have sailed with Anne.

Margaret and Anne, who will circumnavigate in 'Søren' and each sail a remarkable 40,000 miles in her. Worlds apart, these two heartwarming, memorable women are invaluable assets to the ship for their enthusiasm, their uniqueness, their loyalty and not least for the money they have invested in the ship through their voyaging.

Steadily the ship's Articles fill with names and the cabins fill with bags and boxes, stores and spare sails. By the time we slip through that Darling Harbour bridge bound for Auckland there are 35 souls aboard and not a cranny left for a cockroach.

The women 'show their muscle' on the main sheet.   IAN HUTCHINSON
From right, Sharon, Tisha, Sandy, Squizzy,
Margaret, Anne, Gabrielle.

CHAPTER FOUR
Strip Jack Naked

With the Eye of the Wind to the east we are bound;
Six days to North Cape and New Zealand we've found.
Steve has his wedding and the grog it do flow,
She's a Colchester Packet, O Lord let her go!

OUR PASSAGE ACROSS the Tasman Sea is a pleasant shakedown and unremarkable as far as the weather is concerned. There is a little seasickness, much pleasure in being on the way at last with the razzmatazz behind, and much keen observation of our shipmates. Ship routines are set up, watches organised, private journals begun and the first friendships develop. With moderate favourable breezes we slowly pull ahead of 'Eye' but not before the first of many thousands of pictures of our photogenic consort have been secured.

North Cape appears where the navigators say it will and we have a wonderful fast sail down the east coast with fresh westerly winds which leave the sea untroubled and bring dolphins to play in our churning bow wave.

We clear customs at Opua in the Bay of Islands. Both ships then move about 10 miles to an anchorage at Motuarohia (Roberton Island) which is where I have my home. This is a very special occasion for me and we mark it with a hilarious inter-ship cricket match on the grassy flat between ocean and inlet. We, on 'Søren', win the day, mainly because my trusty German Shepherd, 'Sindbad', runs off with the ball whenever I am at the crease thus enabling me to chalk up extra runs while the fielders try to catch her! German Shepherds really are intelligent!

Later, in Auckland, 'Søren' is the venue for the wedding of two previous crew members: Steve and Vivienne, and although the event goes off really well, I remember Steve's party of the night before much more clearly than the wedding itself.

About six of us, led by the redoubtable Andy, aim to give Steve

'Søren Larsen' and 'Eye of the Wind' in the Bay of Islands, New Zealand.   N.J.W. SNELL

a bachelor night to remember. By about 2300 we are mellow after visits to three bars. Andy suggests Fort Street, a well-known red-light area. The idea is adopted unanimously and we are soon installed as patrons of a strip joint where I remember only very expensive drinks and one very beautiful stripper who eclipsed the others completely. But the clientele are too few and perhaps too tame so the management gives us free tickets to another of their establishments and ushers us onto the pavement.

Do we want more of the same? Andy assures us we do — his plans are laid! So we tumble into a new den; a rather more upmarket place and much busier. The drinks come, at God knows what price, and we watch a succession of girls 'strut their stuff', as they say. Steve is very merry by this time and only just in control of his motor muscles. Andy makes his move.

He has chatted to a very vivacious girl (many seem bored to death) about his scheme and now she cajoles Steve onto the stage with her where she succeeds, slowly and with considerable flair, to strip Steve in unison with her own act. It brings the house down and is side-splittingly funny because Steve just cannot care less and happily does as the girl prompts. When he is down to his socks she lets him off. The wild applause is as much for her skill as Steve's efforts! I hope she enjoyed it as much as we did.

The final part of Andy's plan fails. It is to produce a photograph of Steve, in socks only, beside the nude blonde girl, at the wedding and blackmail Steve for a bottle of rum! But the club manager is adamant: no photographs. Pity!

As the only person, from either ship, who has ever been around Cape Horn or across the Southern Ocean, and being amongst the more meteorologically knowledgeable, I give a talk to the crews in a dark, old wharf-shed which has been converted into a small theatre. There I discuss the possibilities of huge waves, tremendous winds, icebergs and hypothermia. My experiences as a skipper of an ocean-going tug down in those waters lead me to believe we could be sorely taxed by the weather, even in summer. The effect of my talk is depressive. The chattering, sprightly crowd who straggled to the meeting, troop out in a very sober mood! I suspect I have prompted a run on thermal underwear and balaclavas. One voyage crewman on 'Søren' decides to go no further although I think his decision was arrived at before my talk.

We gain a wonderful replacement: Cath, an Irish doctor. Here is a lady to warm the heart, with eyes to turn it over and a lilt to soften it to melting! A valuable addition too, not only because she is a doctor but because she has sailed with us before and knows the ropes both figuratively and for real. I am overjoyed to see her back aboard but then, to be sure, I always did have a soft spot for a pretty colleen. Perhaps it's my Manx heritage!

Sadly we lose another wonderful young woman at the last moment due to a rare medical condition (which later proves to be quite treatable in fact). Joss is a tall, strong, purposeful Australian with an irrepressible good humour, and a bent for practical jokes and aphorisms designed especially to get reactions. A lady who lives life rapidly and fully. We will miss her stumping and stirring and seamanlike ability but hope to have her back aboard later when we reach the Atlantic.

We will miss Johnny too, although he had signed on only for the Tasman crossing. A true man of the Australian outback, he had seemed, when he peered over the rail in Darling Harbour. Tanned, country-clothed, mild-mannered but wild eyed was Johnny and he paid his fare in cash! Just what have we here, I thought. Well he has turned out to be a born sailor, happy as a sand boy up aloft and a very quick learner, but his forte is music. Johnny not only plays almost any instrument (he brings clarinet, guitar and harmonica with him) but he can inspire and teach others to play too and will direct us all with eye-swivelling, body language, quick instructions between bars and scribbled sheets of music, chords or words. He is magical and tireless. As long as there are pupils or players he is there. James, our young Australian deck hand, artist and guitarist is particularly sad that Johnny cannot continue with us, because his presence raises the musical potential on board immensely and James feels strongly that we should make more music.

A couple of verses of 'Johnny's Gone to Hilo' make a suitable valediction:

> *Johnny's gone what shall we do*
> *Way down Hi — lo*
> *Oh Johnny's gone what shall we do*
> *John's gone to Hi — lo*
>
> *Oh Johnny's gone and left us flat*
> *Way down Hi — lo*
> *Oh Johnny's gone and won't be back*
> *John's gone to Hi — lo.*

Good luck Johnny.

Sailing day arrives warm and bright with a multitude of relatives, friends and well-wishers. Princes Wharf in downtown Auckland is thronged. Last minute gifts are showered on us so that the deck looks like a market place. Six bales of wool appear for shipment to Liverpool. They are each about 8 cubic feet! Where the hell am I supposed to stow them? The crowd continually fill the gangway, deck and deckhouse. The ships and crews are blessed by Maori

Søren Larsen leaving the wharf at Auckland   IAN HUTCHINSON

and Pakeha alike while video machines record it, cameras click and whirr. Anne scribbles furiously and I try desperately to get crew aboard and visitors ashore. Kisses, hugs, tears. More kisses snatched on the gangway. Finally the break is made; the farewells become waves and shouts, cheers and dabbing handkerchiefs. We swing off the berth, followed closely by 'Eye'; yell a heartfelt three cheers for Auckland and motor slowly up stream to the Harbour Bridge where we turn and begin to get canvas set. Both ships sail grandly down harbour together, 'Eye's' dark tan sails contrasting with our white ones and pleasing to the heart and eye of many a cameraman I'm sure.

A few tiny figures are still waving from the head of Princes Wharf as we sweep past Devonport and clear the inner harbour.

Running eastward in the 'Roaring Forties'   BRIAN BROEKE

CHAPTER FIVE
Whimpering 40s and Roaring 50s

And now we are crossing the Pacific wide,
The weather is foul and fair winds we're denied,
The Old Man is cursin' and swearin' below,
She's a Colchester Packet, O Lord let her go.

WE DO NOT SWEEP VERY FAR past Devonport. We anchor barely 10 miles from the city for the first night, south of Waiheke Island, in the Hauraki Gulf. This is partly to give the newly-boarded voyage crew time to settle in and be instructed in ship's routines and safety procedures while we have their undivided attention and partly to await an expected wind shift which will favour us. There is the problem of stowing that jumble of goodies off the deck too.

'Eye' heaves up early morning and we follow about midday in squally rain and the wind nicely in the west and still backing. As we round Cape Colville in the late afternoon we furl the t'gallant with a strong sou'wester developing. It is a stirring beginning. The land fades in curtains of rain and a pale, ragged sunset on 28th October.

The next day we run 207 nautical miles, one of our best days for the whole passage it turns out, with a living gale giving us a taste of what to expect in the coming weeks.

Seasickness is sorting the able bodied from the infirm and the cooks are having a quiet time considering we are 35 souls on board, but that will change.

From East Cape, which is only a flashing light for us, we shape a course to pass close to the Chatham Islands and even think of calling there, but southerlies force us away so we set our hearts on the dreaded Horn and enjoy the fresh but now failing breeze.

At the end of the first week we have covered 1000 of our 5000 miles to the Horn and everyone has settled in, discovered each others foibles, learned the routines, gained their sea-legs, decided which is the best seat in the galley and discovered how best to appease the cooks and the mate.

Navigation classes are underway and some of the newcomers are getting to grips with the intricacies of the running rigging. Each watch one of the permanent crew walks the deck, for half an hour or more, with a straggle of voyage crew muttering and mumbling behind trying to learn and memorize where everything is made fast and what it does. If Chris is part of the watch there will be some confusion because he will explain that the buntlines shouldn't be rigged like this or that he can't see why the t'gallant should have a downhaul, or...

'Chris, just shut up and learn what we do have.'

'OK, OK. I'm just trying to give people something to compare with but...'

Chris is a sea historian or nautical archeologist and very knowledgeable but his attitude is rather negative. He's a darkly good-looking Londoner but the corners of his mouth are down most of the time. When they do turn up his face is transformed and feelings towards him take a positive leap. He is publications secretary to that august body: the British section of the International Association of Cape Horners. If we complete the passage round the Cape under sail he (and everyone else on board) will be eligible for membership and this he fervently desires. If we have to use the engine he will be insufferable. Meanwhile we all have to learn how to deal with him. Fortunately he is a good shanty singer and we all enjoy that.

On the third day out we make history. Our eldest male voyage crew, Dudley, sits a university Masters degree examination in English Literature. He wedges himself in a corner of the chartroom which is out of bounds to everyone for three hours. The Old Man was sworn in as invigilator before we sailed so he sees that it's all done properly. Dudley is a retired New Zealand farmer. He's very pithy, ('November 5th is the day the only person with an honest ambition got into parliament.') straight and clear-headed, and obviously more literary than your usual farmer. He's thin and stubby and struggles to keep warm on deck, which is hardly surprising since he underwent heart bypass surgery only a few months ago. But there's a lot of life in Dudley yet.

Another week finds us only 200 miles further on. Down here in the 'roaring forties' latitudes the westerlies refuse to utter a sound. In their place we have whimpering easterlies and can make little progress. We tack down to 48 degrees south, then back to 42, but the breeze remains steadfastly light and easterly for eight days. It's very frustrating and Tony begins to mutter about how much diesel we can use and Chris has the corners of his mouth almost dropping off his face.

It's pleasant enough and we are neither wet nor cold. We observe Armistice Day with a nice ceremony on the poop deck where 'Eternal Father' is sung, a minute's silence maintained and grog served all round, while we fly the ensign at half mast. Another day horse racing is the indulgence with everyone rigged out as if we were attending the Melbourne Cup. One of the wool bales, which have found a home in the library as the nautical equivalent of bean bags, is rigged out too, as a huge dice which we trundle or flop about the deck as part of a game devised to simulate horse racing.

It takes us over a week to overhaul 'Eye', who got a 40-mile start on us originally. We are in radio contact three times a day so have been painfully aware of our long stern chase. One day we sight her from our cross trees and the next afternoon we creep close enough to send a boat across, which livens up the day no end.

We both reduce sail and lay our topsails to the mast in order to slow down and make a lee for launching the rubber dinghy. It's not rough, but sloppy enough to require care. Seven of us get to sample afternoon tea aboard another ship for a change and can take photographs of our own ship. We have a good half hour 'gam' and return with stories of strawberry cake and bring some Earl Grey tea for Margaret who is hooked on the stuff. It's been a very pleasant interlude.

Their weatherfax machine has been producing the same depressing maps as ours of course, so Chris (the 'Eye's' mate) and myself commiserate and moan but can see no way past the ridge of high pressure which is giving us the light headwinds.

Meeting at sea with 'Eye of the Wind'.   IAN HUTCHINSON

As we pile on sail again and slip past we get off a few good shots with our funnelator just to keep our hand in for greater efforts later in the voyage, and we capture the attack on video.

Derek is onboard specifically to make a video of the passage to Montevideo, (strange pun) although he is attatched to a watch too. He's everywhere, and already has shots from aloft, from the bowsprit, in the galley, at the wheel and at dinner, as well as having started a series of personal interviews, at least one of them in someone's bunk. The afternoon with 'Eye' has afforded some new angles and ideas and the water balloon action is right up his alley.

Derek is unmistakeably Cockney. It's not just the barrow boy accent, but the rough eloquence, tall stories, exaggerated body language and rapid repartee that mark him. He's right out of Soho. He's getting good results with his small video camera though. There's a little gathering at his cabin door each evening when the generator is on and he can play back his 'takes' through a television screen wedged and lashed beside his bunk. He is a professional camerman but it's his first attempt at film making complete.

He's a professional drinker too and on several nights already

I've had to ask him to reduce the noise level when the lubricated raconteur in him has got out of hand towards midnight.

'But J-i-i-i-m,' arms thrown wide,'I'm just tellin' 'em abaht the time I was a pro' wrestler, see, an' this geezer he jumps up...'Derek leaps up.'He jumps up an' clocks me wiv 'is brolley' His eyes go wide, brolley comes crashing down, brows crease and mouth grimaces in mock pain.

'But it's bloody midnight Derek, and the place is supposed to be quiet after ten,' I remonstrate in an exaggerated whisper.

'Yeh, but nobody minds a good story Jim. Tell yer wot, I'll just finish this one an' then I'll climb into the ol' ferret an' skunk.' (=bunk!)

The audience have got the message even if Derek hasn't and one by one gather their books and clothes and move away.

''Ere then, 'ave a quick one wiv me before yer go Jim'. He pours one for himself but not for me because he knows damn well I'm still on watch. 'Sorry abaht the noise, Jimmy boy. Didn't realise the time. Good fing yer stopped me.'

Incorrigible but irrepressible. In different circumstances his stories are side-splitting and fabulous. Derek is a larger-than-life character as quick witted as a pack of monkeys. I think he might even outwit even Andy his cabin mate. Perhaps Joel, the deckboy and youngest person onboard understands Derek best because he's cut from a similar piece of cloth. He's no public storyteller, mind you, but he has an oddly aphoristic manner for a youngster and his last job was as a Soho 'barrer boy'.

Joel joined in Sydney and is slowly coming to grips with life onboard his first ship, but he is not very sociable and lies in his bunk listening to his walkman much of his free time. You wouldn't have caught me in my bunk when I was 18 unless I was getting much needed sleep. He has a passion for jazz, which I share, and he lends me tapes and his walkman sometimes. Incredible little devices with glorious sound but they turn people into half-deaf and dumb zombies.

Sounds are so important on a ship; from catching the faintest of calls on the radio, to hearing a change in the note of the wind in the rigging or detecting tiny squeals aloft, denoting the need for attention. Hearing the first call from someone overboard or in difficulties aloft can be a matter of life and death. Fear, anxiety, calmness can all be detected quickly by tone of voice. A good watchkeeper, or lookout, uses his or her ears as well as eyes. Sound carries particularly well over water. On a dark night the presence of an unlit vessel can often be detected by sound: voices, creaking spars, the rustle of a bow wave.

I recall such a case in the Gulf of Aden when I was watch officer on a cargo liner. We were ploughing steadily eastward at about 15 knots on a very dark, still night. The sky was a mass of stars which reflected in the dark water so that sea and sky merged indefinably. Out on the bridge wing I thought I heard a faint sound, a creak perhaps. Then definitely a voice, almost ahead. I yelled at the helmsman to put starboard helm on, and as the masts began to sweep across the stars I also heard shouts and saw the black outline of a sail faintly lit by the red glow of our sidelight. Within seconds the sail of the dhow (for that is what it was), with the peak of its lateen sail above my eye level, came flapping past not 30 feet off. A close shave. There was plenty of noise from the dhow as it careened past in our considerable wash. What if I had not heard those first faint sounds? I suspect everyone had been asleep on the dhow until the noise of our approach had awoken someone and caused that first cry of alarm, so sound played more than one part in the event.

The 'Eye' is well astern now and it seems she will stay there. We are pulling away at 10 miles or more a day in these lighter conditions in which we expected her to be the faster ship. She can spread more sail area than us in proportion to her displacement, but complains of weed growing on her hull very quickly. I noticed a fringe of it just below the water line when I was over there last week. At night we reduce sail so as not to get too far ahead. This is a joint venture. But that gets boring and eventually Tony and Tiger (the 'Eye's'skipper) agree that we should press on providing we maintain regular radio schedules. It has been a slow passage so if there is wind we'll just go for it.

We do: in a big way. Our first real blow, with winds over 50 knots, sends us bounding 212 miles in 24 hours and has us floundering up to our armpits and more, at the braces on the main deck. The lifelines rigged around the deck are vital now as are the waterproof covers lashed over the fore and main hatches. We struggle aloft, to furl everything except the lower topsail and two staysails, and fight the mainsail on this first attempt to take in a third reef in the new sail. Later we struggle to get it off her altogether.

The sea is stupendous. Heaving in long relentless lines out of the west its crests are as high as the foreyard. Its flanks are densely streaked with torn foam and the tumbling, roaring crest shot through with beautiful but chilling, translucent turquoise. 'Søren' lifts and lurches over these awe inspiring escarpments of storm-driven sea. Her bowsprit sweeps up and up, searching for the ragged dark clouds flying overhead and then as she lifts her stern up the long weltered slope, that bowed spar tears a ragged line down the sky, down the sea, until it seems we must run under. Down it goes, the deck so tilted that it feels we must all be thrown forward down the slope. The ship rushes trembling forward with a mighty bow wave and in a smother the crest of the sea courses along the ship and tumbles, spouts, crashes aboard in the waist, sluicing about, swirling to the hatch-tops, while that diving sprit slows, hesitates and begins a slow, grand sweep skyward again. With the rise, water cataracts from the scuppers leaving the unwary hanging to the lifelines, their feet relentlessly gathered by the flood of escaping water, and the next great crest remorselessly advances. From the exposed wheel, right aft, its slope seems incredible, its bulk at once monstrous yet marvellous, its march inexorable. But we lift to it again and again and an exhilaration runs through us, so that wild yells mingle with the roaring wind. It is a primeval and tumultuous scene, at once elating and humbling.

A great gale in the wide reaches of the South Pacific is something to be remembered and even in a well-found ship it is fraught with danger. Richard, a hefty New Zealander, is caught with only one handhold as the ship lurches wildly as a wave surges aboard. He is torn from his support and smashed against the main fiferail, head first. Cath shows her mettle and skill in extremely difficult conditions and Richard reappears some hours later with eight stitches, and a high regard for our medical team. Squizzy, Sharon and Andy are all certificated nurses. Dudley has suffered some bad bruising too, after being thrown across the saloon and Russ, the boisterous, roisterous Hamilton entrepreneur nearly meets his end.

Cameras have been much in evidence all day, but Russ, determined to get a shot of a big sea coming aboard by the mainmast, unclips his safety line and crouches on the poop, down by the lee rail, waiting, waiting. A big sea rears and 'Søren' slides bodily down to leeward, scooping in a tremendous sea, flooding the poop deck right to the skylights and completely submerging Russ. Fortunately he has his feet jammed under the mainsheet, a rope that runs along the deck here, so he emerges seconds later very white faced and shaken as well as thoroughly soaked. His camera is ruined even beyond the magic of Andy, who does get a flash and a bang from it some days later, but they are death throes.

''The big wave' – 'Søren Larsen'   BRIAN BROEKE

So we career eastwards towards the Horn, exhilarated but a little chastened by our first storm.

Russ doesn't take too long to recover his usual strident manner. He is a no-nonsense, pragmatic, man-of-the-world; politician and salesman. It is a powerful mix. There's no denying his pitch when he switches into sales mode — which he sometimes does when there is nothing actually to sell. He's a party man too (and I'm not talking about politics) and loves to swap yarns over a few beers, or regale us with his salesmanship techniques (he's embarrassingly candid about methods he's used) or use his persuasive powers to initiate a sing-song. He's a keen, self-made Kiwi lad, our Russ, still with plenty of action ahead of him.

I think he might safely be labelled 'male chauvinist' too and this aspect of his character leads to one memorable clash. Mabel, a buxom American, who is a professional pastry cook with a strong scent of women's liberation about her, also has a penchant for — wait for it — bellydancing (another powerful mix!) She has posted her intention to give a lecture entitled 'God Was a Woman'. The day and the time arrive and in the library there is standing room only.

I should explain that everyone is encouraged to give talks and a list is hung on one of our notice boards where the subjects can be listed against any chosen day. I frequently talk about meteorology or my experience with Greenpeace. Tony has given a series of lectures about the resurrection of 'Søren' from an abandoned hull to her present state. John has enthralled us with his account of his world circumnavigation in an open Viking ship and Chris has spoken about the Association of Cape Horners, and so on. Russ has had his day when he gave us the story of his life as a salesman (with demonstration.). Now it is Mabel's turn.

She begins very seriously (which is not typical of Mabel) making the point that early humans probably revered the female because of her ability to demonstrate creation through childbearing, which would seem miraculous if the male contribution was not understood. There are one or two ribald remarks from the audience about this but they die in the face of Mabel's seriousness. She consults her notes and goes on to give some idea of the wide range of archaeological evidence that has come to light, indicating goddess worship stretching over a 20,000 year period. This is a huge chunk of human history. The finds range from China to Britain although concentrated in 'Old Europe' and the Middle East. Interesting stuff and after a few queries she goes on:

'The fertile agency of the female principle was probably revered as a model of how the whole of nature worked. Makes sense to me. Never did go for the idea that Zeus birthed Athena from the top of his head!' Mabel is warming up and her more usual breezy self is showing through.

'So far, no one knows just how the change to a male god paradigm happened but it seems to be connected with the development of agriculture and complex social organisations. Perhaps men assumed dominance over land, tenure and labour.'

Someone suggests that the discovery of the male contribution to childbearing must have had a profound effect on how male viewed female.

Someone else points out, amidst laughter, that we can't pursue that point with 'innocents' like Joel and Margaret around. Even more laughter ensues at the suggestion that Derek might be embarrassed too. Mabel eventually resumes:

'By biblical times male dominance was almost total and it seems to me that the Bible is an historical document written as the mythology, the glue, for a certain, very patriarchal people and...'

'Oh, come on, that's too much.' Russ' interjection is strident. 'You can't bandy about with the word of God. The Bible is revelation and nothing to do with male dominance. It doesn't put down women and you can't just hypothesise its revelations away because God is thought of as a male.'

'Take it easy Russ. Mabel's giving us a talk on how she sees it.'

'Yeh, but he's got a point...'

There's a hubbub for a few minutes until I call for shush. Mabel picks up her notes...

But Russ has his dander up and, arms buttressed on his thighs, head forward, eyes fierce, he's not going to let the Bible be reduced to a mere historical document. I suspect Mabel has Russ's objections 'all figured out' as she might say in her Colorado vernacular, so now she sits back and lets the discussion rage around her. Waves of argument flow around the diminuitive library slopping over into laughter and expostulations. Russ becomes so het up, or frustrated, that he ups and leaves but hurls a rock as he goes about women usurping God's word, which raises more waves. By the time Mabel's talk gets back on course it's the change of the watch which removes most of her audience. Mabel's last word — 'Wow!'

There are storms above and below decks but we weather both and both leave us with great topics of conversation.

CHAPTER SIX
The Way of a Ship

And now we are sailing the Pacific blue;
The crew are complaining there's nothin' to do,
So all hands on deck the mate he do blow;
She's a Colchester Packet, O Lord let her go!

SHIP ROUTINES MUST BE maintained whatever the weather or however interesting the lectures. At the heart of good seamanship lies the routines of handing over the watch, of regular maintenance, of proceedures for setting and taking in of sail, of fire and man-overboard drills, of checking the compass error; the list is a long one. The captain lays down 'Standing Orders' which outline his demands in terms of general discipline, standards of navigation, safety responsibilities and of the circumstances in which he must be called. Under these orders the mate organises the ship's routines: the watches, the meal times, maintenance of the hull, rig and equipment, cleaning duties, lectures and even when you can have a shower! It's quite a job and it's with the mate that the buck stops too. There is a suitable forebitter about this, or perhaps it could be used as a short-haul shanty:

If the ship begins to roll, Call the Mate,
If the cook runs out of coal, Call the Mate,
If the Old Man goes to bed,
If you see a squall ahead,
If you need a sounding lead, Call the Mate!

If the sailing lights are out, Call the Mate,
If your latitude's in doubt,Call the Mate,
If the wind begins to howl,
If the crew begin to growl
If the anchor comes up foul, Call the Mate!
If you need a hand on deck, Call the Mate,
If the gangplank is a wreck, Call the Mate,

If the capstan's on the blink,
If a drunk falls in the drink,
If you don't have time to think, Call the Mate!

These verses come mainly from a little book published by Chris and his 'Shanty Crew', but the words are older and anonymous, and there are many more verses. Perhaps the writer was the mate himself.

In fact the mate passes some of the responsibilities to other crew members. On 'Søren' John looks after safety equipment. James maintains the emergency fire pump and ship's boat, Garry and Elmo are responsible for the rubber dinghy should there be a man overboard. Everyone has some responsibility and occasionally I change them around so that everyone gains experience.

Each watch has a certified officer in charge (Tony, John and myself), two permanent crew and, with our present complement, five or six voyage crew. On this passage we are working four hours on and eight off so that if you do the forenoon watch from 0800 to noon, you also do the so called first watch — 2000 to midnight. The watches are arranged like this:

Midnight—0400	Middle watch
0400—0800	Morning watch
0800—Noon	Forenoon watch
Noon—1600	Afternoon watch
1600—2000	Evening watch
2000—Midnight	First watch

The passing of time is marked every half hour throughout the day and night by strokes of the ship's bell, which is right forward; hanging on the forestay in fact, on 'Søren'. At the change of each watch eight bells are struck in four pairs. Then the first half hour of the new watch is marked by one bell; the first full hour by a pair of strokes; one hour and a half by three bells (a pair plus a single stroke) and so on. It's a time honoured system and bells struck on a ship at sea have a unique tone as nautically redolent as the cry of an English gull.

With 21 voyage crew I have also arranged for a group of

dayworkers. These good folk (five or six of them) start at 0700 and their day ends with washing up after the second sitting of dinner. They usually heave a sigh of relief about 2100. Their recompense for this long day is 'all night in'. Every five days this group moves onto a watch and the forenoon watch takes over the dishcloths, dustpans and toilet brushes.

In wild conditions the galley duties become something of a nightmare and a dangerous one at that. With the ship lurching violently and the galley deck awash with an inch of swilling seawater, overflow from the pan of stew, a mashed up packet of cigarettes and odd potato peelingss, it is no mean feat to get boiling water into six cups of Milo, two of coffee and one of tea. Then the milk runs out so you have to mix up some more while three hungry watchkeepers are passing their plates for a second helping of that stew which turns your stomach every time you look at it! Or for the evening meal there are those bloody stairs to negotiate with scalding pots of curry or oven dishes of roast potatoes. It needs a cool head with eyes in the back thereof, and at least two pairs of arms and legs.

Pancakes by Tisha  TALLSHIP 'SOREN LARSEN'

A few people seem to have all of these. Take Val for instance. While the others in her group are cursing and crashing about she seems quite calm and in control. When she is in the galley the water boils when it's needed, the dishes stay in their drying rack and the sink never quite overflows. She's just organised, that's what it is. Small, trim, quiet mother of two grown-up children, Val is fun loving, reliable and yes, organised. On deck she is a valuable member of her watch because she just does what is asked of her. No fuss, no complaints about the cold or wet; she just does it. I'm not sure just what 'Søren' gives her back for her efforts but in her eyes I believe there's a romantic mote along with a fairly lonely look so she probably finds satisfaction in the teamwork of passage making across wide oceans, the release from unromantic suburbia. There must be a gill of seawater in her eight pints of blood, too.

Sharon is good in the galley too (the permanent crew, except for Tony, all do their stint on galley duty), but her organisation is more belligerent. She fixes the pots and dishes with a frosty stare from her usually soft brown eyes and sort of dares them to move or spill. I think she occasionally sticks her tongue out at them. Anyway things usually go smoothly when she is there.

Gabrielle not only manages, but also seems to add a little flair. Perhaps the table laid in an unusual way or a new tea cosy she's knitted will appear. Her beautiful waist-long hair might be arranged in a new way or she will find an unusual piece of music for the tapedeck. (If Squizzy hasn't already found 'Pomp and Circumstance'!)

Gabrielle is a gentle Australian. Primarily an artist, she has also been a village store-keeper, farmer, teacher, keeper of a weather station, housewife and mother of six children who now help to urge her to adventures. Her graphic art has a dash and liveliness to it. Sparing in detail, nevertheless it captures its subject admirably. Perhaps that is just her shipboard style.

John is ruthlessly efficient when it's his turn to wash up; Andy does it with flair, clatter and patter. With James it's like a fairground side show but the result is very thorough. Mabel is professional and when Russ is there we all know it! Most of us just grin and bear the chore although the galley is always a lively, bustling place and there is often an opportunity to look into the cook's lovely eyes. Galley duty is not without its compensations.

On this passage a practice has developed whereby the dayworker group, on the last day of their stint, make the evening meal. This gives the cooks a break. Theoretically that is. In fact they spend this free time either answering queries: 'Where do you keep the dried figs?'; 'Have you drunk all the cooking wine?'; or in a terrible suspense, expecting a gas stove to explode or the electric mixer to fly to pieces (it does!). We end up with some amazing dinners from these gang efforts and often served in some spectacular manner.— Indian meals with the relief group in saris and turbans; Italian with suave, formally attired waiters.

The daywork spell can be a lot of fun although it includes the mundane tasks of sweeping, polishing, dusting and scrubbing too. Not all the dayworkers are needed for every task, of course. They work out their own roster, so that an individual might be, for instance, on cleaning only one day and on galley only on another.

The watches revolve around tasks interspersed with spells lying in the sun (ha, ha!), trimming sails, maintenance work and cups of tea. There is always someone at the wheel of course (no auto pilots here) and always a lookout right forward. Every hour, day and night, one of the watch does a 'round'. This involves a check around the whole ship with a view to safety and security of ship and crew. So the 'round' includes checking for cooker gas leaks, seeing that hatch covers are secure, retrieving any loose equipment, inspecting all three heads and showers for water leaks, ascertaining the amount of water in the bilge, seeing that lights are not left on unnecessarily and checking the level of diesel fuel for the generators.

This thorough scrutiny of the ship is concluded by filling out a voyage crew log book kept in the chartroom. The course steered, wind, sea and weather conditions are entered on the hour plus remarks ranging from sail handling to dolphin sightings to Marti's gastronomic feats. Even four-letter words appear without censorship. A copy of the remarks column would make enlightening, if bizarre, commentary on the voyage:

Two whales sighted quarter mile off. John says they are sperms. Only saw them twice.

Marti had four helpings of pudding!

Wind backing. Braced yards at 2030.

Bloody cold. Long johns next watch I reckon.

James reciting hilarious Banjo Patterson poems.

Can't get the hang of the carrick bend Jim is teaching us.

Bugger — lost my woolly cap overboard!

Found Margaret asleep with her light on AGAIN.

Took in t'gallant at dusk, also fore topmast staysail.

Luverly dinner — Tish and Squizzy do it again.

Crossed 50 S at 2100 — drinks on Chris tomorrow. Should cheer him up — and us.

The stars are out after three days of cloud. Fantastic sight.

'Eye' was 70 miles behind at the radio sched. but she's doing eight knots.

Bare, disconnected bones, but in a way it's all there. This log book is the main reference work for anyone keeping a journal and the navigational and weather details are transferred to the mate's log book, but its remarks columns are reserved for nautical matters.

The wheel, lookout and roundsperson are normally changed hourly but the intervals pass quickly for the other members of the watch. There is usually some sail trimming and often sails to be set or taken in too. At night there are star indentification sessions, shanty singing, story telling or some instruction in the deck house, and maintenance is often carried forward by day. Perhaps some scraping and painting, or making baggywrinkle. There are knots and splices to learn and there's always time for a look at the chart.

Each watch has some daily tasks too. The morning watch washes and scrubs the decks and cleans up the galley so that the dayworkers have a fresh start, the forenoon watch polishes all the

Ian bread-making

brass on deck, and the middle (or graveyard) watch makes the bread.

There is hot competition to produce the best loaves and the middle watchkeepers are allowed to devour one small loaf before they turn in, just to check the quality (and because they are rarely present at breakfast when everyone else devours their share).

Sometimes this 0400 bread ceremony is accompanied by sacramental whiskey too, especially if Andy is on the 12 to 4. Then the life histories roll and the worlds affairs are put to rights; then the escapades of the last port are replayed and those for the next planned. By perhaps 0600 the bottle is empty and the 4 to 8 can clear the wreck and report that Andy is snoring normally.

The ships routines are frequently assailed by the weather. Occaionally there is an 'all hands' call when many things need to happen at once. Perhaps a black squall is rushing on us and sail must be reduced quickly. It's a matter of:

'Let's have you, and don't stop for your boots.'

It only happens when it's pitch black and pissing down with rain of course. Figures stumble and lurch from the deckhouse struggling into oilskins, grabbing for the lifelines and listening for orders.

'Upper tops'l downhauls.'

'Aye, aye, ready on the downhauls.' John's stentorian voice answers Tony's command.

'Lower away. Ease the braces.' The rippling creak of the yard coming down is almost drowned out by the rising wind and other shouts.

'Get the middle stays'l off her. And the outer jib.' Groups of drenched crew struggle forward.

'In the lifts. Clews and bunts. Stand by upper tops'l sheets. Haul taut and make fast the braces.' John's bellows get results. There's a brief flapping aloft as the upper topsail is gathered snug up to its yard by clewlines and buntlines.

'Make fast clews and bunts. Up and put a stow on it.'

I see Nigel swing first into the weather shrouds, his gleaming face fleetingly caught in the red glare of the sidelight and his dark shape is quickly at the swooping yardarm. Others follow past the ruby light: Marti, John, Darryl, Cath, and the sail is quickly frapped with gaskets, secure against the worst the wind can do.

There are two dark, swaying shapes busy furling the middle staysail up against the fore mast, balanced on springy footropes.

'Hey Elmo, ease the halyard!' It's Sharon yelling down, answered by Elmo's bass organ holler:

'O.K. li'l darlin'.'

'We'll need an extra gasket out here.' James is yelling from the end of the jib-boom where he and Ian are lashing down the outer jib against any possibility of being torn loose by wind or sea. Out there the roaring bow wave and the dolphin striker tearing through the wave crests lend an inspiring sense of speed and power to the ship. As the two of them scramble back along the foot-ropes James lets out a whoop:

'Dolphins!'

Right under the bow the two luminous shapes streak to and fro, leap and plunge and streak again.

'Clew up the course!'

No time for dolphin watching. The Old Man wants more sail off her. There are a dozen pairs of hands available now so it's not difficult although this largest of our square sails can get out of hand if you're not careful. I make sure each buntline is manned and each clew doublemanned.

'Ease your sheets. Haul away clews and bunts. Smartly now,' I yell, as the sail hesitates, bellied out against the forestay. 'Belay your clews. Heave away the starboard bunts. He-e-e-ave.' I lend a hand with a line manned by Val and Charlie who lack weight, and finally the sail is reduced to a bundle of canvas bunched under the big yard.

The squall is nearly on us. I check with Tony and he doesn't want to reduce sail any more so I can send most of the extra hands below. The watch plus John, Marti, Ian and myself can gasket the course. No need for everyone to get colder and wetter.

A swathe of light sweeps from the deckhouse door as the gang tumbles back in, and I glimpse cups of steaming drinks being passed around. Margaret has been busy.

As I swing into the shrouds the wind arrives with sheets of icy rain. 'Søren' heels to it and the squall almost pushes me up the ratlines. Then it's the big step over to the foot-rope hanging under the yard, and work my way out to the yard-arm. No niceties in furling with the rain trickling down my spine, feet and hands freezing cold. Just free the gaskets from their coils hanging from the jackstay and pass them round and round yard and sail, hauling the wet canvas up snug on the spar and tightening each turn, then move onto the next gasket. I have to wait then for Joel who is working inboard of me. Glancing down I see the two dolphins still streaking ahead of the bow wave which is now blazing with phosphorescence. The dolphin striker ignites a ribbon of green fire to chase the flashing torpedo-like creatures, as it tears through the wave tops. What a sight.

But those cold trickles are insistent so we are soon swinging down off the bulwark capping onto the solid deck.

'Thanks John, Marti; the watch can handle her now.'

'No problem Jim. Have a good watch.'

The deckhouse door streams light again briefly, then slams. I begin to check around the deck making sure ropes have been coiled, headsail sheets secured, braces taut, before reporting back to Tony who has been by the wheel all this time keeping an eye on the helmsman and no doubt having a look at the radar from time to time. The squall has done its worst for now, although the bloody rain is still sheeting down.

'We'll leave her under reduced canvas for a while. There'll be more squalls by the look of the radar. I'll hang on here while you get into some dry gear and put a position on the chart.'

I scramble below at Tony's bidding and return in five minutes well swaddled up, sou'wester crammed on, towel round my neck under dry oilskins.

'O, nine, five. Anne's got the wheel now, Ed is on lookout and Dudley is away on a round. Bit late but never mind. James is making a brew for the watch and Sharon is rigging lifelines forward, with Dick I think.'

'O, nine, five it is. Thanks Tony. Do you want a call if there are any more squalls?'

'Only if you think you need to reduce sail more, but with two reefs in the main and only the lower tops'l spread she should handle anything up to 40 knots. Better give me a call if there is a wind shift though, but I don't expect that until about midday.'

As he ducks down the chartroom ladder he looks at the log.

'Still making eight knots or more. Should be a good day's run. Good night.'

'G'night Tony.'

James soon appears with the hot drinks, Sharon reports the lifelines rigged and Dudley finishes the round so all the watch except Ed are gathered by the wheel. James suggests a song before the skipper gets to sleep.

'What'll it be? Spanish Ladies?... Rio?... Santiana?'

N.J.W. SNELL

'Give us Paddy Lay Back.'
I down some hot coffe and begin one of our favourites:
> *'Twas a cold and dreary mornin' in December,*
> (the others yell *'December'*)
> *An' all of me money it was spent*
> *(spent, spent,)*
> *Where it went to Lord I can't remember,*
> *(remember)*
> *So down to the shippin' office went*
> *(went, went)*
> *Then the roaring ranting chorus:*
> *Paddy lay back (Paddy lay back)*
> *Take in yer slack (take in yer slack)*
> *Take a turn around the capstan, heave a pawl*
> *(heave a pa-a-a-wl)*
> *'Bout ship stations boys be handy (be handy)*
> *For we're bound for Montevideo round the Horn.*

We are sung out after six or seven verses and a good deal warmer.

The rain has been driven away too. Nothing like a song to cheer things up.

Such 'all hands' calls, as I have described, are rare. More often the watch on deck will call just the permanent crew dayworker, or perhaps an extra hand or two unfortunate enough to be sitting in the deckhouse at the time.

In rough conditions I often allow the watch to shelter in the deckhouse , but fully dressed for deck work at a moment's notice. Sometimes the older voyage crew get a night watch off, which is much appreciated. I have to be careful with Anne though. If I leave her in her bunk without prior arrangement and something unusual occurs — a passing ship, a big school of dolphins — then I receive a dressing down couched in very straight Australian terms. Anne just hates to miss anything.

There are other events which prevent the routines becoming irksome. Birthdays are always celebrated with vigour. The cooks always produce a custom-made cake and someone makes a special card which, with crew signatures and messages, forms a fine memento. I've seen cakes decorated with ships, sextants and aeroplanes; cakes with a can of beer or other unmentionable surprises hidden in them and one cake in the form of fulsome breasts, cherries and all! The ingenuity is boundless. There is normally a party too of course and the tradition at sea is that the drinks are on the celebrant.

Then there are occasions like St. Patrick's Day, the Melbourne Cup, or the day 'Søren' completes her circumnavigation. Each such is an excuse for some dressing up, a special meal, a tot of grog on the ship and always some singing.

Almost without fail the 'Søren Larsen Song' is called for and sung with great gusto. It comes from a seafaring film, but James has adapted the words for our ship.

> *All that I own are the clothes on my back*
> *And the tools of a sailor's trade;*
> *A fid and a palm, a few needles, a spike*
> *And a knife with a good clean blade.*
> *I've a berth in the foc'sle, a seat on a bench*

It's another birthday.

TALLSHIP 'SØREN LARSEN'

> *In the galley where I can feed,*
> *And a hook for to hang me old oilskins on*
> *What more can a shellback need?*
> Chorus:
> *We are the Søren Larsen crew*
> *We come from everywhere,*
> *Choose any point on the compass you like*
> *You're bound to find us there.*
> *Born in a gale in the roarin' forties,*
> *Entered in the log,*
> *Sent up aloft to the upper t'gans'l*
> *And christened with navy grog.*
> Second verse:
> *I've been up in the riggin' with Marti and John*
> *When the howlin' winds do blow;*
> *I've bunted the tops'l with Nigel and Jim*
> *With the boilin' sea below;*
> *I've hauled on the braces with Elmo,*
> *Damn near drowned in the same big wave,*

There's Yankees, Canadians, there's Kiwis and Pommies,
All bloody good men in a shave.
Chorus.
I've crossed both Atlantics and doubled both Capes
More times than I can tell;
I've fought the big seas in a parish-rigged barque,
Froze off Cape Farewell;
I've cursed the calm in the Doldrums,
When you'd swear the wind was dead;
Laid to off the Horn in a westerly gale
That would blow the hair off your head.
Chorus.

This, together with 'Colchester Packet', are the ship's favourites. They are roisterous affairs at party time but can be heard quietly rendered too, by the watch gathered aft on evenings, when the Southern Ocean weather does not intrude on the watch routines too much.

CHAPTER SEVEN

Suns and Satellites

'Both mate and cook and passenger bewailed their
*   fearful plight.*
They worked out calculations thro'both the day and
*   night.*
"When you know where you are"said they, "there
*   is no need for fright".'* — Anonymous.

The log line is tangled, the sextant is bust;
The chart is a mess and the clock's full of rust;
The mate's in a flap, where we are he don't know,
She's a Colchester Packet, O Lord let her go!

THE SOUTHERN OCEAN RUNS clean around the world. It is
bounded by Antarctica to the south and marked, to the north, by
the two great continental headlands: the Cape of Good Hope and
Cape Horn; and by Tasmania and Stewart Island, New Zealand.
Over this vast oceanic girdle flies the great west wind system
known as the 'Roaring Forties'. Here sailing ships can run eastward
the world around hampered only by some small islands: Kergulen,
St Paul and Amsterdam; Auckland, Campbell and Macquarie Islands
below New Zealand.

Here the greatest speeds were achieved in the commercial square
riggers, the wildest conditions encountered while 'running their
easting down' with the strong, favourable winds. There is dispute
over the exact speeds and the wildest weather but it is safe to say
that runs in excess of 400 miles in 24 hours were attained, while
winds of 80 knots and seas over 80 feet (24 metres) high were
encountered.

Here too, giant icebergs drift and vast areas of fog develop over
the cool tongues of Antarctic water which penetrate northward.

Although these inhospitable waters can be used to good
advantage when sailing eastward, it is an area fraught with danger,
not least of which is navigating accurately. Skies are sometimes

overcast for weeks, precluding celestial navigation, so that the ship's position can only be estimated by 'Dead Reckoning', (a term which derives from deduced reckoning). This D.R. position is arrived at using four factors: the course (direction) on which the ship is heading, the speed, the leeway caused by the wind forcing the ship sideways, and the set and drift of the body of water through which the ship is moving.

The course as steered, more or less accurately, by the helmsman is recorded hourly and also at every alteration. The navigator must correct this compass heading for deviation caused by the ship's own magnetic field, and variation due to the earth's magnetism.

The speed is also recorded hourly and is obtained from a 'log', which these days is in the form of an impeller attached to the hull underwater. But for more than 300 years seamen went through the process of 'heaving the log' every hour of a sea passage, and there were two important spin-offs from it. Firstly the present day 'log book', in which all the navigational details are recorded, was originally the book in which the hourly 'log' readings were entered. Secondly, a ship's speed is quoted in 'knots' (nautical miles per hour) and this peculiar term stems directly from 'heaving the log', as we shall see.

The principle upon which 'the log' operates is simple enough. If someone jumped overboard holding the end of a long coil of rope while the ship was making a speed of 1 nautical mile an hour, then after 1 minute 1/60th of a mile of rope would have run out. If the ship was making 5 miles per hour then 5/60ths (or 1/12th) of a mile of rope would have gone overboard. Conversely, by measuring the amount of rope which went out in a minute, the speed could be calculated.

It is not very convenient having people leaping overboard every hour so a triangular piece of wood is used, weighted along one edge so that it floats perpendicular to the sea surface, and attached to the long line, the 'log line', by a three-legged bridle. The log line is wound onto a wooden reel which ensures free running, and the timing is started when a distinctive mark pays out over the rail. This mark is about 100 feet from the log itself. To keep the length of line within manageable bounds the timing was done over 30 seconds rather than a minute.

Now a nautical mile is the distance on the earth's surface subtended by one minute of arc (1/60th of a degree) at the earth's centre. In about 1560, when the log was first used, this distance was thought to be about 5000 feet. So 5000 feet in 1 hour was about 41.7 feet in 30 seconds. Sailors being practical fellows, they used 42 feet which was 7 arm stretches of rope or 7 fathoms, (the word derives from the Scandinavian word 'favn' which means 'armful'), and they tied a knot in the line at these 42-foot intervals to save measuring each time. In the 18th century new calculations showed the earth's circumference to be larger than previously estimated and the nautical mile was reckoned to be about 6100 feet. This meant the knots needed to be 51 feet apart, but practical considerations were important so an extra fathom only was added making the knots 48 feet apart. Since the seamen would not budge from this the cunning makers of sand glasses (for this was before watches were available) manufactured 30-second glasses that ran out in 28 seconds. Mathematical reason was restored.

Nowadays the length of the standard nautical mile is 6080 feet (or 1.825 kilometres) which means our knots should be 47.3 feet apart. 'Get knotted,' says our practical seaman. 'Eight armfuls is good enough for me.' And so the standard log line is still marked in 48-foot intervals and timed for 28 seconds.

Practical 'Jack' added an important refinement to the log for his own comfort and safety. He attached one leg of the bridle to a hole in the triangular 'log' with a wooden bung so that a sharp jerk would disengage it, allowing the log to be much more easily hauled back aboard. Without this device, on a ship cracking on at 15 knots or so, our intrepid seaman would have been in danger of disappearing over the stern as he tried to stop the line when the sand glass watcher yelled his 'stop!'

Just to add a final confusion we made a log on 'Søren' which ran for 15 seconds and had knots 25 feet apart. It gave results very close to those recorded by our — wait for it — 'electronic' log!

For reasons which should now be obvious the speed of one nautical mile per hour is called a 'knot'.

Now just in case you think this is all very complex, let me quote from a gentleman, Marcus P. Vitruvius, who wrote in about 20 B.C.:

'... a useful invention of great ingenuity handed down to us by our ancestors, which enables us ... to know how many miles we have travelled.

'An axle is carried through the side of the vessel and on the projecting end a wheel, 4 feet in diameter, is fixed with paddles on its circumference striking the water. The inboard end of the axle carries a drum with one cog projecting beyond its circumference. In contact with this is a case holding another drum having 400 cogs at regular intervals, so placed as to engage the cog of the axle drum. The second drum also has a cog projecting beyond its circumference. Above in an outer case, is another drum which revolves in a horizontal plane and has teeth in it which engage the cog in the side of the vertically placed drum, so that one revolution of the latter turns the horizontal drum to the extent of one tooth until its circle is complete. Tubes must be fixed in the horizontal drum in which round pebbles will be placed. In the outer case containing the drum one opening will be cut, having a pipe affixed through which, when a tube comes over the opening a pebble will fall with a ringing sound into a brass receptacle. Thus, the paddles strike the resisting water and being driven forcibly backward will revolve the wheel, and the wheel will turn the axle and the axle turns the drum. Each complete revolution the tooth on the first drum strikes one of the 400 teeth on the second drum. When, by the action of the paddles, the wheel has revolved 400 times it will move the horizontal drum forward one point. As often as this drum brings a pebble to the opening it will let it drop through the pipe. Thus, by the sound, can the speed be judged and by the number of pebbles the length of the voyage in miles be shown.'

The description is almost as incredible as the device. Note that this device had been 'handed down by our ancestors'!

By my reckoning, the mile measured by this ingenious 'log' was 5026 feet long which is a pretty short mile, but not bad for 20 B.C.

Looked at another way the word 'mile' derives from the Roman word for a thousand. The mile was a thousand paces of a Roman legionnaire. Now this was reputedly about 4,800 feet. If the circumference of the Vitruvius paddle wheel is reckoned at 12 feet then the pebbles would ring out every 4800 feet. Not bad! The Roman legions must have been an astonishing sight loping along at 4.8 feet to the pace. Perhaps a pace was really two steps.

I'm not sure about the pebble log in rough conditions. Perhaps there was one on each side of the ship and the navigator then added the pebbles to get his distance travelled!

We must return to our Dead Reckoning. The third factor is leeway. This is the angle between the ship's fore and aft centre line and the wake which is tracing elusive scrawls back over the heaving waves. Leeway is of necessity a calculated guess at best.

Finally, because the ocean is always on the move, carrying everything with it, we need details of these movements. Unfortunately they are somewhat irregular even though there is an overall consistency. For instance in the Southern Ocean there is a drift to the eastward of the surface water of about 10 miles a day, increasing to 20 or 25 in the Drake Passage between Cape Horn and the Antarctic Peninsular. Again an educated guess is the best we can do with this drift, using average figures collected over the years and taking weather conditions into consideration.

To recap then: the four factors involved in working up a D.R. position are course, distance run by log, leeway, and set and drift. All are subject to some uncertainty, as outlined, so the result can be widely in error. However, with experience, a sailing ship making say 150 miles a day should be able to plot its estimated position at the end of the run to within ten miles. This means a position possibly 100 miles in error after ten days without celestial observations, or 300 mile after a full crossing of the Pacific.

Fortunately it is unlikely that the errors will accumulate in this way. More probably some will cancel others but nevertheless errors in reckoning the D.R. are known to have caused hundreds of shipwrecks and obviously many more such disasters will be unrecorded.

The small mid-oceanic islands are a terrible hazard to a ship relying upon Dead Reckoning. Although a sighting of such an island can pinpoint the ship's position, there will be many hours and days of uncertainty and anxiety, scanning the horizon or listening for the sound of breakers at night or in poor visibility. The navigator must be humoured at such times.

Not many complete ocean crossings are completed with totally overcast skies, although I ran 15 days with solid overcast once. When the sun breaks through, the moon shows her face or the clouds defer to the morning or evening stars, then the navigator is happy and may even be heard humming a tune.

Every observation of a celestial object (heavenly body is an

The author 'looking for stars'. IAN HUTCHINSON

alternative term, with wonderful connotations!) results in a position line on the chart, and any two such lines cross to define the ship's position. Since 1772, when the forerunners of both the modern sextant and chronometer were first carried at sea together, it has been possible to obtain a position line with an accuracy of about one mile. This is the major reason for Cook's charts being so much more accurate than any before his time. Celestial navigation has developed through the 19th and 20th centuries with improved sextants, even more accurate chronometers, and simpler tables for computation, but on unchanged principles. Such navigation is a pleasant blend of art and science. The artful part is the handling of the sextant, in obtaining accurate readings with the ship plunging and yawing, waves obscuring the horizon and driving clouds only allowing glimpses of sun or stars. There is a nice skill and deftness needed to handle these complex, interacting factors and there is much satisfaction to be gained from their mastery and in making successful landfalls.

For a million times over two centuries, the navigator has stood with legs braced apart on the heaving deck, sextant clutched firmly in his right hand while an assistant waits by the chronometer for the urgent 'stop', when the sun's edge touches the horizon in the telescope. For as many times the satisfaction of the carefully plotted position lines on the chart has been gained.

The advent of 'satellite navigation' using man made objects (the Venus connotation is lost!) and electronic computing, has been a quantum leap for the navigator. The weather has no effect. The position is known to within 600 feet (or better) continuously, and the ship's track can be followed on an electronic chart if desired. Safe navigation is assured.

Unfortunately there is no joy in this; no satisfaction. The leap has been, like many a similar leap, a technological triumph but a human disaster. The digital display at once destroys endeavour, atrophies skills, and scuttles satisfaction. It also distances the navigator from his real world and reduces him from artisan/scientist to a square-eyed accountant of sorts. This is not rhetorical, old-fashioned prejudice. The change in attitude towards navigation, the loss of sensibility towards the way a ship makes its way over the globe under the celestial sphere, is profound and impoverishing. There is a growing 'join the dots on the chart' mentality and a pointless concern with whether the 'box' is showing 7.3 knots or 7.4.

There are specific circumstances where such immediate digital accuracy can be invaluable. Should someone fall overboard, for instance, then a couple of quick entries on the G.P.S. (Global Positioning System) touchpads will result in the course and distance to the accident position being continuously displayed. Irrespective of visibility this should enable the captain to get his ship back to the victim in the minimum time and with previously undreamed of accuracy. It is also conceivable that in bad visibility the G.P.S. might make the difference between wreck and safe passage through coral reefs. On the other hand the continuous knowledge of the ship's position can, and does, lead to bad decisions. Because you know how to proceed to a destination does not mean you should proceed there.

A case in point concerns a yacht approaching New Zealand, a few years ago, in very bad and overcast weather. The eight crew were very tired, seasick and one had an injured shoulder. The skipper decided to make for a small harbour through a difficult entrance on a rocky coast with storm-force winds blowing almost directly onshore. This decision was largely prompted by the fact that the yacht had a satellite navigation system. When approaching the coast, the yacht became unmanageable in the violent winds and irregular high waves caused by the proximity of land, with the result she was wrecked on an offshore rock and only the skipper survived. I contend that without the satellite navigation system the skipper could not have made the decision to close with the land in that area in such conditions. This is not an isolated example.

The sea demands prudent seamanship in making navigational decisions and G.P.S. attitudes are eroding such prudence by divorcing the navigator from the elements. Unfortunately this is inevitable just as a decay in a person's arithmetical ability is inevitable when they use a calculator. Of course there is no compulsion to abandon celestial navigation or good seamanship when a G.P.S. is installed, but my experience is that 'the box' is so seductive and persuasive that attitudes change rapidly and dramatically. People become lazy and less astute.

We are so easily lead by technology. Even more alarmingly we accept the loss of job satisfaction so readily.

On 'Søren' our G.P.S. seduces us all a little and a few totally, but we have an active group of would be celestial navigators at my daily lectures and three budding professionals so the sextants are kept busy and there are long discussions about position lines, altitude corrections, hour angles and other such niceties, and much enthusiastic star identification on the night watches. By the time we get to the Horn there are six voyage crew capable of taking reasonable sights and plotting the position from two such observations. The chartroom is frequently a hive of activity with well thumbed almanacs and plotting sheets passing between three or four navigators.

At twilight there are sometimes four observers 'shooting' stars and planets, dodging each other as we manoevre for suitable positions from which to search the heavens, and all muttering and jotting down angles and times on scraps of paper. The art of celestial navigation is alive and well on board this ship.

Ian is particularly insistent to get to grips with the basics of navigation. His is a scientific mind that needs the theory behind the calculations. This is scarcely surprising as he is something of a scientist, in charge of our scientific programme which has three facets: surface water sampling, solar intensity measurements, and sea water temperature profiling down to half a mile or so. This last is mainly required if we get close to any icebergs. Ian is on deck frequently with his solar box of tricks, whenever there is a prolonged spell of clear sunshine; but the sea water sampling is a complex affair requiring at least three operators. The two who handle the sample bottles wear one-piece plastic overalls (they are quickly dubbed 'the condom gang'!) because the samples must not be even minutely contaminated. The samples must be taken from water that the ship has not touched, so Ian's undoubted ingenuity (abetted by Andy's) is called into action and a system

Ian and Cath making the sea-water tests.   TALLSHIP 'SØREN LARSEN'

of lines and blocks is rigged from the jib-boom end so that the weighted bottle can be 'dunked' ahead of the ship, stoppered and recovered without touching either hull or rig. It goes direct to the tender touch of a 'condom-ed' figure. It is then sealed and chilled for delivery to a laboratory at the end of the voyage where it will be used for measuring the iron content of sea water across this little-traversed part of the Pacific.

So Ian is often fully occupied in his off-watch time and can be found pouring over his navigation problems in a corner of the chartroom, long after his bunk should have called him. This stocky Englishman has a quirky sense of humour with a ready laugh and can be a rather surprising leprechaun at times. He's happy aloft and has served on 'Søren' often enough to be a very able-bodied voyage crew. He is our self appointed ship's photographer too and is happy juggling lenses, cameras and lightmeters. A man of many parts.

Charlie is another character with a special interest in navigation. He's brought his own sextant and navigational computer which, after considerable keyboard manipulation, spits out bits of supermarket cash register paper with hieroglyphic results. Perhaps Charlie has adapted one of his business machines from his New York real-estate office. Charlie has a belligerence about him that stems from inner-city 'Big Apple.' A conversation with him is something of a sparring match. He stands square-on, eye to eye with you and there's a dare-me glint there. His views are firm and you get them straight. He's a yachtsman so feels comfortable at sea and there's a romantic streak that brought him on this once-in-a-lifetime voyage. There's nothing to buy or sell here either so he just enjoys himself.

This ocean is a cradle of navigation. Polynesians were crossing wide tracts of the lower latitudes, successfully, long before Magellan ventured across in 1520. They had a detailed knowledge of the stars' movements, the rising and setting of celestial objects, currents and seasonal wind patterns, so they were real navigators although they did not possess any celestial measuring instruments as far as we know.

The ongoing debate over the migration of the Polynesians to New Zealand and Hawaii, both thousands of miles from their nearest neighbours is intriguing but doomed to be speculative unless we are willing to accept orally transmitted legends as recording real events in memorable fashion. We are enamoured of the written word, feeling that something committed to print surely has a truth unmatched by the spoken word. But the printed word can lie more readily in one sense: the author does not have to face the reader. In reading about subjects which are familiar to me I frequently detect both errors of fact and 'slanted' truths especially when the full truth is unpalatable. Deception and prevarication lurk even in 'scientific' journals. In advertising there is a whole lexicon of deception.

Never mind, the Polynesians made their stupendous open boat voyages, and probably the Chinese before them. The widest of the oceans was their compass. Cook marvelled that these 'natives' ranged across an area stretching over 4000 miles from New Zealand to Hawaii and a similar distance from Tonga to Easter Island, with dialect differences no greater than between Scot and Devonian in his own country.

Others crossed this ocean between Magellan and Cook, but the latter expanded knowledge of its limits and its myriad islnds in masterful fashion and without the contingent arrogant conquest indulged in by many explorers from Europe.

Cook, was probably first to sail from New Zealand eastward around the Horn in 1774 following a track much like ours, although in 1773 he had sailed far to the east of New Zealand and almost unbelievably down to 71°S before recurving to Easter Island and warmer climes (to the great relief of the crew, I'm sure). Cook was the explorer and navigator 'par excellence'.

On that second voyage he carried the first practical chronometer or seagoing clock ('his trusty watch') which gave him the ability to find longitudes accurately, something impossible until 1767 and extremely difficult and mathematically labourious even then. The chronometer was such an important step forward that its inventor, in England, John Harrison, received £22,000 from the government — about £6 million today.

The story of the second sucessful sea-going chronometer is worth re-telling. It was with Bligh on H.M.S.*Bounty*. When he was cast adrift by the mutineers in 1789, the chronometer remained aboard and was taken ashore at Pitcairn Island when 'Bounty' was finally burned. The mutineers were undisturbed for 18 years until the whaling ship 'Topaz', Captain Folgier, called looking for water. Among the inhabitants he found only one original mutineer, John Adams, who gave him the chronometer to carry to the British authorities as incontestible proof of 'Bounty's' fate.

The valuable timepiece was apparently stolen from Folgier and, after changing hands several times in Chile, it was brought to England by a Royal Naval captain in 1843, still in working order. It now resides in the museum of the Royal United Services Trust.

The accuracy of chronometers did not improve for 150 years after Cook's voyages, but they became very trustworthy and widely available in the first half of the 19th century. Before the advent of radio time signals at least two chronometers were carried on a ship, gimballed and cosseted against shocks, and an officer (originally the captain) wound them religiously at a fixed time every day. In all my time at sea in commercial ships the second mate undertook this task at 0800 daily and had to report its completion to the captain without fail.

As navigator on a yacht in the Solomon Islands in 1978 I decided to check my newly aquired watch against the chronometer on a New Zealand naval ship lying at anchor nearby. On the bridge I was puzzled to find the two chronometers, in their glass case, showing totally different times, until I realised both had stopped.

'Never use them nowadays', explained my petty officer adviser. 'No need, the Sat. Nav. does it all.'

After twenty odd years of chronometer routines it was like a slap in the face. The Navy didn't wind their chronometers anymore! The ultimate symbol of that quantum leap.

CHAPTER EIGHT

South and East

Oh we're bound to the east ;yes we're bound round the Horn,
And soon yer will wish that ye'd niver been born;
There'll be rain and then sleet, there'll be ice and then snow,
She's a Colchester Packet, O Lord let her go.

OUR TRACK ON THE CHART has lost its meandering style now, and drives purposefully down through the 50°'s towards the Drake Passage. This is the 420-mile-wide body of water between the rock bound South American Horn and the ice bound Antarctic peninsular. The persistent (usually) westerly winds drive the surface water through this funnel at 15 to 25 miles a day and depressions swirl through in swarms. One day there are seven 'low' centres in and around the Drake Passage on the weather facsimile chart from Valparaiso.

Grey overcast skies and biting winds become our daily fare and thick, steaming, milky brews of Milo become the staple mid-watch treat at night. What comfort in hands clasped around the hot mug and the almost scalding liquid coursing down the throat? There has to be suffering in order that joy may be appreciated.

We are welded into a real crew now. We know each others' strong points and weaknesses; who is most useful aloft and who needs cuddles when they are cold and wet — and who doesn't. We can get around the deck at night and handle the lines without vision-shattering torches and we know who can produce the best bread (and the worst). Perhaps most importantly we know who needs early calls for watch and who sleeps lightly or heavily. We even know how loudly we can talk or sing, around the wheel, without waking the Old Man.

There is great satisfaction in this quiet team work, in the routines, in feeling confident and happy with the ship and about shipmates. Almost every day there are minor crises: the handle breaks off the starboard head pump, the water maker breaks down, a buntline carries away, it's too rough for Joel to do his one-armed press-ups, or Andy loses everything from his word processor when the generator fails temporarily. The mate might forget to call Anne for a lecture, or morning tea is made with water at less than a rolling boil. But we can handle such crises (except the last!) and they lend more pleasure to the steady routines of watch keeping, meals, sleeping and domestic duties.

A traditional sailing vessel is a wonderful venue for teamwork and human encounters. Isolated, entirely dependent on crew skills and perspicacity, the ship demands attention, alertness and vigilance, and these obligations must be shared because they are continuous. The handling of a sailing vessel is very labour intensive too and often includes an element of danger which puts real edge on co-operation from team members. Aloft, furling a sail in gale force conditions, it can be disastrous if someone on deck casts off a buntline instead of a clew. You may forgive them but only if the flogging sail doesn't knock you off the yard. There are many circumstances where lives depend upon the helmsman too, and we all learn to sleep and rest leaving our lives in the hands of the watch on deck. There may be fog, ships to be avoided, ice bergs and there are the ever present forces of wind and sea to contend with. So a ship demands a team commitment if she is to carry us safely to port. Once away at sea, the ship is our master and we must, perforce, serve her well.

Not everyone is equally able bodied of course, but as long as we recognise our own, and others', shortcomings there is little danger in that. Margaret and Anne never go aloft for instance, but they have become staunch helmswomen. Joel lacks experience, but he's strong and has no problem with heights. Sandy, Mabel and Robert lack confidence at this stage but can be relied upon to undertake any task with care and intelligence. If you need a hand quickly don't ask Chris R because he'll discuss the job first. Potentially, the most dangerous person on board is the keenest. Vince is so determined to experience everything to the full that he will over reach his capabilities and jump to tackle jobs he cannot handle alone. He's a raw-skinned New Zealander and dedicated to 'Søren' and the concept of this Cape Horn passage. He cannot understand Chris's apparent lack of enthusiasm. It frustrates him so much that sometimes I fear the belligerent streak in him might leap out and try and knock some sense into Chris. But it doesn't and the potential for danger is only realised in a minor way. In fact Vince proves his metal and ability later when, after breaking a finger in a slip on deck and having it tended and splinted by our fair doctor, he gamely tackles work aloft after only a few days of frustrating semi-idleness. Vince is as keen as they come.

Darryl is another keen, but much younger, Kiwi. His enthusiasm is tempered with experience gained on New Zealand's sail training ships; a 148-foot barquentine and 105-foot topsail staysail schooner. He's quick and able both aloft and on deck and is a good team worker. It's good to have his energy to hand on your watch. The Irish have a strange effect on him though. He becomes vague and preoccupied and suffers a temperature rise whenever a female of that race is in sight.

Slowly the outside temperature drops and when we reach our furthest south, at 58° 25' some 300 miles before we reach Cape Horn, it is just above zero centigrade. The sea is a few degrees

Cath, the Irish doctor, working on the t'gallant yards   IAN HUTCHINSON

higher at 4°C. Cold enough; especially when fingers have to tie in reef points and the like. Gloves are a hindrance then so the fingers are exposed to the biting wind. It's painful.

What sort of men were they that brought their ships around this cape in winter and with none of our comforts. Heaters, gas stoves, good food, dry(ish) bunks and waterproof oilskins were unknown to them. Sometimes, coming the other way, it took weeks to beat around the Horn with hours at a time spent aloft trying to tame wet, icy canvas with only a cold, flooded deck to come down to and a sodden mattress for rest.

Hypothermia had not been invented then, fortunately. Men died for sure, but it was usually violently in a big sea sweeping the deck or being flung from a yard by flogging canvas.

In November 1878 the barque 'Ben Vorlich' was running hard for the Horn, close to our present position, when she was totally overpowered by a huge sea. The helmsman saw the monstrous wall of water coming and ran from the wheel. As the sea swept over the stern it smashed everything before it and carried seven men straight overboard. Two others were flung from the foreyard into the sea. Nine men in one wave. After days of back breaking toil the remaining crew got the severely damaged barque under sail again and made port. This sort of experience was all too common although the number lost in that one wave must have been exceptional.

The ability to recover from such a disaster under great difficulties was a measure of the toughness of those men too. It is almost inconceivable that such Herculean tasks could be performed in such appalling conditions by men deprived of what we now consider as basic necessities: sustaining fresh food, warm clothing and shelter.

Here is an extract from Captain James Learmont's *Master in Sail*, detailing the incredible effort he and his crew expended in saving their ship the 'Bengairn', which was lying over at 60 degrees after their cargo of coal had shifted in heavy weather in the Tasman Sea.

'On deck the scene was one of desolation; as the big combers came along they swept everything before them overboard. From the minute she heeled over it was really a terrifying sight, a fine ship on her beam ends with the seas battering the whole of her starboard side as she lay helpless, unable to escape from their fury as they stripped her of everything that was moveable.

The ship was to all intents and purposes in her death throes, but we had to save her if possible in order to save ourselves. All the boats on the lee side had been swept away, and with the heavy list you could have walked outboard on her weather side, so it was useless to think of trying to lower the one remaining lifeboat.'

Captain Learmont goes on to describe the damage to hull and a hatch, both of which were allowing tons of water to get below and further endanger their perilous situation. They spent hours securing spare sails over the hatch which was half under water. He continues:

'With darkness coming on and the gale unabated I decided to cut the topmast backstays and let the top hamper go. As soon as the seizings were cut on the mizzen the topmasts doubled over above the cap and the whole lot went in a mighty crash. Frank was like a Trojan as he wielded saw and axe, encouraging his helpers in forcible language.

'The loss of the tophamper on the mizzen relieved the ship considerably so I decided to cut the main away as well. This action eased the leverage for in all, on each mast, topmast, topsail yards, topgallant yards and masts with royal yards would weigh about 40 tons. Mustering all hands on the poop I fed them with what food we could get, which, as the galley was washed out, was bottled stout and Australian biscuits.

'I didn't see my wife for two days.... As our quarters had been completely gutted she managed somehow with the help of the apprentices to get herself and the children up into the charthouse.

'By way of the sail locker, all hands got into the after hold and started to move the coal over from starboard to port by means of a basket and trolley. On account of the heavy list the incline was such that a tackle was necessary to pull the trolley up to windward.'

After a paragraph concerning the problems of raising steam in a boiler to get pumps going, he goes on:

'Night and day trimming went on with only brief stops for food and drink. Once I felt we were reasonably safe, with the improvement in the weather, I decided that the crew would do better if they had a rest. I was afraid of going to sleep myself, so I called for a volunteer to stand with me while the rest had a sleep...'

After a short rest, pumping was continued but they were faced with a new danger.

'...the broken spars that were hanging over were cutting the lower rigging at every movement and I was afraid that if they sagged further the jagged steel might pierce her underwater, which would finish us, so I decided to get clear of them somehow. With the mate I went aloft which was more like crawling than climbing on account of the list. On the lower cap we were over the sea...

'With an axe I cut the wire brace runner that was holding the wreckage and as soon as I got it half way through the whole lot went.

'Working night and day at trimming the cargo and at the pumps we were gaining ground. I was at both jobs along with the crew, hungry, dirty and sleepy. The passing of days had not meant anything to me but now I realised it was *five days* since the cargo shifted.' (My emphasis).

The last paragraph ends:

'By this time we had secured the yards on the foremast and set some sails. At last she was answering to her helm. As Sydney was our nearest port we set course for there.'

I can happily report that they made Sydney and, by God did they deserve their success.

Self reliance is another necessary attribute for those who cross oceans under sail, even today. We must be prepared to tackle repairs of every conceivable kind: machinery, rigging, sails, masts, spars, even galley equipment and radios. We must minister to personal injuries too although we are fortunate on 'Søren' with a doctor and three registered nurses to cover that sort of emergency.

I once had the misfortune to be the 'medico' on a ship when a seaman smashed his hand and wrist in a fall. It was a frightening and shocking job to put it all together again and stitch the terrible wound even though I did have good equipment and advice, by radio, from a doctor.

The man only recovered the use of that hand several years later. I have had to remove teeth too and I can do without a repeat of that performance. This voyage I am a victim as Cath has to fill a cavity for me when a sizeable filling disappears with a mouthful of dinner.

Major emergencies such as the 'Bengairn' suffered are impossible to prepare for of course, except in a very general sense. We always rig lifelines along the open decks in bad weather; taut ropes stretched between strong points at waist height. Above the bulwarks on the main deck we have more horizontal lines stretched to help prevent anyone going overboard should they be swept off their feet by a big sea. Everyone on deck wears a rope safety belt at all times this passage, and the clip at its extremity is clipped to the lifelines or a strong point of the ship's structure. (Margaret causes considerable mirth when she comes to the wheel and on being advised to clip on straight away, she clips on to a spoke of the wheel.) At the first sign of bad weather we close and clamp down all deck openings and cover them with pre-formed wooden shutters and canvas covers. Similarly all deckhouse windows are shuttered and barred. We have also fitted an immensely strong steel beam over the weakest part of the deckhouse, bolted to the ship's structure on each side, to fortify this large deckhouse against the onslaught of the huge seas we can expect down here. We have prepared as best we can. 'Søren' is very small compared to a ship such as 'Bengairn', but we are also more buoyant without her heavy cargo which was the root cause of her problems. We also have much better survival equipment although its value, this far from normal shipping routes or aircraft flight paths, would be doubtful if it was not for the proximity of 'Eye'.

Between 1850 and 1920 there were hundreds of ship losses in the Southern Ocean and especially off the Horn, but there were some amazing rescues too. Perhaps the best description of such a rescue comes from Captain Frank Shaw in his book *White Sails*

83

and Spindrift. It makes incredibly splendid and moving reading. The barque 'Dovenby' is running towards the Horn in terrible weather when they sight another vessel low in the water with almost every sea washing right across her. Shaw is an apprentice at this time under an irascible Captain Fegan.

'It never occured to our indomitable captain to abandon this distressed vessel to her fate. He was crude, he was tyrannical: he lacked most of the saving graces; but the sea he had learned to despise — though reverently — had toughened him to such a pitch that he refused to admit the possibility of failure. Whatever Irish bog had bred him, it had established within him an indomitable fibre; and I think it was his violent courage that made him the autocrat — not always fair minded — that he was. The fierce fighting lust within him demanded some outlet, otherwise he must have collapsed from apoplexy. Hard weather gave him his best opportunities; fine weather found him afret with boiling juices within that soured his fiery soul'.

The mate, Mister Perkins, is another memorable character.

'He could drive men until they dropped and still stand on his feet. He could brow beat recalcitrants, kick them into the scuppers if needs were. He insisted on a scrupulous cleanliness in all parts of the ship. He hated the Royal Navy bitterly — I don't know why, unless it was because of an ingrained inferiority complex, of which we knew nothing in the last part of the 19th century — and I remember one occasion when the ship's cook accidently dumped a can of slush into a spik-and-span warship's gig lying alongside, Mister Perkins solemnly took him aft and gave him a tot of rum from his own private bottle!'

Captain Fegan gets the 'Dovenby' into a position about half a mile to windward of the sinking 'Minotaur' and the first act in the rescue almost spells disaster.

'When Fegan was satisfied the ship was in position he threw her into the wind; her fore and aft canvas slatted frantically as all way was checked.

'Watch your chance Mister' he trumpeted. 'Good luck'.

'Aye, aye sir,' grunted Perkins. 'Take the weight on your capstans!'

The capstans clanked; as the boat lifted its keel from the chocks the ship shuddered, leaned viciously to windward, and then took in half the Cape Horn sea. It seemed no less. The men at the capstans were hurled into the scuppers. The boat settled back into its chocks. The boat crew ... jumped as one man for the mizzen stay, swinging up clear, like monkeys. The lifeboat filled. The ship shook herself, stuck her bowsprit down into a wave trough, and stood on her nose. She performed a score of fantastic gyrations. But, the moment the shock of the watery assault lessened, Perkins had us into the boat bailing with all our might... and at the next attempt the boat was lifted and swung out. Then it became a furious fight to save her from being stove against the side. We who had jumped in had all our work to keep her fended off, with stretcher, boathook, and oarloom. There was no quick release gear. I seem still to hear the mate's poignant cursing as he struggled to unhook the after tackle block; jamming his fingers, tearing his clothes, being slammed wildly by the slackened falls. My job was to unhook the for'ard tackle; the blocks seemed to weigh a ton. Always as I tried to manipulate the awkward thing, the scend of the sea taughtened the tackle and forbade it. 'Shove your knife through the ... thing!' raged the mate, his voice reaching me in low whispers. I was reaching for it when the tackle block unhooked itself and the boat was free.

'...As soon as we emerged from the ship's shelter the weight of the wind sent us along, and Mister Perkins ordered a reefed sail to be set. That was a feat of no common cleverness. But this ex-North Sea cabin boy could have sailed a scow around the world, I think. We got up the diminished sail, and the boat plunged ahead, tearing the waves to foam and froth. Occasionally a high wave towered as if about to swamp us, and had a weak man been at the steering oar — Perkins disdained the rudder, which the sea might easily unhook from its pintles — we must have broached to and been overwhelmed... We were a handful of men fighting the sea, defying it with our puny artifices. Never have I felt so insignificant.

'...Exposed there in the boat the cold was indescribable - ice clogged my jersey, my bootless feet were like frozen marble.

'While we were crossing that half mile or so of ugly water — soaring high to see the wreck ahead, swooping deeply until it felt as if we could never lift again, with spindrift slashing everywhere, and the boat itself appearing to spin in giddy circles — Captain Fegan — crafty seaman — got the 'Dovenby' underway again and, as soon as he saw we were clear of such scant shelter as the low hull afforded, worked the barque down to leeward of the 'Minotaur'. This in itself, with a harassed ship, was no trifling feat of seamanship especially considering how short handed he was with almost half his crew away in the lifeboat. But he knew that for the boat to attempt to return against wind and sea was an impossibility; whereas, down to leeward of the wreck, we might stand a fighting chance. So, using his skill and definite courage, he took the roaring fabric across the wreck's stern, and wore her round on her other side. It meant loosening canvas, setting it, and furling it again; everything there being ice-bound; but he did it. In all the bright lexicon of windjamming there was no such word as 'fail'!

'Meanwhile we threshed on, until Mister Perkins deemed it well to douse the sail and rely on oars. The boat almost capsized at that juncture; indeed, I still have a breathless feeling that she did capsize and roll clean over. She shipped very heavy water, which ridded her of spare oars and the water-breaker and several sections of the bottom boards. Perkins bailed and steered at the same time, handling his long steering oar whaler fashion, with amazing adroitness. He was a man of numerous faults, but he was a deep-sea sailorman.

'...we got the boat within close hail of the hard-set 'Minotaur'. Mister Perkins was railing at the crew now they were pulling hard. He used language that might have set the sodden timbers on fire. Had he employed similar words on 'Dovenby's' decks he would probably have been brained with a belaying pin, but no one cared; indeed his savage ferocity of word and act was afterwards praised by us as showing the calibre of hard-case man he was!

'To approach her from the weather side must have been fatal — any wave might have swung the boat against the hull and bilged it irremediably. Mister Perkins was not a tyro — he steered for us to pass under the squatting stern. To leeward was a considerable tangle of wreckage. Although the masts were cut away the action of the sea had kept them close alongside; a rope was fouled to serve as a painter — a wire rope that could not be cut. The spars pounded the hull. It was not easy to discover a passage in the curdled debris through which the boat could approach with safety to herself; but sea-wise Perkins discovered it. I have a vague impression of fending off loose wreckage with a boathook, then of clawing a hold into the chains. I remember the 'Minotaur's' captain yelling: "Hurry — hurry — she's all but gone!"

'"Come on then!' said Mister Perkins. "How many?"

'There were 28 men and boys; and it was impossible for our boat to receive them all and guarantee safe transit. The unfortunate Minotaurs had to see to themselves to a great extent; all our effort was required to keep the boat from disaster. Indeed, we were once washed clean onto the wreck's deck over her low side; but by some miracle of deep-water juggling, we scraped clear again.

'Jeffreys was sent to join me in the bow, to fend off as I received our salvage, which came down, man by man, the first one grasping our painter and taking a hitch with it. Just as he slithered down the rope — he was frozen so that he could hardly move — the painter tore apart. He went overside; I grabbed him; got an arm, hooked his hand over our gunwhale, then fetched him in like a sack of coals. His face was piteously blue, but his stiff lips said 'Thanks mate!' He was pushed underfoot; we took in the next one; a boy, one of our chummy mates from Iquique; but he was so far gone with exhaustion that he didn't even recognise us. We carried no restoratives in the boat. The salved people had simply to crouch in the swilling seawater that half filled us, and make the best of it. Maybe the feeling that out of almost certain death had new hope come, warmed them.

'It was a wild, senseless scrabble actually. Details do not stand out clearly; everything was so breathless and so intensely cold and uncomfortable. I felt as if my arms were dragged from their sockets a score of times. I was hit, kicked in the face by the boots of men coming down the line that was thrown to replace our broken painter. I remember reaching over to grab one man who'd jumped at the wrong moment and missed the mark — the suction alongside was dragging him under; I had hold of his pants-seat and a wrinkle of his shirt and I swore I'd hang on 'til hell froze over! Jeffreys spared a hand just as I was being dragged over to join him; his bull-like strength swung him in, the lurch of the boat aiding human effort, and the man's fingernails raked down my face from temple to chin. I didn't feel the pain until much later, when I thawed out!

'"Look alive!' Perkins was braying ceaselessly as he worked his oar like a scull to keep the bow close in; since it was now not possible to use the pulling oars because of the loose wreckage on which they might break — and we had no spares.

'One of the 'Minotaur's' men lost his hold of the rope as he slithered down and he fell betwen boat and ship's side. A wave pyramided over him, and there was a fragment of timber in its foamy crest. It hurled itself at the submerged man and sank him — I saw a thin tinge of red appear in the curdled water, nothing more.

'But when another missed the boat — a slim boy — and fell into the sea, to reappear on the other side, having passed clean under the keel — Rhys, elderly, rheumaticky as he was, owner of a weak heart, jumped over the side after him, hanging on to the gunwale with one tattooed hand and the boy with the other, until Chamberlain and Macauley got their hands under his armpits and brought him back.

'When 14 people had come thus, Mister Perkins funnelled his hands to hail the 'Minotaur's' captain.

'"Full load — we'll be back!' he yelled undramatically.

'The captain waved his hands stiffly, but he gave us a one man cheer. So we cast off, backed out... and settled for the return voyage. It was impossible to step the mast or set even a rag of sail, but such of the salved as could move insisted on double-banking the oars, and we slugged along towards our ship, jockeying wildly in her new position.'

the yard and he's probably yelling a crude joke over the wind to Garry whose wide grin can be seen from the deck. An inspiring crew for sure. Sandy, Cath, Darryl, Rob, Ian, Vince and Chris all do their bit aloft too. There is no shortage of hands.

Most of the labour of setting or taking in sail is performed on deck where the controlling lines are led. Out on the yards it's a matter of releasing the sails from their gaskets or manhandling the canvas up onto the forward part of the yard so that the plaited gaskets can be bound around yard and sail tightly. On 'Søren' this is a comparitively simple task because the multiple buntlines hold the sail very quietly under the yard. The more normal and simpler-to-rig buntline system allows large sections of sail to remain bagged out with wind which can cause much cursing and finger wrenching labour when furling. In either system broken buntlines allow parts of the sail to fill with wind and flog in strong winds. If such breakages occur when you are on the yard there is some danger until the sail can be smothered. At such times the oft-quoted maxim, 'one hand for yourself and one hand for the ship' is quite worthless. In truth there are very few jobs aloft that can be done with one hand. Many require at least three. Marti and Elmo spent a couple of hours making a yard arm repair yesterday. Elmo lay along the yard, his legs and elbows lending security so that his hands could manipulate tools, while Marti sat on the footrope, leaned on the brace and wielded hammer and chisel seemingly as comfortably as if he was in a work shop. Challenging work.

For many people onboard there is challenge in just getting the ship around the Horn. It's the toughest thing we can ask of the ship and ourselves. It's an initiation into the special ranks of the ultimate sailor. No matter what conditions we may meet, doubling the Horn is a fabulous achievement under sail. A feat to stir the spirit of grandchildren, just as Margaret, granddaughter of a sailing ship master, has been stirred. She is approaching the Horn, with a deep, abiding anticipation which will be exchanged for an enriching fulfillment that will be with her always. Gabrielle too has a special connection with the dreaded Cape. One of her ancestors was master of the ship 'Cromdale', which in 1892 came very close to ending its career amongst icebergs in this region.

Yard-arm repairs

We could choose to freeze off Cape Farewell, or risk shipwreck in coral and shark infested waters. We have rejoiced and felt the adrenalin course with wonderful feats of seamanship and tricky ship handling, but nothing can quite match the feat of taking our ship down and around this storm bound, southern most finger of land. Square rig sailors hold it firmly as the mark of final fulfillment.

We get fog and we are south of the charted line denoting the extreme limit of icebergs. The radar is malfunctioning (Andy is busy with pliers and screwdriver while Tony looks on grimly) so the lookouts are instructed to look and listen more intently than ever. Val, a heavily disguised Auckland mother of two, accepts the admonition to look for icebergs as if they are an everyday suburban occurence. She will be utterly amazed if we do sight one.

I will never forget seeing a huge old berg down here a few years ago from the 1200 ton ocean-going tug 'Greenpeace'. We were lurching along in dense fog when we spotted a target on radar at about 12 miles. Plotting showed it to be stationary so I altered course to have a look. At about 300 yards we saw it. Faint and insubstantial, it materialised first at sea level but grew writhing up through the fog until it was above the masthead. I never did see the summit. The weathered, icy cliffs were deeply indented with bays, coves and caves, the surfaces scoured smooth and peaks rounded by wind and waves. An awesome ice island adrift from the Antarctic for perhaps years slowly decaying as the currents swirled it eastward across this wild Southern Ocean. It was almost a mile across. No chance for a square rigger running her easting down in a gale of wind to avoid such a berg. No sign, with the strong following wind, until the lookout cry 'Ice ahead!' At 300 yards there is only time (half a minute at 15 knots) to realise the awful certainty of destruction and death, to utter a final oath or quick prayer. Perhaps time to spin the wheel but there would be no way to avoid such a mile long barrier in those conditions. How many ships suffered such a fate? Not a few, I fear.

David Bone in his *Brassbounder* gives a vivid description of meeting with ice in fog aboard a homeward bound barque, the 'City of Florence'. She is sailing gently when the fog closes in about day break. The captain is below asleep with the mate in charge. He orders the hand-cranked fog horn to be set up right forward and one of the crew — Dago Joe — is sounding three blasts at intervals to indicate that they have a fair wind. Welsh John, another seaman, thinks he hears another fog signal.

"A horn, I tell 'oo!...Listen!...Just after ours is sounded!"

R-r-ah!...r-r-ah!...r-r-ah! Joe was improving.

We listened intently...'There now,' said John.

Yes! Sure enough! Faint rasps answering ours. Ulrichs said three: two I thought!

"Don't ye 'ear that 'orn, ye dago fiddler", shouted the bo'sun.

"...'ere! Hup there, one of ye, an' blow a proper blast! That damn hoodlum. Ye couldn't 'ear 'is trumpetin' at th' back of an area railin's!"

John went on the head; the bo'sun aft to report.

'A proper blast. The Welshman had the trick of the wheezing gadget. Ah! There again!...Three blasts, right enough...She would be a square rigger running like ourselves! Perhaps we were making on her. The sound seemed louder...it came from ahead.

R-r-r-r-r-ah!...r-r-r-r-r-ah!...r-r-r-r-r-ah!

...R-r-r-r-eh!...r-r-r-r-eh!...r-r-r-r-eh!

The mate was now on the alert, peering and listening. At the plain answer to our horn he rapped out orders. "Lower away fore an' main t'gans'ls... let 'em hang, an' lay aft an' haul th' mains'l up! Come aft here one of you boys, an' call th' captain. Tell him it's come down thick. Sharp now!"

'I went below and roused the Old Man.

"Aye...alright" he said, feeling for his seaboots. "Thick eh?...tell the mate t' keep th' horn goin'!...A ship ye say?...Running eh?...Aye! All right... I'll be up..."

'I had scarcely reached the poop again before the Old Man was at my back. "Thick, b'God," he said rubbing his eyes. "Man, man! Why was I not called before?"

'The mate muttered something about the mist having just closed in... "Clear enough t' be goin' on before that," he said.

"Aye,aye! Where d'ye mak' this ship? Ye would see her before the mist cam' doon, eh?"

"Sound that horn, forrard there," shouted the mate. "Keep that horn goin' there!"

'John pumped a stirring blast... "R-R-R-R-AH!...R-R-R-R-AH!...R-R-R-R-AH!"

'We bent forward with ears strained to catch the distant note.

"...R-r-r-eh!..." At the first answering blast Old Jock (the captain) raised his head, glancing fearfully round.

"...R-r-r-eh!...r-r-r-eh!....."

' "Down hellum! Down hellum! DOWN," he yelled, running aft to the wheel! "Haul the yards forrard. Le' go port braces! Let 'em rip! Le' go an' haul!...Quick Mist'r! Christ! What ye standin' at?...Ice! Ice, ye bluidy eedi't! ICE! Th' echo! Let go! LE' GO AN' HAUL! LE' GO!"

'Ice! The mate stood stupid for an instant — then jumped to the waist — to the brace pins — roaring hoarse orders. "All hands on deck! Haul away there! All hands! On deck men — for your lives!"

After frantic activity the ship lies stopped, heaving gently to the swell with everyone peering into the fog nervously but vainly. Suddenly they see a cold, white, luminous sheen low across the bows.

'At the first glow the Old Man started - his lips framed to roar an order - no order came!

'Quickly he saw the hopelessness of it; what was to happen was plain, inevitable. Broad along the beam, stretching out to leeward the great dazzling 'ice blink' warned him of a solid barrier, miles long perhaps. The barque lay to the wind, at the mercy of the swell, drifting dead to leeward at every heave! ... On the other tack perhaps? There was a misty gap to the south of us; no 'ice' blink there... If she could be put about?...No, there was no chance!...To gather speed to put her about he would have to bear off towards the brightening sheen! Already the roar of the swell, lashing at the base was loud in our ears...There was no room! No searoom to wear or stay!

' "Embayed!" he said bitterly, turning his palms up. "...'all hands aft an' swing th' port boat out!"

'The port boat? The big boat? Had it come, so soon, to that? More than one of us cast an anxious look at the broad figure of our master as we ran aft.

'Madly we tore and knifed at the lashings, working to clear the big boat. She was turned down on the skids (the fashion of thrifty 'limejuicers') bound and bolted to stand the heavy weather. We were handless, unnerved by the suddenness of it all, faulty at the task. The roar of the breaking water spurred us on... A heave together!...Righted, we hooked the falls and swayed her up. The mate looked aft for the word. 'Aye', said the Old Man. 'Oot wi' her, an' try tae tow th' heid roun'! On th' ither tack we might ... 'He left the words unfinished! Well he knew we could never drag 3,000 tons against that swell.

A wild outcry turns our eyes forward. Dago Joe (forgotten on the lookout) is running 'aft. his precious horn still slung from his shoulders. 'Arretto! Arretto! Arretto!' He yells as he runs. 'Arretto Captain!' waving his arms and signing to the Old Man to stop the ship! Behind him, over the bows, we see the clear outline of a small berg — an outflung 'calf' of the main ice! There is no time! Nothing can be done! Small as the berg is — not the height of our lower yards — it has weight enough to sink us, when aided by the heaving swell!

' "Quick with th' boat, there!" yells the Old Man. He runs over to the companion way and dives below, jostling the second mate who is staggering up under a weight of biscuit bags.

'In a moment we have closed with the ice and are hammering and grinding at the sheer glistening wall. At the first impact the jibboom goes with a crash. Then the fore t'gallant mast — yards, sails, rigging — all hurtling to the head, driving the decks in. A shelf of solid ice, tons weight of it, crashes aboard and shatters the fore hatch. Now there is a grinding scream of buckling iron, as the beams give to the strain — ring of stays and guy-ropes parting at high tension — crash of splintering wood! The heaving monster draws off, reels, and comes at us again. Another blow and...

' "Vast lowering! Hold on! Hold the boat there!" The Old Man, coming on deck with his treasured papers, has seen more than the wreck of the head! He runs to the compass — a look — then casts his eyes aloft. "Square mainyards!" His voice has the old confident ring: the ring we know. "Square mainyards!... A hand t' th' wheel!"

'Doubting, we hang around the boat. She swings clear, all ready! The jar of another blow sets us staggering for foothold! What chance?... "A hand t' th' wheel, here." roars the Old Man. Martin looks up goes back to his post.

'A man at the wheel again! No longer the fearful sight of the main post deserted; no longer the jar and rattle of a handless helm! Martin's action steadies us.... We leave the swinging boat and hurry to the braces.

'A "chance" has come! The power of gales long since blown-out is working a way for us : the ghastly descendants of towering

Cape Horn greybeards have come to our aid!

'As we struck, sideling on the bows, the swell has swept our stern around the berg. Now we are head to wind and the big foresail is flat against the mast, straining sternward!

'It is broad day, and we see the "calf" plainly as we drift under stern-way apart. The gap widens! A foot — a yard — an oar's length!...Her head till swings!

' "Foreyards! Le' go an' haul!" roars the Old Man. We are stern to the main ice. Already the swell — recurving from the sheer base — is hissing and breaking about us. There is little room for sternboard. "Le' go an' haul!" We roar a heartening chorus as we drag the standing head yards in.

'Slowly she brings up... gathers way...moves ahead! The wind has strengthened; in parts the mist has cleared. Out to the south'ard a lift shows clear water. We are broad to the swell now, but sailing free as Martin keeps her off! From under the bows the broken boom (still tethereed to us by stout guy ropes) thunders and jars as we move through the water.

' "Cut and clear away!" roars Old Jock. "Let her go!"

Aye let her go!...We are off...crippled an' all... out for open sea again!'

What a dramatic episode, what an incredibly lucky escape. How fortunate that we have such a wonderful writer to pass on the story.

The number and extent of icebergs varies very widely from year to year and although December and January are the months when the northern limit of bergs is furthest from the Horn, they can be encountered in any month. Captain Nelson of the four-masted barque 'Auchencairn' had several bergs off the pitch of the Horn in December 1895.

In winter the ice can be a major hazard. Richard Dana in the classic *Two Years Before the Mast* describes how his ship spent over a week looking for a way past an immense field of ice floes and bergs to the west of Cape Horn.

The fog clears for 'Søren' with a rising gale and again we roar along, the wind moaning through the rigging and those long swells

Great sailing in the southern ocean – Søren dips her lee rail   IAN HUTCHINSON

heaping up into vast marching hills and valleys scrawled with foam. Their crests begin to crash and topple down in cataracts of white water. The main deck is constantly flooded, the galley awash. Wet, glistening oilskins sway from hooks around the masts below and there are drips and oozings in many cabins as the ship's fabric stretches and groans to the sea's onslaught. We marvel (I have never ceased to do so in all my time at sea) at how our ship escapes those devastating onrushes of the crests, how she rises to every sea, shrugs off the invading water, carries us safely over this wild, heaving wasteland. She swoops down into the troughs, like the mighty albatross, and appears unscathed as the next crest assaults.

There are birds galore. Sandy, our sturdy Stewart Island 'bird watcher', is entranced and excited by the variety and their wonderful dexterity in the storm-force winds. Cape Pigeons zip past, sometimes almost close enough to touch; compact, plump little birds, with a unique dappled upper-wing patterning. They frequent all the oceans of the world and seem to love ships. The huge Wandering and Royal albatross seem, by contrast, almost disdainful and stare with unblinking, unrelenting eye as they curve past the stern, hang in a gale as if it were a mere breeze and then wheel away and stoop along a ragged trough with a wing tip threading delicately the fretted surface. Up they soar again to speed across the bow and away into the rain and spume. Their cousins, the mollymawks (crazy bird name which stems from the Scandinavian for 'painted gull') only slightly less impressive in flight, are better dressed. The Black Browed variety is almost sinister with their 'mascara' eyebrows; the Grey Headed, a lovely soft-plumaged creature and the Bullers almost gaudy with their striped bill. All have black upper wings and back so they are not easy to identify specifically, at a distance. We have endless arguments about them, but never tire of watching.

Shearwaters, petrels and prions weave and dart among the large birds and, like butterflies, the storm petrels dodge and flutter down on the torn surface of this tremendous sea. Legs dangling, they touch the surface and seem to bounce, springing and flitting as if engaged in a game on a summer pond. Surely theirs is the most amazing adaptation to these wild conditions. They can weigh only a few ounces yet defy the worst the elements can muster. And these tiny feathered tufts of life dance and socialise a thousand miles from anywhere.

I have seen them nesting at Deception Island in the South Shetland Islands: bleak, cliff-face nests in freezing conditions with their chicks no bigger than a hen egg. The Storm Petrels (Mother Carey's Chickens to sailors) are an unsung wonder of this amazing world.

Sandy staggers back aft following her bird observing stint from the safety of the deckhouse top. Her eyes are bright and she grins with typically repressed delight. But the lilt in her voice betrays the intense pleasure she feels at having counted and recognised 25 birds in her 10 minute check. This nature-loving young woman has taken to the sea like one of the birds she so admires. Her own nest was in the salt-rimmed bush of Stewart Island, looking out on the Southern Ocean, and probably her parents had a fair slash of the sea in their blood too as do most of those hardy islanders. She will become a permanent crew on 'Søren' one day.

The storm force winds do not persist. Within a day they are down to a comfortable gale and soon we are wishing for more wind as our daily runs drop to 130 from 180 or 190. Poor Chris is frustrated by the short duration of the wild conditions. He wants a 'proper' Cape Horn dusting and was beside himself during the week of adverse light winds we had earlier. When we crossed the 50th parallel of latitude he bought eveyone a drink and appeared briefly on deck naked as a bizarre celebration. Soon afterwards he organised an interesting celebration of our first month at sea: the Dead Horse ceremony.

When sailors signed on a ship in England they were given their first month's pay in advance, ostensibly to equip themselves for the voyage and to give their families some subsistence. In fact it usually went to the boarding house master who had delivered them aboard and supplied them with a few bare necessities if they were lucky. So 'Jack' felt that for the first month on the ship he worked for nothing. The end of this 'slavery' was marked by the Dead Horse ceremony. They made a canvas or sacking effigy of a horse which was paraded around the deck, hoisted to the main yard arm to a special shanty and cut down by the youngest member of the crew. If they were lucky the Old Man would dish out a tot of rum but, if not, they had the satisfaction of knowing that their slavery was now fully paid for, (though at a pittance).

On this occasion Chris makes the stuffed horse and leads us in the parade and shanty:

> Chris: *Oh, I say ol' man yer 'orse will die*
> All Hands: *An' we say so, an' we 'ope so.*
> Chris: *'Cause the wages here is none too high,*
> All: *Oh, poor ol' man.*
> *We'll sink 'im down with a long strong roll,*
> *An' we say so, an' we hope so,*
> *Where the sharks'll have his body an' the devil 'ave his soul,*
> *Oh, poor ol' man.*

Joel stretches out on our yardarm to cut away the dangling 'horse', which falls overboard to wild cheers. Tony breaks out the rum bottle to complete a memorable episode. Chris is delighted.

With about 1200 miles to go to Cape Stiff (as British seamen called Cape Horn), 'Søren' is settled to strong, steady westerlies which give us daily runs up to 190 miles. It is cold, but not freezing, the deck remains awash but we manage to keep the galley deck reasonably dry now and although the water maker is not very efficient in such cold water, we each get a shower every third or fourth day; the crew of 'City of Florence' must be squirming in their graves. Elmo has manufactured two canvas gutterings for the deckhouse and the rainwater so collected is in demand for washing clothes.

This is running our easting down in fine style. Spirits are high, watches seem to pass quickly, the 'navigators' have reached the exciting stage of trying their skill with the sextant whenever the overcast skies will permit, and Mabel has her class of would-be Spanish conversationalists in regular session. Every day we speak by radio to 'Eye of the Wind'. Voyage crew take over some of the radio sessions so some very unprofessional remarks and conversations pass on the airways. Details of the latest birthday party, or of successes and failures in bread making, comparisons of bird and whale sightings and on a couple of occasions we even have singing into the microphone. Tony and I cringe in mock embarrassment at this unreserved levity but it is excellent to have the contact since we are now about 100 miles ahead of 'Eye', and good to encourage the relaxed atmosphere on board.

Fog closes in some days, but the radar has succumbed to Andy's dexterity so its (almost) all-seeing eye lends us some relief from tension. Vigilance is still needed though because 'growlers' and 'bergy bits' do not give good echoes yet could cause us grievous damage should we collide at seven or eight knots. Fortunately the nights are steadily getting shorter as we angle southwards with less than six hours of blind darkness. When we get to 58°S the night will be scarcely four hours long at this time of year, and not even pitch dark at that. In mid winter the reverse would be the case and a shudder racks me just to think of tackling this passage then.

CHAPTER NINE

Cape Stiff

We're roundin' the Horn with a gale from the west,
The tops'l is goosewinged, we've furled all the rest.
The sea's runnin' high and the rum's runnin' low,
She's a Colchester Packet, O Lord let her go!

UNDER GREY SCUDDING CLOUD we carry our circle of seascape towards the bottom of the habitable world; the southernmost promontory of the South American wedge.

On closer inspection this trailing sweep of land turns out to be a vast jigsaw of islands stretching over a thousand miles along the western side of the Andean backbone, sweeping steadily eastward and finally hooking to the north east where Magellan's Tierra del Fuego drops to the sea at Cape San Diego. Even there, across the treacherous, tide swept strait of Le Maire, graveyard of many sailing ships, there is another final island — Staten Island, the last shard of the shattered archipellago. But to the southward too, standing on a sunken shelf off the battered coast, there are a handful of fragments: the Hermite Islandsand southernmost of these is Horn Island upon which stands the infamous Cape itself: a steep conical bluff of spray blackened rock in 55° 59'S. This is the mark.

Yet, in truth, that underwater shelf of 40 to 70 fathoms, bears another pinnacle jutting up into the wild sweep of the Drake Passage some 35 miles further south: the islets of Diego Ramirez (Digger Ramrees to the British shellback). No place on earth could be more storm bound than these fragments of land, pounded by the world's biggest seas — rising perhaps 80 feet from trough to crest at times — scoured by sleet-laden, hurricane force winds and assaulted by huge Antarctic ice bergs. Fearsome rocks to the men of the sailing ship era. How many of them came to a terrible end there?

Yet these rocks and all the salient islands, headlands and bays of this region were dicovered and named by men in very small and generally ill-equipped vessels by our standards. The Drake Passage is perhaps the most oddly-named, for the man never did pass through it. Drake used the Magellan Straits (between Tierra del Fuego and the South American mainland) in 1578, and was driven south by storms when he emerged into the Pacific. He landed on an island, which he named Elizabeth Island, remained several days in a fine sheltered anchorage and collected food in the form of berries, and water and firewood. Historians believed he had landed on Horn Island because Drake reported that from its seaward cliff he could see no land to the south. This is surely a mistake. Drake's description is vivid and detailed and does not describe Horn Island at all. In any case, since the weather was fine, he would have seen Diego Ramirez had he been peering southward from Horn Island.

Felix Riesenberg in his book *Cape Horn* makes a persuasive case for an island some 250 miles west of Cape Horn being Drake's 'Elizabeth Island', although this position is now occupied only by an underwater bank of black sand and rock — Pactolus Bank, reported by a ship of that name in 1885. The depth there is 67 fathoms minimum but the surrounding depths are over 2,000 fathoms. The Andean mountain chain is volcanic so it is possible that Elizabeth Island sank to become Pactolus Bank. Reisenberg was a Master Mariner and knew the Drake Passage well. His research is thorough and his retracing of Drake's probable track from the original log books is seamanlike and impressive. Drake's 'island is an intriguing mystery but certainly he didn't pass through the strait which bears his name, and may not have been within 250 miles of it.

The Cape itself was named in 1516, by a Dutchman called Schouten, who hailed from the town of Hoorn, still a bustling little harbour on the Ijsselmeer; and the Le Maire Strait was his too after the man who had the vision and wherewithal to equip the ships and send Schouten on the long, arduous expedition that first rounded the cape. Le Hermite was a Dutchman too, but over 100 years later. Meanwhile in 1619 two fine Spanish seafarers, the Nodal brothers, turned their attention to exploration (much to the relief of the English I suspect because the Nodals had captured and destroyed dozens of British merchant ships). They cicumnavigated Tierra del Fuego, passing westward through Drake Passage, discovering the Diego Ramirez islets and naming them for the cartographer they had on board.

Later came Darwin in H.M.S. Beagle and that ship's name graces the chart in the intricate channel between the Land of Fire and the scatter of islands southward.

At this outpost of the world then, we have the names of Englishmen, Dutchmen and Spaniards on the chart, with the Portugese-born Magellan pre-eminent in the name of the deep but tortuous strait between his Tierra del Fuego (named for the many fires the native people made) and the South American mainland.

I have not been in the Magellan Strait but the Beagle Channel is very beautiful. Its dark, turbulent waters reflect glaciers and snow-capped mountains which are clothed below, to the water's edge,

Cape Horn to the Falklands   AUTHOR SKETCH

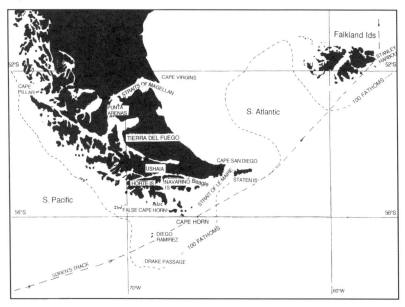

in beech forest which is richly green in spring turning bracken-russet with the approach of winter. Here, tucked in a deep bay and frowned upon by the rugged mountains, lies Ushuaia, the southernmost port in the world.

This Argentinian outpost is totally subjugated by its natural setting. It is incongruous that any sort of settlement should exist amidst such primeval grandeur. This wild channel, through a maze of lofty islands, seems too desolate, too savage, to allow a haven for humans. From a couple of miles off, Ushuaia seems a mere brush stroke on this spectacular canvas. Ashore it is a somewhat ramshackle affair with streets terminating in forest or petering out in impossible gradients.

In fact it is a town grown from a mission station. After Darwin's reports on the natives of the area English missionaries set out to civilise the naked (they were extremely hardy!) heathen folk. They were so successful that by 1925 there were none left to civilise. They were extinct! European food had reduced their hardiness and European diseases had done the rest.

Darwin saw his most primitive people there in the Beagle Channel and was, in a sense, responsible for their demise. Was it indeed the survival of the fittest?

All the early explorers came here in ships similar in size to ours, but with very inferior equipment. Their rigging was hemp instead of wire, their sails flax, they had no refrigeration, no heating and storage facilities were primitive. But they had stout men and plenty of them. Magellan had one man to every two tons of carrying capacity of his ships; we have about one soul to four such tons. Even that is not a fair comparison because Magellan's water was stored in casks which take up enormous amounts of space compared with our steel tanks. He had to carry rope, sails and repair equipment for several years rather than months. His ships were armed too so powder, shot and the guns themselves had to have stowage space, as did the small arms. We have to imagine ships such as ours but crammed with twice as many people in half the space. Most of them lived in what we would call squalor, and slept wherever they could.

The captain had his cabin in the aftercastle; a superstructure built up above the maindeck. The steering was controlled back there and a clear view could be had of the whole length of the ship and her sails. Other officers and dignitaries were housed aft too. That tradition has come right down through the centuries of sail to 'Søren', where the captain, myself and the engineer (a reflection of the importance of engineers even in square riggers!) all live right aft, adjacent to the chartroom and steering position. The rest of the permanent crew live forward in the fo'c'sle (abbreviated from forward castle) and the voyage crew occupy what was originally the cargo hold. They share two or four berth cabins, small but snug.

Our bunks, a locker or two, some pictures and a few books; these form our personal sanctuary onboard. Strangely, for most folk it is enough, and these snug little berths with creaking woodwork and massive oak beams can have more meaning as our 'space' than many a home on shore. There is a wonderful womb-like feeling to even a damp bunk when you come below from a wild, lurching and cold world on deck. There's a perverse pleasure, even gleefulness, in rigging some device to deflect or catch the odd persistent drip from the deck above your bunk. The discomforts and dangers are real, and very close, but the satisfaction in dealing with them is the more intense for that. Its fabulously cosy to wedge yourself into a bunk in a sleeping bag and listen to rain drumming on the deck and hear the muted sea voices surging against the three-inch-thick oak hull planks.

Simple but intense experiences which can only be appreciated after having the wind in your hair, rain in your face and hands busy holding onto life. A ship like 'Søren' gives us these opportunities daily down here in the Southern Ocean. We are more healthy in body, mind and spirit for them.

Perhaps I romanticise. Cold rain and spray are not pleasant and danger is best when it is past. We are not looking for discomfort and danger, (some on board go to great lengths to avoid spray in their hair that's for sure!) but they are both here in considerable measure and we are not diminished by facing them. It is surely the very essence of ocean sailing that we expose ourselves to forces which can discomfort and overawe us, even possibly destroy us, but with skill and determination, care and (in our case) teamwork we can use these forces to make our desired passage.

Each small success along the way; each wheel trick, each furling of sail, each mug of tea delivered safely to the man at the wheel, is a significant component of our overall success. Each of these minor triumphs has a wonderful potential for personal satisfaction. Perhaps it is these satisfactions, and their mounting sum, which are the happiest prizes for making such a voyage as ours. There are sights to see, ports or islands to visit, new friendships, skills to learn, but all these can be had in much easier ways. Only on a wind-ship can you have them and derive the tremendous satisfaction of having earned them by your own efforts.

We have not made port yet, however. All is grey and cold and we are in iceberg territory so the nights and patches of fog are un-nerving. There is always doubt about the ability of radar to pick up small 'growlers' which may be almost awash or at best just a foot or two above the surface.

Here, west of the Horn, the limit of icebergs sweeps well up into the Pacific to about 46°S although nearer the land it dips down and runs clear of Cape Horn itself at this time of year (December). The limit line is drawn using all reported berg sightings for the past 100 years, but some bergs undoubtedly drift unseen. There have been extaordinary years when icebergs have been seen in vast numbers off the Horn.

In 1892 the full-rigged ship 'Cromdale' rounded the Horn on March 30th bound for Europe. About 300 miles eastward she came up with a huge mass of bergs lying across her path. It took her a whole day to work clear and her master reported that in all his roundings of the Horn he had never seen ice like it. He reckoned the biggest berg to be 1000 feet high, which is fantastic, but this was confirmed by independent sightings from other vessels in later months.

It has been mandatory for many years to report any ice seen at sea but the sailing ship era was virtually over before radio transmissions were possible at sea. Since the Panama Canal was opened in 1914 the Cape Horn route from Australia into the Atlantic has been little used so sightings have been few and far between.

Laying aloft in a thick fog   JAMES PARBERRY

We receive the positions, by radio from New Zealand, of three large bergs south-east of us but with the added warning that these are simply the reported ones; there will be others not seen, by any ships and too small to be observed by weather satellites which can only 'see' a berg if it is at least a square mile in surface area.

Icebergs are, by their very nature, illusive. How do they finally disintegrate for instance? I have made several voyages to Antarctica and on each occasion the first icebergs we sighted were large and not accompanied by disintegrating 'calves', as small bergs are called. Later, further south, when the bergs were more numerous, signs of decay were very apparent.

As a berg drifts northward into water above 0°C it will begin to melt (bergs are formed on land from compacted snow and are therefore fresh water). As the volume decreases the surface area will get proportionally greater so that melting will become more rapid since there will be more surface in contact with the sea, compared with its mass. This surface also becomes very convoluted which will enhance melting even more. Also, erosion at sea level (due to wave action, and clearly visible on older bergs) will eventually cause large chunks to break off. Could it be that a critical stage is reached when melting is so rapid that the berg is surrounded by an envelope of fresh water, which will no longer support it with its head above water, so to speak? Certainly it is my impression that, having drifted into warm waters these bergs have a catastrophic death rather than death by attrition, which is the commonly held theory.

The Antarctic continent is unique in having several vast ice shelves formed by huge glaciers all feeding to the sea in one area, and coalescing while being inexorably forced seaward. The Ross Ice Shelf, the biggest, lies in a huge bight of land — the Ross Sea — and is over 400 miles wide at its sea face which is over 300 miles from the coast. The ice cliffs fronting the sea average 100 feet high and although they extend 600 feet or more below sea level they are well afloat. Chunks continually break off, often very large chunks, and these are the renowned tabular icebergs of the Southern Ocean. The largest I have ever seen was three miles long, one mile wide and over 100 feet high. It was awesome, but bergs over 90 miles by 25 miles have been reliably reported This is almost unimaginably large: 2250 square miles is twice the size of Western Samoa or Stewart Island, or half the size of Wales. In winter most bergs are trapped in the sea ice which surrounds the continent (doubling its size) but when freed in summer they drift slowly north and west, averaging about five miles a day, until they reach the Antarctic Convergence. This is the boundary between the very cold Antarctic water (below 0°C) and the warmer Southern Ocean. The transition is often abrupt and usually marked by increased bird, fish and mammalian activity. Here the icebergs swing with the Southern Ocean drift towards the east, and their demise is assured because of the increased sea temperature. In the Atlantic, however, bergs commonly reach 40°S and occasionally even 30°S, so our anxiety about icebergs will not end when we round the Horn.

A sharp lookout is maintained and whenever fog is present an extra watchkeeper is stationed at the radar. Sleet and rain are common too and both affect the radar adversely.

Thermal underwear is playing a large part in our lives now. Woolly caps and balaclavas of every colour appear and some folk wear two at a time, plus an oilskin hood. There is no problem keeping warm so long as you can keep the inner layers dry, but often this is not possible. On one occasion, freshly on deck for a night watch, I decide to brace the yards a little to a slight wind change. As usual, I take the lee braces while the watch haul to weather. 'Søren' chooses her moment and scoops half a wave aboard over the lee rail, washing the braces overboard and submerging me to the shoulders as I hang on grimly. My one-piece oilskin does its best but there are some trickles, and my feet are cold and wet for the rest of the watch.

With the ensuing roll most of the water surges across the deck and half submerges the gang at the weather braces too.

'Shit! The course brace is overboard.' It's Mabel, our Colorado stalwart. Sharon, small but determined, sits with feet braced against a bulwark staunchion, hauling the long heavy rope back onboard while Mabel coils it. The task complete, both squelch aft to take over the watch.

'I just HATE wet feet.' Mabel's complaint is true enough no doubt, but her glowing, circular-spectacled smile is in no way extinguished. Mabel is buxom, but now, with thermal clothing, numerous jumpers and oilskins she is decidedly 'roly-poly'. Her arms hang at 20 degrees to the vertical and her oilskin jacket is more than fully occupied!

Sharon, who is the only female permanent deck crew this voyage (I'm not forgetting the cooks!), asks Mabel to relieve the lookout and a yellow-clad penguin-like figure waddles off down the reeling deck while Sharon organises the rest of the watch.

'Rob, how about taking the wheel?' Rob pulls his oilskin hood tight, peers into the dimly lit binnacle then turns to Andrew who is waiting patiently to be relieved.

'One — zero — five; and she's pretty wild,' he intones loudly and clearly. 'Swinging 20 degrees either way sometimes.' He spins the wheel a full two turns as he shifts his considerable bulk down to leeward.

'Got it.' Rob's voice is soft. Andrew is not satisfied.

'One — zero — five,' he almost yells it.

'Yep, one — o — five.' Rob is louder this time. Satisfied, Andrew comes over to me. 'One — zero — five, and Rob's got her now.'

'One — o — five. Thanks Andrew.'

It's an age old system of wheel relief that ensureS the handover is correct and that both helmsman and officer know it.

Charlie comes aft, having been relieved by Mabel, so I tell Tony, who is in the chartroom putting a position on the chart, that the watch is fully relieved.

'Thank you. My watch can go below then.'

'Yahoo, that's it men. Have a good watch you guys.' Marti and the old watch clump away to the cosy deckhouse.

Sharon organises Val to do the first round on the forthcoming half hour and I send Elmo off with Dudley and Richard to check the headsail sheets.

'Could you organise coffee for me Chris? I ask. 'What about you Rob?'

'Yep, thanks'.

Chris E. knows how we take it and returns with big mugs in just a minute or two. The previous watch will have had the water boiling. Chris E. is a thorough sort of chap. A large Australian used to careful, painstaking work as a land surveyor. He's not outwardly enthusiastic so needs to be drawn out. He's got a good head on his shoulders and a deep rich voice which give his opinions a resonant forcefulness.

Sharon sits beside the binnacle, huddled down to conserve warmth and avoid the strength of the wind.

'What does the weatherfax show Jim?'

'Should remain much as it is for the rest of the night with a front passing tomorrow. More rain with that and the wind'll go back to the southwest. Probably have to wear ship again. Do you want to go and change? You got pretty wet at the braces.'

'I'll wait till they come back from the headsails, thanks.'

Sharon is not physically tough but she's firm-willed and purposeful, a good organiser and likes to know what is going on. She and Elmo are very much in love but an odd couple with more than a foot difference in height and probably 50 pounds in weight; Sharon is the lighter I hasten to add. They met aboard 'Søren' over two years ago and are inseperable. They almost pine away if I put them on different watches.

Elmo returns from the foredeck now.

'Foretopmast stays'l sheet is chafed again. Usual problem. We've doubled up on it.'

I know he'll have made a good job of it.

'We'll change it tomorrow when we wear ship,' I decide.

'Good idea. How's Li'l Darlin'?' He touches Sharon's shoulder.

'Bloody wet, and not very warm.' She turns soft brown eyes up to him.

Elmo laughs, hauls her to her feet and envelops her in wet oilskins.

'Elmo get out of it', she expostulates, struggling away, 'you're soaking bloody wet!'

'Go and change before you have a domestic dispute.' I encourage.

'Thanks.' Sharon marches off giving Elmo a mock-fierce shove in passing. He laughs again.

'The watch can take it easy in the deckhouse, Elmo, but make sure they're ready if we need them in a hurry. Sharon has organised the round, but check that someone relieves the lookout on the half hour.' In this cold, sleety weather we are changing wheel and lookout half-hourly.

I often send Dudley into the deckhouse when he's finished his trick at the wheel. His circulation is not the best and for all his lined oilskins and big mittens he gets cold easily and recognises the danger. In fact most of the older watchkeepers readily accept a spell in the deckhouse to warm up, but I'm sure it must be trying when the time comes to brave the wild world on deck.

Shantyman Chris is revelling in the harsher conditions. 'This is a bit more like it!' He wants to suffer the dreadful conditions of the sailing Cape Horners of old. Well, perhaps not too dreadful but bad enough to really feel as if he's one with them. I can sympathise with him; there's a fierce intensity to his ambition to make a 'proper' rounding of the Horn under sail. He is constantly and acutely aware that we might use the engine for some emergency thus ruining his chance of becoming a member of the International Society of Cape Horners. If he were to fall overboard I can imagine him agonising over his own rescue if it meant using that infernal machine.

Chris is absorbed in nautical history and archaeology, about which he is encyclopaedic. He can, and does, hold forth on these subjects at any moment, day or night, if you so much whisper the name of a ship, wreck, or sailor town. Should you interrupt with a question or remark, he is as if deaf, or you get: 'That's as maybe but...', and on he goes! Extraordinary. If you attempt a light-hearted interruption Chris will continue talking seriously and without pause.

As a shantyman he has a great knowledge of the historical

background to these work songs. He is a member of a professional shanty group in England who specialise in singing in authentic old time manner and with un-expurgated lyrics. I remember him, on another ship, refusing to continue with a shanty when someone complained about his Anglo-Saxon expressions.

He has a rather sour demeanor and rarely expresses pleasure. But some of us like him in a grudging sort of way. He is very predictable and a romantic of the first order under his dour mien. The occasional smile and sparkle in the dark eyes are delightful, perhaps because we see them so seldom. He is a plumber when he's at home in London and distrusts anyone whom he suspects of considering themselves of higher social status.

Among the distrusted ones is cabin-mate Andrew who is a white-maned Anglo American of rather haughty disposition. He has a B.B.C. diction with a Boston overlay, and a nice turn of phrase often delivered along the barrel of a decidedly Roman nose. He is definitely a rung or two above plumber status. Andrew was a ship's officer briefly in his youth, has a house on an island off the Maine coast, an apartment in Boston and collects fine ship models and paintings. Rounding Cape Horn will be the consummation of his lifelong affair with things nautical. He is a large, heavy man with an imposing presence, an authoritative manner and an excellent sense of humour. He also has a fine store of reminiscences from a lifetime of travel and well-remembered encounters. Standing squarely at the helm of a square rigger running her easting down to the Horn, Andrew is a happy man.

Most of us are in fact. We are now within 300 miles of the 'mark'. Although the Valparaiso weatherfax looks horrific and is so complex as to defy any predictions, the real weather is very moderate and the sky holds no threat. Force 6 breeze (25 knots) from the west, moderate sea, long westerly swell (about 400 feet between crests and 15 feet in height) overcast and cold, but clear. 'Eye', some 100 miles astern is suffering light head winds. Well, the weather chart is pretty strange.I reckon we should be off the pitch of the Horn on the 8th December, but I've no sooner given voice to this opinion that the wind eases. We are now under full sail except for a precautionary reef in the main. Full sail down here at 58°S where we had imagined we would be blasting along in a 'Beaufort Hooley' (as Marti would say) and under a mere scrap of sail. The appropriate verse of 'Colchester Packet' even went so far as to predict it.

The weather Gods have been very easy on us. We have been shown what they can call up but the wild conditions have never persisted long enough to convert wild into ferocious, awesome into terrifying.

When a great wind blows long enough over the ocean, waves are generated that outrun the forward motion of the depression that is the wind's source. These waves are termed 'swell' and in the Southern Ocean they can be very long: up to 1500 feet perhaps and 40 feet high trough to crest, and they are of regular formation. Since the depressions travel from west to east and in the southern hemisphere the winds blow spirally into the depression in a clockwise manner, it follows that on the equatorial side of the depression the winds will be from the westerly quarter. The swell generated is therefore steadily being augmented by this area of westerlies which is itself steadily following in the wake of the swell. Now the depressions follow one another at irregular intervals and along similarly irregular paths and they can be very complex entities, but when two or more follow each other closely the generating and sustaining forces can build the largest swells to be found anywhere. Since the depressions travel at speeds greater than most vessels can hope to attain (20 to 45 knots) they will overtake a vessel running eastward and, in the vicinity of Cape Horn will, in all probability, pass close to the southward. The result is that winds up to 60, 70 or 80 knots may be experienced and these, still from the westerly quarter, will raise a set of local waves known as the 'sea'. These seas will be perhaps 30 feet or more in height but of comparatively short wave length — perhaps 200 to 300 feet. Imagine then the seas superimposed on the swell both travelling generally eastward, but by no means in the same direction, and at different speeds. It is a devilish brew. Waves of many shapes and sizes will result and occasionally peaks will arise of perhaps 80 feet and so steep that the crests will tumble forward.

Here is the genesis of the Cape Horn 'Greybeards'.

But this is not all. There is another ingredient to mix in the cauldron. A wave's effect can be felt at least one and a half wavelengths below the surface so our 1,500 foot swell stirs the ocean down to over 2200 feet, or 370 fathoms. This depth can be found from 140 miles west of the Horn to 90 miles south, reducing to less than 70 fathoms within a 70-mile radius of the Cape. When these long waves begin to 'feel the bottom' as sailors say, their energy is transformed so that they become shorter and higher. Now you can imagine something of the possible enormity of the Cape Horn seas.

Listen now to a brief description from a woman who only just escaped with her life in such seas. There were three people on board the yacht 'Tzu Hang', running towards the Horn in 1957, but only Beryl was on deck at this time.

'She was getting used to them [the seas] now, but the wind still blew as hard as ever...A wave passed under 'Tzu Hang' and she slewed slightly, Beryl corrected her easily, and when she was down in the hollow she looked aft to check her alignment. Close behind her a great wall of water was towering above her, so wide that she couldn't see its flanks, so high and so steep that she knew 'Tzu Hang' could not ride over it. It didn't seem to be breaking as the other waves had broken but water was cascading down its front, like a waterfall. She thought 'I can't do anything, I'm absolutely straight.' This was her last visual picture, so nearly truly her last, and it has remained with her....Then she found herself floating in the sea...'

The yacht was thrown end over end, dismasted and left a waterlogged hulk but, almost miraculously, they saved her and made port. Fortunately they were not assaulted by further such monstrous waves.

Here is another pen describing a Cape Horn 'rogue' wave, this time in a big cargo carrying square rigger:

'At midnight the wind was howling slaughter, and stout Old Jock, dismayed at last at the furious sea upreared against him, was at last forced to lay her to....Intent on the work [reducing sail] we had no eye for the weather, and only the Captain and steersman saw the sweep of a monster sea that bore down on us, white crested and curling.

'Stand by,' yelled the Old Man. 'Hang on for your lives, men! Christ! Hold hard there!'

Underfoot we felt the ship falter in swing — an ominous check in her lift to the heaving sea. Then out of the blackness to windward a swift, towering crest reared up — a high wall of moving water, winged with leagues of tempest at its back. It struck us sheer on the broadside and shattered its bulk aboard in a whelming torrent, brimming the decks with a weight that left no life in the barque. We were swept to leeward at the first shock, a huddled mass of writhing figures, and dashed to and fro with the sweep of the sea.'

'Søren Larsen' fills her decks with ocean often enough but she lifts her buoyant stern over every wave, and just as well with our helmsman standing only six feet from that stern and totally exposed, although secured with a safety line. One such wave as described above could change our lively ship into a shambles and probably maim or kill some of us.

The combination of sea, swell and shallow water can wreak havoc in lesser oceans too; even in the North Sea. In June 1984, aboard the fullrigger 'Sorlandet', and barely 40 miles from the Danish Coast, we suffered the effects of a strong west-north-west gale blowing over an old swell from the south west which was running into water of less than 20 fathoms. We were staggering southwards under lower topsails and staysails, shipping heavy spray overall, but no solid water had come aboard. The sea was about 20 feet high and very uneven with crests crashing about heavily. The watch on deck were all huddled aft, with just two voyage crew braving the main deck, in the shelter of the deckhouse, for a breath of fresh air. There were about 50 voyage crew below and many were seasick as this was only the second day of the voyage.

Suddenly that falter in the pattern of the ship's motion, followed by a windward lurch down into a steep trough. While her momentum was still downward the next wave seemed to rush forward and build in fury. It smashed against the steel plating of the starboard side with such shocking force that many people below thought we had collided with another ship.

Indeed the steel plate bulwarks were bent inboard the whole length of the main deck (100 feet) and every supporting stanchion was buckled as if struck by a massive solid object. The sea swept aboard viciously, tore liferafts and spare spars from their lashings on top of the deckhouse and threw them in a crazy jumble to leeward, smashed the solid wooden ladder giving access to that deckhouse top and filled the lifeboat hanging in davits on the lee side of the quarter deck. The two voyage crew on the main deck were simply engulfed and flung violently to leeward. The boy lacerated his hand on the main fiferail as he desperatelysought to prevent himself going overboard. The girl ended up jammed under a lee stanchion with a broken leg and shoulder. One wave!

We have suffered no such disasters and no matter that a few people are disappointed not to have seen the ultimate in Cape Horn weather; Tony and I are more than ordinarily happy to have crossed the widest of oceans unscathed.

Cath breathes a sigh of relief too. She's had one or two threatening accidents to cope with but her expertise and resources have not been overstretched. Medicinal rum cured all minor ailments, the aloe plant in the galley soothed a few others, and Tiger balm massages were our wonder drug. Cath's touch of the Blarney was her secret weapon. We give thanks for both a kindly Neptune and an Irish doctor.

Now, at 58°25'S, 146 miles below the latitude of the Horn, Tony feels we have sufficient sea room and orders a new course for a position just south of the Diego Ramirez Islets. Suddenly we realise the mark we have been steering for is very close.

The afternoon of December 8 is grey and threatening. There's heavy overcast with a biting wind and the barometer is falling. But excitement is rising with our midday position a scant 35 miles from the islets. After 42 days and 6000 miles of sailing this 35 miles seems incredibly little. On the track chart in the saloon the noon position seems right there at the tip of the land.

All afternoon there is activity with binoculars, mental calculations, speculation and frequent checking of the speed, but it is 1600 hours before the welcome cry from the fore crosstrees — 'land ho'.

'Where away?', the Old Man yells.

'Fine on the port bow'

Within minutes there are 35 souls on deck; some scrambling aloft, others impatiently scanning the dull horizon where the outstretched arms are pointing. Yes, eventually even the weakest eyes can see the two faint dark bumps curtseying on the unsteady horizon — Diego Ramirez — outposts of the Horn.

Tony wears a quiet smile. It has been a long passage, much longer than anticipated, but his ship has stood the strain well and been thoroughly tested. Spars, sails, hull and fittings have all come through unscathed and, with only one or two minor injuries his crew have been safely delivered this far too. Fresh water, although rationed, has been adequate, food has lasted well and now the navigation has been proved accurate. The passage is not finished yet, but this is a major milestone for him especially. The 40-day run, land to land, is the longest either the ship, or Tony, has ever made.

He has been keeping watch as well as having the captain's responsibility. All our lives are in his hands in a very real way. He could carry too much sail and damage the rig, he could carry on running too long in bad weather rather than heaving-to, thus endangering us all. His decision (taken after consultation with Tiger) to run on ahead of 'Eye' means that if they got into difficulties we would not be able to assist them readily because we would have to beat back against the westerlies. There are dozens more non life-threatening decisions too, such as the water rationing, which affect morale, which is extremely important on a long passage. Tony doesn't make his decisions lightly so his mind is heavily engaged even off watch.

It's a lonely job being captain. Not that Tony hides himself away, or is an introvert, but the final responsibilities he cannot share. He must stand just a little removed, be just slightly autocratic, for the effective maintenance of alertness and seamanlike discipline onboard.

This necessary attitude augments the loneliness. Traditionally a ship's master was the very personification of autocracy but those days are past fortunately. Tony manages his ship well. Firmly in control, no nonsense, but he's able to join in the fun too; the singing, the social flux. Recently he's been reading Villiers' *The War With Cape Horn* to his watch each evening and then dispelling the horror of the harrowing episodes by leading some shanty singing.

Slowly, we haul the islands up over the horizon and since the weather continues to moderate we alter course to pass within a mile or so. Rugged is the only way to describe the Diego Ramirez islets standing brazenly in the full sweep of the wild west winds and suffering the onslaught of the worlds' greatest seas. Chile lays claim to them; even maintains a tiny military garrison there, huddled in a few huts in an eastward facing bay. We hope they are suitably impressed to see a square rigger swinging past under full sail, but if they are they don't say so when they call us by radio. They just want our name, nationality and port to which we are bound. Very formal although Mabel thoroughly enjoys the lovely flow and roll of Spanish when she talks with them.

If they are not excited, we certainly are and there's much singing and jollification on deck. The famous homeward bound shanty 'Rolling Home' gets an airing and one verse is very topical:

Bullies, sweat yer weather braces,

For the wind is freshnin' now,

And we're roundin' Digger Ramrees,

To the north our ship will plough.

We'll be up with the mighty Cape tomorrow morning with any luck, but we are ready to celebrate now. So Gabrielle's new flag goes aloft for its first airing and looks good. She has worked on it for days, after she and James settled on the design. The name of Tony's company is 'Square Sail Pacific' and he wanted the flag to reflect the name. Finally it is a square blue flag with a large white square-sail in the centre; simple, clear, smart. House flags, as they are technically called, go at the mainmast head, ensigns right aft or at the end of the gaff (at sea), and courtesy flags — the ensigns of the country the ship is visiting — go on the foremast.

Gabrielle has made a Falkland Islands ensign too, during this passage, so she can almost claim to have served a flag maker's apprenticeship. We also toast Tony for getting us here, we sing of the Spanish Ladies of South America and of 'Eye' who reports on the evening radio schedule that they have found a favourable breeze, although they are nearly 200 miles astern. I devise a new verse for 'Colchester Packet' which is bellowed across the Drake Passage.

> *The Eye of the Wind's comin' up from astern,*
> *She's doin' eight knots but no cause for concern,*
> *'Cause we're doin' ten with the t'gallant stowed,*
> *She's a Colchester Packet, O Lord let her go.*

We don't stop at one verse, of course, or one shanty. I hope the ghosts of the Cape Horn seamen lingering here appreciate their modern counterparts giving voice to their old favourites. Those old timers would have been happy with our weather, that's for sure.

Reluctantly people take to their bunks. The mood is gay but everyone expects to be called in the early hours and there are still watches to be kept. Daybreak is before 0300 in this high latitude — it's almost midsummer.

The night watch continue with songs and many a story. No one can relax. Questions fly and I tell of my other voyages this way, none of which have been in really stormy conditions. I explain that even here, in summer, statistics have it that on only about nine days a month will there be winds of gale force or more, so there's nothing abnormal about conditions today. I'm in the middle of a yarn about the worst seas I've ever encountered (in the Great Australian Bight) when, in the first faint flush of dawn I see, under the main boom, the unmistakable dark cone of the world's greatest cape.

'There it is!'

My story is never finished!

Cape Horn in sight   IAN HUTCHINSON

Quite quickly other land appears fanning out on the port bow, and from the chart we can confirm Hoste Island with False Cape Horn at its southern tip, the Hermite Islands all overlapping themselves and, as the light grows, the mountains of Navarin Island show too; mountains which frown to the north on Ushuaia across the Beagle Channel.

Land. Suddenly lots of it. But there's no mistaking the Cape Stiff of the British sailors who coined this familiar title with a nice flare for double entendre.

'Call all hands! Get the kettles on and tell Andy we'll need the rum before breakfast! Yes — everybody. We're the first people to see Cape Stiff from the deck of a British square rigger for 55 years. Can't have anyone sleeping through that! I'll call the Old Man.' I think some of my watch would prefer to contemplate the scene quietly and by themselves!

The deck sprouts crew. Some, clutching blankets, take a quick look and dive back to their bunks for another hour, others clutching hot mugs of coffee and cameras stand in knots peering forward with sleepy eyes and the oncoming watchkeepers (for it's almost 0400) struggle into jumpers and mittens, seaboots and balaclavas against the chill.

By 0500 everyone is on deck, and it's 0520, December 9, when the Cape is due north of us. We send up a mighty cheer and Andy pops the first champagne (not very traditional but there are no

Master and owner Tony (left), with Andy, and Cape Horn,   IAN HUTCHINSON

objections). Tony produces a specially minted Cape Horn lapel badge for everyone and Tish and Sqizzy unveil the biggest, most beautifully decorated fruit cake I've ever seen. It has the same striking design as the badges: royal blue ground, light blue compass, white albatross and circular inscription — 'Søren Larsen — Cape Horn — 91'. What a beauty! It was made in Auckland and must have been brought onboard in the dead of night. I had no inkling of its presence and I can smell a fruit cake at 20 paces. It goes down really well with the traditional tot of rum that Tony dispenses. He has a wide smile this morning. He's waited many years for this moment. Now he asks for a minute's silence in remembrance of all the sailors who passed this way and especially for those who did not return. It's a nice gesture and there are some wet eyes. Since Schouten named Cape Horn thousands of seamen have perished in these waters, hundreds of ships met their ends. Our festive mood is somewhat chastened by these thoughts and the colourless day. Grey, heavy clouds; but high enough to clear the Horn at 1400 feet. A dull sea running steadily from the southwest driven by a cold and rising wind.

There are enough white caps to liven the scene a little, but the land is forebidding, crouched on the horizon; the Horn itself a dark wedge of bare cliff; a dismal sentinel. There is some disappointment that we are not rounding in storm force conditions, or that there is no fanfare of trumpets, but Sandy has it right:

'I reckon we've sneaked past the dragon while he's snoozing, and who would want to wake a dragon?'

Chris parades in a special Cape Horn tee shirt and shivers for an hour or more to claim empathy with the ill-clad sailors of old. He also presents similar shirts to Tony, Joel and myself; a thoughtful memento. Soon afterwards I find a new personal card on the galley noticeboard designating Chris as a 'Cape Horner'. He came fully prepared. He's certainly cheerful today.

Joel has the wheel as we enter the Atlantic. I'm not at all sure that he fully realises the uniqueness of the occasion, as he has no background of seafaring, but I hope he will remember it always. As a lad, I would have been beside myself with pleasure and pride to be aboard a square rigger around the Horn (I still am!) never mind at the wheel. Perhaps Joel is too but if so, he's playing it very 'cool'.

Tony is outwardly calm too, but his emotions must be in tumult. He's had a vision of doubling Cape Horn for so long and here he is in his own square rigger! It's a sublime moment for Margaret thinking of her grandfather passing this way and how amazed he would be to see her here peering at the dark cape. Gabrielle's great grandfather of the 'Cromdale' will be twitching in his grave no doubt. Let's hope we don't meet with the vast fleets of icebergs that great ship experienced.

I've been this way twice before but this time, under sail, it is different and very special. This time it feels like the culminating point of 40 years at sea. There's a powerful sense of fulfillment.

The ultimate 'photo opportunity,' Chris R.   IAN HUTCHINSON

CHAPTER TEN

Another Ocean, Another Ship

The Eye of the Wind's comin' up from astern,
She's doin' eight knots but no cause for concern,
'Cause we're doin' ten with the t'gallant stowed,
She's a Colchester Packet, O Lord let her go.

SØREN LARSEN IS THE FIRST British square rigger to double Cape Horn in those 40 years. The last such ship to pass this way was 'Joseph Conrad', a small full-rigged ship skippered by Alan Villiers and crewed by a gang of more or less teenaged boys, undertaking what was to be the last real sailing adventure in square rig. It was an enterprising and exciting voyage which was wonderfully documented by Villiers in his book, *The Cruise of the Conrad*. They rounded the Horn in 1936. 'Joseph Conrad' was an iron ship. Goodness knows when the last British wooden square-rigger rounded!

'Eye of the Wind', weed infested and struggling in light winds, is still some 200 miles west of the Horn, and they are praying for some north in the wind because they are rather close to the Chilean coast. They are determined to claw their way along though and a little over two days after us they do, at last, make it past Cape Stiff and it's our turn to return the congratulations they gave so unstintingly to us.

We are still in contact three times daily so we know what weather each other is experiencing, what sails are set, whose birthday it is, even what's on the menu. Sometimes we get voyage crew to chat and question each other which helps to keep the joint venture alive.

It was a difficult situation for Tony and Tiger when 'Søren' proved consistently the faster ship. Previous experience had indicated that 'Eye' would be the faster in light winds and 'Søren' when conditions got wilder. But 'Eye' has dropped steadily astern, presumably due to her growth of weed. Later in the voyage we discover just how much fun it is to sail in really close company. After both ships had dry-docked in Lisbon 'Eye' was a match for us, especially in light conditions.

She is a beautiful old ship, this consort of ours. Her black hull and tanned suit of working sails are a delight to the eye and heart. Her decks and brightwork are always clean, her rigging well maintained and smartly finished with leather chafing pieces where protection is needed, fancy ropework, neat seizings and so on. A well turned out lady. Tiger, her skipper, has lived aboard for many years and has set an enduring high standard and style. 'Eye' has had a great deal of loving care expended on her since Tiger and a group of friends bought her in 1973 at the end of her cargo hauling career. She was built in Germany in 1911. At 132 feet extreme length she is about eight feet shorter than 'Søren', while beam and draft are each two feet less. All told 'Søren' is the heavier vessel by perhaps 60 tons, with heavier masts, spars and rigging too.

'Eye of the Wind' photographed off Tristan da Cunha   IAN HUTCHINSON

Both vessels have a very successful record, over more than a decade, of adventure cruising for people from every walk of life, both sexes and any age. 'Eye' has been based in Australia for many years exploring Tasmania in summer and cruising the Pacific in winter while 'Søren' has made Auckland her base port since 1988, also making winter cruises to the Pacific Islands.

Now, both are back in the Atlantic. As the homeward-bound shanty has it:

> *Now we're in the ol'Atlantic,*
> *With t'gall't no longer stowed,*
> *With our lee cathead a-divin'*
> *To the land — Lord let 'er go!*

The Atlantic, home waters almost, for 'Eye' is registered in Faversham in Kent and 'Søren' in Colchester in Essex; ports facing each other across the wide Thames estuary.

We may be in our home ocean, but it's the wrong end of it and the winds are not very welcoming. They turn fresh northerly so that we cannot steer for the Falkland Islands. We have taken a week longer than expected to get past the Horn which will reduce our length of stay in port. A small drama arises over this.

All hands except the helmsman are called to a meeting in the main saloon, the hold. Tony puts it to us that we must be in Montevideo by December 21. There is to be an official naval welcome and several people have flights on the next day. Even allowing for a good passage we will only get two days in the Falklands, less even, unless we motor the remaining 250 miles. He asks the voyage crew to vote on wether we should motor or persist with sailing at the risk of having less than a day in port. Tony is clear that he thinks we should start the engine, and the vote goes his way, although it is not unanimous of course. Chris leads a small band of 'sail-at-all-costers', but they accept the vote....

'Well I suppose we have rounded the Horn under sail...'

Our four cylinder B & W Alpha diesel is duly fired up and put into gear for the first time in 46 days.

Grant gets fired up too and becomes a 'real' engineer, bustling about with oil can in hand, crescent spanner gleaming from his rump pocket and ear muffs like an insignia of office around his neck. Not that Grant has been short of things to do. Apart from running the main engine an hour or so a week to 'keep her sweet', his work has been a steady flow of maintenance and repair to generators, water maker, toilets, steering gear, galley stove and tools. He's had almost every night in his bunk and thus been the only permanent 'idler', as dayworkers were called in commercial square riggers; usually bos'un, carpenter and sailmaker. Grant is very visible when he's around. A big man with a heavy tread, big hands and no-nonsense opinions. It's his first voyage on 'Søren' although he's covered thousands of miles in his own yacht, many of them single-handed. He's not always very diplomatic towards unseasoned voyage crew and although we all use expletives at times, (except Margaret), Grant's versions have a rather hard edge to them; real Kiwi timber mill stuff. He's quick to tackle jobs though, and his bright dancing eyes and ready laugh are reassuring. He's not as tough as he seems.

Almost everyone picks up on the sense of urgency imparted by the steady rumble-thump of the big diesel and the jerky motion of the ship into head seas. The talk is all of the land, of money and postage, of purchases to be made and even of hairdressers. The saloon table is festooned with shore clothes being checked over and de-moulded. The navigation lectures, Mabel's Spanish lessons and pin-rail diagrams are all abandoned. Small lapses in ship's routine discipline occur. There's an unsettling capriciousness in the air. Sailors call it 'The Channels', with reference to the common outbreak of frivolous behaviour that appears onboard British ships as they approach the English Channel after a deep sea voyage.

Into this bubbling ferment of activity and anticipation drops a minor grenade. 'Eye' has decided to sail to Port Stanley and disregard time factors. Chris is immediately beside himself. We, on 'Søren', are transformed into second-rate sailors, no-hopers, while 'Eye' becomes the only square rigger worthy of the name. His fear is that 'Eye' might be eligible for Cape Horners Association status and we may not. Oh dear! Chris does not let up on us for the rest of the passage. In fact he still mentions the ignominy of our last day's motoring in letters to me a year later. He determines to transfer to 'Eye' in Port Stanley. He will sail aboard a 'real' ship.

At first most of us find his attitude amusing because of his terrible seriousness and because two weeks ago he was fulminating about 'Eye' holding us back.

'They're not really trying to keep pace. If they were decent sailors they'd clap on a bit more bleedin' sail.'

His persistent grumbling and pessimism eventually cause protest though, and I try, unsuccessfully I fear, to quell his diatribe, which strains our friendship temporarily.

Fortunately the high spirits onboard are unquenchable. His thunderous scowl and mutinous mutterings are treated rather like unwanted interference behind a favourite radio programme: tuned out by lending one's ear ever more intently to what one wishes to hear.

Dick drops another, though somewhat less catastrophic bombshell.

'The rum's run out!'

But he knows who most needs humouring on board!

'I've saved you the last bottle, Jim,' he whispers conspiratorially.

Dick has been our happy barman this last month or more, beginning with his spell off-duty after his head injury. It's a self-appointed task requiring an hour or more of his free time each day, much of it spent struggling to extract bottles or cartons from the hidden recesses of the bond store behind the main engine, or the jumbled confines of the overfilled laundry recess. He's a typical case of a person finding a niche in a team. Dick is a practical Kiwi, a small businessman from the country who can not only turn a strong hand to anything but can see where the hand is really most needed. He would be a good man in a real emergency I reckon.

Dave is another such. Ruddy faced, jovial and of considerable girth, he reminds me of John Bull except for the very Australian banter. Unlike Dick, he does not understand or appreciate the qualities that Margaret displays. Dave is a good man to have on your watch, ready and able, strong, and of happy disposition. If you have him on the tail of a t'gallant brace the spar is in some danger from his efforts.

The rock-bound south-eastern coast of the Falkland Islands looms out of a grey misty morning on December 12. We are motor-sailing almost parallel to the lie of the coast through water strangely green and murky after weeks of the blue and indigo clarity of the open Pacific. It is almost as if the British have imported some English Channel water with which to surround their far-flung possession. The promontory which marks the entrance to Port Stanley juts eastward, with a surge of white water at its foot and many a rock, fringed with kelp writhing in the backwash. We are not used to having the dangers of land so close aboard. After 47 days at sea we are extra wary in our approach, checking bearings, the compass error, the anchors and steering gear, supressing our excitement with professional purpose and routine.

It is a wild, primitive land without a single sign of human habitation. Sea birds abound. Not the albatross and prions of deep water, but gulls and terns, shags and penguins of the littoral. Everyone is busily occupied or scanning this low hummocky land and its creatures when — BLAM! — the air is literally rent, devoured, by a pair of black, hurtling military aircraft. They bank away with their awful inner fires crackling and roaring at us. They become black specks in a few seconds. We are left open mouthed. Round they come again to scream just feet above the masthead it seems. The explosion of their passing is unbearably loud and shattering. Most of us can't help cringing a bit and everyone registers amazement. Then the decks erupt with grinning, laughing, shouting people.

'Did you see that?'

'Woweeee!'

'What a welcome!'

Indeed this is a Falkland welcome especially for us. Bizarre I think. Bizarre and shattering, incongruous and inappropriate; but I'm in a minority of one. Well, the birds are on my side. There's not one to be seen for 20 minutes! Later, in a bulging pub, we meet the incredibly youthful men who were flying the two Phantoms. They might be 20, but I doubt it. They buy Drambuie in £5 tumblerfuls! The invincible charioteers of the British Empire; crikey!

We receive a visit from 'Albert' too, a lumbering reconnaissance Hercules, who gives us a more civil welcome by human voice on VHF. Certainly it seems our visit here is not to pass unnoticed.

RAF Hercules welcomes us to Falklands   IAN HUTCHINSON

Lookout on the bow of 'Søren Larsen'   IAN HUTCHINSON

CHAPTER ELEVEN

Winsome and Wistful Islands

The next place we're bound for is Port Stanley town,
With the 'Eye of the Wind', but we've left her hull down,
Then it's off to the Plate boys to test the vino;
She's a Colchester Packet, O Lord let her go!

WHEN WE OPEN the outer portion of this fine harbour, Port William, a heavy launch ranges alongside with the pilot and our agent on board.

'Mornin' Capt'n. Welcome. We've been expectin' you this past week. Tony Davies, your agent.'

Silence; confused silence.

'But I'm Captain Tony Davies.' The skipper has a silly grin.

'Well now Captain, there's a coincidence for you! Just call me Taffy then!'It's no joke — they have identical names.

An abrupt turn to the south between rocky headlands brings us into the long narrow harbour of Port Stanley with the town strung along the centre part of the southern shore of this landlocked, drowned valley. It's a southern version of the Shetlands. Smooth, worn hills clothed in peat, bog, gorse and grey outcrops with never a tree. The water is cold, dull and wind scarred. It's a wild hostile beauty which clutches the heart, has pale, grey, unflinching eyes and a firm, cold handshake. The harbour is remarkable in its long fingerlike formation (three miles by less than half a mile), its windswept beauty and for what it contains. Most notable, because it presents itself first, is a monstrous, weird, floating commercial port. Next are the wrecks and finally the town.

The pilot guides us to the queer floating wharf which is a leftover from the Falklands war. The whole structure is anchored to the sea bed and attached to the shore only by one long metal roadway like a huge ship's gangway. Six huge pontoons are locked together to give a working platform many acres in extent on which a complete port complex is built. Warehouses, generating plants, services for workers, fire fighting systems, repair facilities, cargo-handling equipment, garages, refrigerated stores and Custom Service offices are included, as well as the whole being surrounded with fendering and mooring bollards which could handle a small fleet of 'Søren Larsens'. There were two such floating ports here at one time, the second given entirely over to troop accommodation, but it has since been sold and towed to New York where it is moored in the East River as a prison. The remaining 'FIPASS' (Falkland Intermediate Port and Storage System) beside which massive steel geometry we appear dwarfed and wonderfully organic, is at least a useful, if anomalous, legacy of the infamous war, but it must surely end its days as the Falklands most monstrous wreck because it cannot be serviced underwater. Perhaps its life will be abnormally extended and it will join the august company of amazing shipwrecks in the harbour. This seawater seems to contain a special preservative because here lie some of the most intact old wrecked ships in the world.

High and dry (at low water) at the eastern end of the inlet sits the barque 'Lady Elizabeth', beached in 1936 after lying afloat, but condemned, in the harbour since 1913, when she was already 34 years old. She is not only still upright and with hull intact but has her lower masts standing and the main yard crossed. Further up the harbour, at the end of a rickety jetty, lies the best surviving example of a wooden, deep water British ship. The 'Jhelum', built in 1849, is largely intact and a wonderful natural museum of 19th-century ship construction. The last remnant of a true American clipper ship lies at Stanley too: the 'Snow Squall', which ended her career here in 1864 after grounding in the Straits of Le Maire; and the well preserved 'Charles Cooper' is the last surviving North Atlantic packet ship and most intact survivor of the roughly 7,000 square-rigged merchant ships built in the United States. Further afield, the Falklands can boast as many as 150 recorded shipwrecks. Undoubtedly there were many more in which the ships perished without trace or survivors along the wild coast.

Chris the marine historian has arrived in his Elysium. He can scarcely wait for the entry formalities to be completed. As soon as they are he's off; camera, notebook and a rare enthusiasm all much in evidence. We are happy for him and relieved to be rid of his carping for a few hours.

Grant is soon off to stretch his legs too but returns after less than half an hour.

'Hey, Jim, there's a yacht berthed on the inside of the dock from Tauranga (New Zealand) and I happen to know it was stolen earlier this year! What the hell can I do about it?'

I suggest some enquiries at the Stanley Police station so Grant heads for town, looking rather puzzled.

The long, steel-clad gangway takes me onto a bleak, windswept road which climbs steadfastly up the harbourside hill to join another exposed, forlorn road running parallel to the harbour but some 200 feet higher. Radio masts slit the overcast sky and damaged, shuttered buildings litter the grey landscape along with concrete and metal debris. Not an immediately engaging prospect, and a chill wind is no help. I am very happy to accept a lift from the first passing driver. If the countryside is not friendly, the driver certainly is.

'From the sailing ship iss it then? Post Office — no problem. Hop in. I'm Hugh.' Probably Huw in fact for there is a Welsh lilt there. 'Aye, my da was from Wales, but there's a Falkland accent too so what 'oo 'ears is a bit mixed like. There are folk from all over 'ere, even some from Noo Sealand. Come for the sheep farming. Iss 'oo from Noo Sealand? Taffy told me the ship came from Auckland.'

'Yes, I am a New Zealander.' I suddenly realise that a Chatham Island sheep farmer would feel very much at home in this landscape. Huw continues, with a sweeping gesture as we trundle along the empty utilitarian strip of tar seal:

'All the aerials, buildings, junk — even the road — are from the war. It changed everything here. Shot us into a noo era — literally!' He chuckles. We pass a section of hillside darkly excavated and strewn with sacks of sods — peat.

'Aye, everyone has some peat. When 'oo builds a house the government grants 'oo a piece of peat land. We still use it for

135

Terrace housing with horse, Falklands   IAN HUTCHINSON

heating 'oo know. It's grand stuff. There's electricity available now but peat is still popoolar.'

Now the first dwellings appear and they are not prepossessing. Bare, glued to the earth in unimaginative rows; no adornments, no curves, no gardens.

'Town is spreading. These are the latest additions,' explains my chauffeur. 'Sort of council houses'. We turn down an incredibly steep hill with a wharf and water waiting to catch us at the bottom. I can see we are in the older part of Stanley now. Roof lines are irregular, colours vary, fences and wall separate properties and a few shrubs crouch behind them for shelter. There are footpaths too and street signs and near the bottom of the hill a shop or two of sorts. Most buildings are insubstantial though, which is surprising in this cool and windy climate.

'The important folk built in stone but timber from wrecks and their cargoes was widely available and it was cheaper, quicker and easier for amateurs.' There is no time for further explanations because we've arrived at my requested destination.

'Thanks, Huw. Saved me a long walk.'

'No problem, Jim. You'll never walk far in Falkland. People iss happy to pick others up.' He is proved right. None of the ship's company get to walk more than a few hundred yards on Falkland roads.

The Post Office has its back to the harbour and faces squarely onto the major intersection with the waterfront road which follows the curving water's edge closely from end to end of town. There's a church and a police station and a low, rambling sort of hotel, 'The Upland Goose', so this is the hub. Nearby, beside the footpath, stretches the impressive three foot diameter iron bound mast of a very large sailing ship. A plaque informs that it is from the iron ship 'Great Britain', used as a storage hulk here for many years but towed, on a submersible barge, to Bristol, England, for restoration in 1970. Designed by the famous engineer Brunel in 1843 as a passenger steamer, she was converted to the world's then largest full rigged ship in 1882 and ended her career like many other vessels, in Port Stanley, after a battering off the Horn.

Sailing ships making the east to west passage around the Horn were often severely battered by the infamous storms of the Drake Passage, losing men and spars and even damaging the ship's structure. Sometimes there was no alternative but to turn back to a safe haven where repairs could be undertaken. Port Stanley was ideally situated. Some years there were dozens of ships in distress at Stanley and sometimes the damage was so extensive that the ships were abandoned to the insurers, or condemned by surveyors. It was rarely feasable to remove the ships from such a remote place so they became storage hulks in the harbour or were simply run ashore as wrecks. The cargoes were reshipped or sold to the highest bidder.

Accidental shipwreck was common on these rocky islands too. They lie on the route between Europe or the east coast ports of the United States and Cape Horn and ships regularly passed on both sides. During the years spanning the Australian and Californian gold rushes Stanley enjoyed an economic boom based on servicing the ships employed in those trades. Victuals, equipment, water and repairs were in constant demand and high prices could be obtained. But fog and mist were prevalent, currents strong and uncertain and navigational aids minimal before 1910; so many ships, not intending to avail themselves of Stanley's services, ended their days in the Falklands.

The Post Office doubles as an unofficial community centre. If you sat at one of the sturdy desks in the main room for a day, you would probably meet everyone in Stanley. The employees spend as much time passing the local news and chatting as they do in business. A good old-fashioned Post Office with helpful clerks and a warm atmosphere, such as would give nightmares to a time-and-motion-study expert.

There is a special issue of stamps for our visit. It's a unique experience to decorate my letters with personalised stamps, so to speak. They are beautiful. The 14p issue shows 'Eye' beside a chart of the Atlantic with our route, and the 29p one has 'Søren' under full sail with an antique compass rose; both very handsome stamps in gold and blue. They are selling well with 'Søren's' crew buying whole sheets and the locals seem interested too, perhaps because we are spreading the word that the ship will be open to the public tomorrow.

The rest of Stanley is visually uninspiring although Christ's Cathedral and one or two other stone buildings are squarely impressive, and the big white telecommunications dish beside Government House is startlingly exotic. Mostly buildings are utilitarian and plain. The wind has too much bite in it for men to spend time on fanciful architecture and the living is too precarious to allow much artistry to flourish. Much more important to have a heavy, draft-proof door than a beautifully carved one; more time spent on making vital farm implements than on stylish garden gates.

There is more money and leisure now than ever before though. The war brought men, money and materials undreamed of, and changed Falkland society irrevocably. When the excitement, fear and trauma of the fighting had passed there were still the men, thousands of them. The business folk (and probably the girls) were busy as they had not been since the Californian gold rush in 1849. The horses and ubiquitous bicycle gave way to four-wheel-drive

Andrew writing home.

Photo: IAN HUTCHINSON

vehicles (which clutter the town roads dreadfully), the building industry went into overdrive, the pubs ran dry.

Now, in 1991, the military folk have moved to newly built quarters miles from Stanley and they are mostly self-contained, so business has slumped again. Prices are high, the Land Rovers are getting old and petrol must be paid for. But not many folk want to go back to the land and the basic lifestyle of the Falklands prior to 1982, although sheep farming is still a major source of income. There seem to be two avenues which hold out hope for prosperity: tourism and oil. The islands have wonderful wildlife and a pristine land and seacape. There are dozens of bird species including three types of penguin, albatross, geese and birds of prey. Sea lions, seals, dolphin and whales all frequent the coastline.

139

There is a fascinating history to research; there are wrecks and the war, which later event has lent the islands unprecedented advertising. Unfortunately (though in all truth fortunate for the wildlife and their habitat) the Falklands are a very long way from Europe, North America or Asia and there are only two tenuous means of access. A small cargo ship, with space for a few passengers, plies rather irregularly to Punta Arenas in Chile; and the R.A.F. fly a supply plane from England once a week via Ascension Island, on which civilians can purchase seats. There is a problem of land mines too. These were laid by the Argentinians and being plastic they are, as yet, undetectable and thus not retrievable. Danger signs warn the would-be hiker to stay away from several beaches and some inland areas. So, in all, tourism is not booming.

Then there is oil. It is a widely held theory that the Falkland's war was not so much a war to protect the rights of a small British community, as proclaimed, but rather to protect oil interests. The large and comparatively shallow underwater shelf from which these islands rise has proven oil deposits. There have not been any attempts to recover this oil as yet, but many Falklanders believe it must happen soon and look to it as their saviour. To judge by the effects of such an oil boom on the Shetland Islands, for instance, the short and medium term results are very disruptive of social structures and people's well being. Long term results are not known. But the argument goes that life in Stanley has been hugely disrupted anyway and that island economics traditionally suffer wild fluctuations, so you take what offers. My birthplace, the Isle of Man, has certainly had economically successful periods based in turn on smuggling, fishing and tourism, with low, even desperate times in between, with each new boom or crash causing upheavals in the local culture. Perhaps the argument has some truth in it.

The oil industry is so gargantuan though and the local population never anything but its slaves. Eventually, and historically speaking very quickly, the oil is finished. The men who own the rigs and ships leave and the locals are left to clean up, count their dollars and the costs to their health and sanity. Perhaps the rusting debris and abandoned rigs will become new homes for the wildlife struggling to recolonise — perhaps.

If the oil men come, this lovely harbour will ring again with the sounds of industry, the old wooden desks in the Post Office will give way to teleprinters (one desk will surely remain in the fine little local museum) and the waterfront will sprout high rise buildings, burger bars, hairdressers and even a strip-joint. The girls (or men!) will have to be hardy. I doubt that even shirts come off very often here except immediately before jumping into bed, for it's a bleak, windy place.

Even the gorse bushes squat down, low and dense for self preservation. This habit makes their blooms the more intense and the splashes of gold across the hillsides are in wonderful contrast to the other muter shades of grey, brown and green. Once out of town it is a beautiful land. Water is everywhere; fresh in the peaty soil; salt in almost every vista. The coastline is fantastically convoluted. Bays, fjords, rocky promontories and islands capture the eye in every direction. Odd lonely farms, one or two lonely settlements and fences are man's mark on the wild scene (and those deadly notices).

There are two main islands: East and West Falkland, separated by a comparatively open stretch of water called Falkland Sound running south-west to north-east for about 50 miles. Each main island measures about 60 by 20 miles.

The group was first seen in 1592 by Captain John Davis of North West Passage fame, but named by Captain John Byron in 1764 when on a voyage of scientific investigation in the ship 'Dolphin'. Its history is as convoluted as its coastline involving settlement by the French, Spanish and British but the changes in jurisdiction were without hostility until Argentina revived a claim dating back to the time of Spanish settlement in the 18th century. There are still place names reflecting the three settlements: Choiseul Sound and Cape Bougainville; San Carlos for the Spanish and Darwin Narrows or Berkely Sound being typical of the predominantly English names.

Our sojourn in Stanley is short: two days, so we only brush the surface and although some groups hire cars to get further afield many of us are confined to the environs of the port. Poor Grant spends much of his time with the police, who had suspected the yacht was stolen but needed a witness for positive identification. The culprits are quickly behind bars but telephone calls and paper work eat into Grant's shore leave.

We get to meet more people than you might expect though, because our open day attracts a steady stream of visitors. Open days are usually noisy, bustling, busy affairs with sightseers getting into every corner, questions galore, and kids spinning the wheel and trying to climb the rig. This time it is unnervingly quiet. The Falklanders just file on board, look, thank us sincerely and file off again. It's as if they are being permitted to inspect the scene of a disaster. The men don't actually bare their heads but I half expect them to. Are they just shy? There are exceptions of course, and the teenagers are almost as brash as anywhere else, but it's an amazingly quiet open day nevertheless.

On their own ground, in the pub, it's better. We get to talk more freely with the locals there in the evening, but they are not garrulous; we have to draw out responses. There are four pubs plus the 'Upland Goose', which is a hotel/restaurant where Tony, Andy and myself enjoy lunch in an ambience that could be upmarket Lake District in England. The other ale houses not only have very English names: The Globe, The Rose, The Victory and The Stanley Arms, but their style is unmistakenly 'old country' too. The clientele ranges right across local society from the Homeric Drambuie-quaffing Phantom pilots to farmers, labourers and the town's young bloods with their girls who drink beer from the world over. There is no local brew. Trade is brisk and our rather loud group intrusions are welcome enough. There is no mistaking us of course, as the cool weather is ideal for showing off our lovely 'Søren Larsen' long-sleeved shirts and padded jackets. Anyway, who can mistake a sailor in from the sea?

Well, you could be forgiven for not recognising Margaret as an erstwhile shellback. While we let our hair down she has been having hers done up. After considerable efforts on Taffy's part a local lady has been located who can fit Margaret into her duties as a housewife, and tow-headed sailor has been transformed into smartly coiffured English Lady again. There are many ways of celebrating a rounding of the Horn.

There is one other noteworthy event. The Governor, William Hugh Fullerton C.M.G, invites all hands to The Residence at the far end of town where it 'resides' quite grandly in a fine garden surrounded by trees. These latter are a mark of considerable distinction in the Falklands. I am shipkeeping so do not attend but from the returning, bright-eyed crew I get mostly stories about the free drinks, the excellent hospitality (probably the same thing!) and considerable detail about one of the maids. Ah, well, 47 days at sea you know! There is talk of a remarkable flower-filled conservatory too. Tony is impressed both with the Residency and the warm reception and the American members of our voyage crew are surprised and happy to find that the Governor's wife, Arlene, is American-born.

Our departure is particularly memorable. The day is bright and breezy with white caps running the length of the harbour. First we motor westward beyond the town then turn and steadily set sail and just as steadily pick up speed until we run past the town centre at about nine knots with topsails straining. With a nicely judged turn to port and smart bracing, we shoot through the narrows and out into a full gale in Port William. Binoculars show the waterfront lined with people, the Residency dipping the Union Jack to us (a bit irregular but very sporting and a welcome sign that our crew did not break too many rules of etiquette when they visited) and four-wheel-drivers following up along the headland. We must make a stirring sight from on shore.

We leave without Chris who is overjoyed to get extra time among his beloved wrecks and to continue his researches at the beautiful little museum while he awaits 'Eye', who is due later in the day. Ed has also decided on another adventure and ships aboard a small Chilean freighter bound for Punta Arenas in the Magellan Straits. He is taking the opportunity to travel in Chile and he's had enough seafaring and watchkeeping for a while. He's a walker and climber and needs to stretch his legs in solitude. Ed is a mathematician. A balding, bespectacled American; professor Calculus of 'Tintin' fame. He's given to flashes of wit and garrulous exposition on all manner of subjects but also to periods of doleful silence and brooding. He is used to many hours of contemplative thinking each day in his shore life and finds the noise on board very stressful: people and ship noise. I have found him sitting in the library in the early hours, after his watch perhaps, absorbed in thought and felt he resented my intrusion. On watch he was happiest on lookout, right forward on his own. Fortunately he has struck up a friendship with Mabel and he has happily joined in most of our parties and shenanigans but perhaps, of us all, Ed has got the least from our voyage. Less than he hoped for anyway, and I am sad about that.

Burial at sea, (see next page)

IAN HUTCHINSON

CHAPTER TWELVE

Ashes and the Silver River

In Montevideo we'll all have a fling,
With bold senoritas we'll dance and we'll sing,
We'll wine 'em and dine 'em and take 'em below!
She's a Colchester Packet, O Lord let her go!

SØREN RACES DOWN Port William Sound and into open water again. There's white water everywhere and the wind howls in the rig. Everyone has been warned to expect rough weather so we are snugged down, stowed and lashed. Before we clear the lee of the land though, we have a duty to perform so we reduce sail and heave to perhaps a mile offshore. Everyone gathers aft and Tony prepares to read the burial service. We have brought with us from New Zealand the ashes of a man who was born in Stanley. His widow has asked that his ashes be scattered somewhere near his home port.

The ensign is lowered to half mast. We are bareheaded. Tony speaks loudly for his words are whipped away by the gale. The grey flying clouds and dark sea match the sombre mood and the Lord's Prayer has a leaden, dirge-like air about it accompanied by eerie organ music supplied by the rising wind through our swaying rigging. The ashes drop quietly as the service ends and John starts to sing 'Fiddlers Green', which has a fantastically poignant effect under these circumstances. We join the refrain:

Wrap me up in my oilskins and jumper,
No more on the docks I'll be seen,
Just tell me old shipmates I've taken a trip mates,
And I'll see them someday in Fiddler's Green.

There are many wet eyes.

Sail is crowded on again and watches set in near silence as we each ponder the significance of life's adventure and the inevitability of our return to the elements. Spirits return slowly; the ship demands our attention. There are scores of Falkland stories to recount too and the anticipation of Montevideo to buoy us; anticipation of things Spanish, flashing eyes and red wine. Mabel's Spanish classes take on a new urgency. The pupils have passed from basic vocabulary and numbers to designing useful phrases such as:

'Donde puedo comprar una cerveza?' (Where can I get a beer)

'Me gustaria alquilar un coche' (I wish to hire a car)

'Queria una habitacion con cama de matrimonio.' (I want a room with a double bed!)

There's going to be no holding back these brave Cape Horners. Men and women alike are going to take Montevideo by storm.

It takes us a week for the run of 1060 miles almost due north in mostly fresh conditions with steadily rising temperatures. Five days out it is positively balmy and layers of clothing are discarded. This is more like it. It takes only a minute to get dressed for a night watch now and no violent cabin-mate-waking struggle into thermals, layers of woollens and oilskins. Orion climbs the northern sky again with Gemini and Taurus. Canopus no longer marks our zenith. There is a proper night again and we cannot look for the flush of dawn in the middle watch anymore.

Bird life changes too. The Atlantic has it's own shearwaters and petrels so Sandy has a new enthusiasm and the bird recognition books are cluttering the chart table again. On meeting the warmer water of the Brazil current which sweeps southward from Cape San Roque along the South American coast, we are witness to a striking display of feeding frenzy on the part of the Mollymawks. Thousands of them cover acres of quiet sea. The passage of the ship sends them paddling over the surface to wheel away in a lovely black and white pageant, but to settle again and peck enthusiastically at some morsel. When we throw small pieces of squid the effect is startling. These handsome Black Brows flock to our wake in their hundreds and eventually compete, acrobatically right under our hands. They skid down, feet splayed, massive wings braking, to stab expertly at the scraps. The air is full of birds but there is never a collision although plenty of argument. A wonderful display for photographers.

The ship's company slowly loses its togetherness. The break in the Falklands and the intrusion of land based worries begins to take their toll as we approach Montevideo. Most of the voyage crew must leave the ship and have itineraries for touring inland or prebooked flights for home, so there are concerns about confirmations and changes of plans. Pan American Airways have gone bankrupt while we've been at sea throwing some arrangements into disarray. There are telephone calls to think about, tax men to join battle with, family concerns. Even the permanent crew catch the disease 'terrafirma instabillata.' The ship begins to take second place. The watch officers have to take great care that people, with their minds elsewhere, do not make mistakes. Fortunately work about the decks is second nature to most now.

The morning of December 21 finds us motor-sailing through the brown, silty waters of the Plate. This huge, shallow estuary collects the waters of two great river systems both rising in the heart of Brazil: the Uruguay; and the more westerly Parana, which is joined by the Paraguay about 650 miles from the sea. Both rivers are major highways for their namesake countries. When conjoined they form the Rio de la Plata (i.e. River of Silver; so named for the volumes of that metal transported from the interior to Spain via this estuary) which hosts two major ports: Buenos Aires in Argentina on the South bank, and Montevideo the Uruguayan capital on the northern shore.

Montevideo was founded by the Spanish in 1726 and grew steadily in size and shipping facilities. It is much easier of access than Buenos Aires because the latter is 150 miles further up the sand- and silt-choked estuary. The Uruguayan port does not only have cargo handling facilities but specialises in ship repair, and many a square rigger battered by the Cape Horn weather, or damaged by ice, limped back to Montevideo to effect repairs or await new spars from England.

There is a long, buoyed channel in the outer approaches and the numerous wrecks marked on the chart show the necessity of keeping between the buoys. The wind falls away steadily until we are motoring with sails hanging in their gear, through thick brown soup, laden with rubbish and dead fish.

The hummocky land rises slowly to starboard and then the city high-rise buildings, insubstantial at first in the haze but growing like a statistician's bar graph and unmistakably man-made. One or two merchant ships pass outward bound and there are small fishing craft in the distance as we throb steadily up the brackish estuary. There's a langour and heat, a faint exotic smell in the air: South America.

Then, quite suddenly, just before midday, our navy escort turns up; a small frigate with waving figures, large ensign and chattering V.H.F. radio.

'Welcome, welcome captain. This is Diego Lamas. We are taking a film of you. Could you set more sail please? We will send a pilot for you and our camera man will circle you. Is that O.K.?'

'Yes, go ahead. It's good of you to meet us. When will we go alongside and to which berth?' Tony is trying for some specific information but that is not a common commodity here.

'The pilot will tell you everything captain'. Diego has excellent English but the accent has lovely Spanish vowels. He is our agent who will liaise between the ship and Spanish speaking officialdom. The photographers circle while we spread our wings in the 'clock calm' and the pilot comes aboard — except there are three of them! Two pilots and an interpreter. All are Uruguayan naval officers resplendent in smart white uniforms with flat-topped peaked caps and plenty of gold braid.

The fun begins almost at once when contact is made with the port control radio tower. There are rapid interchanges in wonderful rolling Spanish, silences, discussions, eye rolling and vivid gesticulating. The liason man finally declares: 'Wait please captain'. We wait, or at least proceed at snail's pace. Half an hour and several V.H.F. conversations later there are smiles and relieved removals of the uniform caps for head mopping.

'We will go to the naval port captain. There is a tug in your place who will not move. The tugs are on — how do you say — strike.'

The brass throttle wheel is given a twist or two, and Grant winds on some more propeller pitch while the crew continue furling sails and preparing mooring lines. Ten minutes into the harbour entrance channel the V.H.F. is strident again. More agitation, expressive gestures and brow mopping.

'Captain, I am sorry, you cannot be at the military wharf. The commandant says the ship there cannot move. We must stop.'

We do so about a mile from the breakwaters, hovering in mid-channel, while the frigate ploughs ahead and disappears. Unbelievably, before we cover that mile there are two more changes of berth while the pilots get steadily more heated. Finally we are ordered to a berth alongside a naval diving tender. The approach is against a very light breeze but we must turn through 90 degrees to lay alongside the tender which is berthed across the head of a basin. The pilots discuss tactics at length and advise variously, port-side to, starboard-side to, anchoring first, not anchoring. Their speech gets more rapid, the arm waving and head mopping more agitated. They have reckoned without Tony. The Old Man is an excellent ship handler and there is no way he will permit these young naval types to play with his ship. A hundred yards from the tender he just takes over. We are all very relieved and go to our mooring stations happily, Tony puts her alongside without even squashing a fender and with our stern swinging two feet from a precious frigate. The pilots first look a little hurt, then alarmed and finally they shake Tony by the hand and say how well everything went. Before we are fully secure a shore official arrives with Diego Lamas to tell us the tug has moved and we must shift to the originally designated wharf. It's unbelievable — but it's Uruguay!

This sort of pantomime develops again on various sets throughout our two weeks in Monte. Organisation is entrepreneurial and results are proportional to the effort put into dialogue. The tugmaster becomes a good friend once we get him aboard to talk. Fresh water hoses are arranged to our advantage only after numerous gesticulating sparring rounds with the port officials who lounge and sulk behind big bare tables in their dockside office, which looks like a converted gymnasium locker-room. Spanish-speaking Mabel soon leaves but I grab anyone I can, who can speak English and Spanish, to help me keep my end up. Diego is ideal if he's around. It can be very frustrating but it's fun too; a battle of wits.

Everyone loves Montevideo. Uruguay may be a third world country with 2500 pesos to the U.S. dollar (it was 25,000 a few years ago so they knocked off a zero and started again!) but these people know how to live. A trip into the city leaves an impression of movement, music, dancing, flashing eyes, swerving cars and careering buses, sidewalk cafes, wine, women and song.

Ah, the women, the girls. They are wonderful dark, smooth skinned creatures with flashing eyes and sultry looks. Sturdy of limb and with strong features. Round in the counter and bluff in the bow too. We spend a fair bit of time eyeing these beauties. What's new with sailors in from the sea? I wonder if the females onboard find the Uruguayan men as delectable?

We do more than ogle the girls. We get to grips with them! One night half a dozen of us make for an all night dance at a crazy disco called 'Too Much'. It almost is. We arrive about 2300 to find about six couples lounging around and a couple of leather-jackets at the bar. By midnight we have had a few beers and are very eager — but no girls. By 0100 the music is getting loud and the cellar is swinging. By 0200 and through until 0500 it is wild. We cram onto the bouncing dance floor with some locals and can they, do they, dance? When the Latin rock really gets going the place is a heaving, swinging, singing melee and the wooden floor is giving under the strain. We sweat our cerveza straight out in the first hour. When we tumble out onto the footpath at about 0500 I am wringing wet. The rain, sheeting down as we run for a taxi, is wonderful.

Joel kept a cool eye on the crowd all night and furtively whispered warnings about 'hoods' who were looking for trouble. He assured me he would be ready to defend us, but to be prepared. Well, Joel is pretty street-wise but I didn't see any skullduggery. Plenty of beer drinking, some marijuana smoking along with some heavy petting on the sofas tucked under the stairs, but no fights.

One young girl kept an eye on Joel too. She becomes a regular visitor to the ship and persisted right to departure day although I believe the object of her desire did not succumb. Patricia (with a beautifully drawn out 'r') helped in the galley and washed clothes for the crew but she slept ashore. Joel hid whenever he saw her coming. We ribbed him about it unmercifully of course.

Diego Lamas is omnipresent, almost omnipotent. He can arrange anything from a free dental appointment for me with the navy, to a box of nuts and bolts, transport, or a visit from the President of the country. He and Andy have daily meetings to keep the worn bearings of Uruguayan services functioning, and they prove to have the necessary skills.

Diego brings his daughter to the ship and every male aboard homes in. She is very beautiful and has the most exquisite features I think I have ever seen. A wonderful dusky complexion, flushed with delicate rose and eyes so dark, so expressive and electric as to send a sort of shiver of light across a room. A truly beautiful girl of 17 with proud bearing and happy demeanour. She will surely be absolutely stunning as a mature woman. Ximena the beautiful.

Montevideo is the end of the Cape Horn leg of our 'Homeward Round the Horn' venture. All but five of the voyage crew have to leave here, and as there are only four joining the Atlantic adventure will be comparatively short-handed. Tony gets us all together on the second morning to review the voyage briefly and formally farewell those who are leaving. Each gets a handsome certificate to commemorate the Cape Horn passage and showing the distance covered: 8,801 from Sydney or 7,449 from Auckland. Tony is at pains to thank everyone for their support and for playing their part in the successful, if slow, passage and he apologises for the very short stay in the Falklands.

Then come the personal farewells which are more difficult. A few are tearful and most leave with a very real sense of loss. Always, aboard the 'Søren', the voyage crew become very attached to the ship and there are invariably special friendships formed. The shared work, dangers and excitements of an ocean passage under sail make for strong bonds. Professional seafarers are somewhat blasé out leaving their ships,. It's the nature of the job.

Seamen have hundreds of acquaintances but usualy only a few close friends, and there is always another ship, although they do have favourites. The voyage crew often know they will never make such a voyage again. In a sense they leave a fragment of themselves onboard, which they will always miss. They may have come to understand, and love, 'the way of a ship in the midst of the sea', and to leave a love is never easy. Much of the farewelling, then, is sad, but the melancholy is short-lived because Montevideo offers so many interesting and diverting opportunities for those remaining and the others are occupied with travel arrangements and the practicalities of changing to land-cruising overdrive.

Christmas Day is very special. For a start it is a day off for everyone (except the cooks). Since some of us only turned in at 0500 after dancing, we do not even emerge until mid-morning, but by lunchtime the saloon and galley are decorated and culinary goodies start to appear while we begin a little parcel opening ceremony. A few days previously we had each drawn a name from a hat to ascertain for whom we should buy a gift. A good scheme — probably Andy's idea. Everyone bought just one gift and there was an upper price limit. The variety of presents and suitability for each recipient are impressive. Books, leatherwear, jewellery, wine, tapes and writing equipment to name but a few and none are duplicated. The ceremony is prolonged and made amusing by every parcel being passed around prior to opening for everyone to guess the contents.

Musical instruments appear, the songsters among us lead songs of every imaginable type (and some unimaginable) while wine and beer begin to flow and the rum bottle is uncorked (perhaps the reason for my prolonged warbling on the clarinet!) so that by the time of the evening feast the cooks could have produced nearly anything and we wouldn't notice. But they produce most splendidly, very ably, abetted by Tisha's friend Clive who has flown from the Middle East to find himself very much a part of the galley team. We do notice their efforts and drink them a heartfelt toast for both this special meal and their unflagging efforts over the past three months. Anne gives one of her sterling speeches, full of admiration for the ship and its master and crew, and exhorting all voyage crew to realise what a unique adventure they are part of. She is a remarkable speaker. Never at a loss for a word, eloquent, clear and from the heart.

Another Christmas treat is the arrival, from New Zealand, of Tony's wife Fleur and their children Natasha and Tristan, together with our ex-cook/now office girl, Kristeen. They bring a huge pile of mail which results in an uncanny silence onboard for several hours. For most of us it's the first mail for two months. The children have some gifts to unwrap, but they are almost surfeited with Christmas since they celebrated in New Zealand and again on the flight. A childhood fantasy come true — a three day Christmas!

Midnight mass in a big old church in the old part of the city is a memorable experience. We thread our way through the narrow alleys and streets which are unusually quiet and empty. A few crackers are thrown from balconies at our chattering group but Christmas is probably an indoor family time, or perhaps everyone is off to mass. Inside, the lofty, pillared nave and solemn organ music extinguish our street-walking exuberance instantly. I sometimes think that churches are designed to tame the spirit, confine it in the wooden pews at floor level while the greater Spirit hides somewhere in those ceiling arabesques, or behind the fabulous trappings beyond the altar steps, all the while watching, judging. I must have a guilt complex. I like churches and cathedrals nevertheless. They are often splendid buildings of inspired design and staggering architectural complexity and they do contain a spiritual presence. Whether invoked by the constant prayer and religious ritual or by the original act of consecration I am not at all sure but you do not need to be very spiritually awakened to be aware of the presence.

On this occasion we have the advantage of not being able to understand a word of the Spanish service so that we can simply absorb the atmosphere, the beautiful fluid, rolling words, the waves of congregation responses both in voice and movement, and the singing. It is enchanting. That's it! A church is an enchanted land albeit a rather sombre, solemn version without elfin pranks. But it is full of magic; there's a wizard, spells are cast, there are fabulous gold and silver chalices , rainbow hues of stained glass, and the essential escape from the 'real' world outside the unassailable walls. Fairies have been banished to glades which our scientifically clouded eyes can no longer see, and our cash-register deafened ears can no longer hear their music, but a cathedral can still supply the magic.

We emerge sobered, hushed and at a loss for words and what to do next. Most suggestions seem too irreverent and self-indulgent so most of us decide to just walk a while even though it is after 0100. It is a good time to re-enter the material world. The haggle and bustle of this old city has ebbed and the summer night has laid a soft hand over the city's hard heart this Christmas Day. Normally you can eat out at midnight or later, and the streets are busy until after 0200, even 0300. Crossing the main streets is hazardous even then because as traffic volume decreases, the speed seems to rise. But tonight the old city, spilling down to the sea and the wharves, is peaceful and romantic. The bright, low, gibbous moon washes the wide esplanade with its grand seaward-facing civic buildings, and gentle moon shadows add a dimension to the architectural geometry. The quiet sea steals just an occasional moonlit glance ashore and finds all well. The military guards at the huge arched entrance to our wharf are mostly asleep and I get only a faint grunt to my 'buenos notchas'. My steps ring on the shining cobblestones and the rail lines of the silent dockside. 'Søren's' spars are ruled sharply like multiple crosses against the luminous clouds, and the moon has transformed the harbour into a truly silver river.

CHAPTER THIRTEEN
Spanish Ladies

In Punta del Este be warned to take care,
For there's gales and there's girls and their skin is so bare;
And they're round in the counter and fine lined below;
She's a Colchester Packet, O Lord let her go!

IT'S GOOD TO HAVE 'Eye of the Wind' with us again. She is berthed alongside so there is more potential for cameraderie than ever before, and for the New Year we have a real get-together party; the first since a dockside barbeque at Pyrmont. Some of us rekindle friendships made there, in Sydney, and fill in gaps from our regular radio contacts — the love affairs and what the skipper said when the voyage crew dropped a pot of paint on the wooden deck. There are joint forays to the local cafes and ethnic restaurants and John makes eyes (and more) at Sylvia, one of two beautiful Peruvian sisters who cook on 'Eye'.

Chris is with us again too and he is invested with membership of the 'Søren's' special hard-case club. Andy, John, Nigel and Marti as founding members see to it that he is initiated properly and with due ceremony. He quaffs the mandatory pint of beer in one go without batting an eye and promptly gives us some fine renderings of a few forebitters and shanties. He is bubbling with enthusiasm and stories of his Falkland wreck hunting, and he plans to travel overland to the far south of Argentina in order to sight a couple of particularly famous wrecks. He has persuaded Rob to accompany him. Although Chris is not grumbling, the 'Eye' must have been something of a disappointment to him because they motored a fair bit of the passage and his watch officer would not allow shanty singing.

Apart from Christmas and New Year days, the ship maintenance work continues but everyone on 'Søren' gets three clear days off, and many go inland. I spend some of my time just wandering around the extensive and fascinating port. The main cargo handling facilities are close by and busy. Everyday there are half a dozen large ship movements ranging from the behemoths of the container trade through run-of- the-mill general cargo carriers to a beautiful 1960 vintage refrigerated fruit carrier which catches the eye like an 'old master' in a room full of 'modern' paintings. None appear to carry the local flag with its golden sun and blue sea. Tugs fuss them into all sorts of angled and awkward docks and lead them, tethered, out to the breakwaters and freedom.

Further along, the old port is decaying and dirty but crammed with shipping. Small local coasters mix-it with hulking deep sea stern trawlers from around the world — Poland, Bulgaria, Spain and Japan — and smaller vessels from the Orient piled with the killer drift nets or seine gear. Crammed together, fender girt, they are busy with every facet of ship repair and maintenance. One or two are all white paint with decks covered with fresh stores. Most are unkempt and dirty and not a few show only rust to the world as if in the final throes of some terrible scabrous disease. Each floating dock, of which there are four, is full, some with two vessels, both overhanging. Gangs of men are busy with propellers, staging and welding gear. The shipyard racket is a constant background of ringing steel, hissing air hoses and the crackle of arc welding.

In another area the active fishing fleet, mostly local, are loading ice, flaking huge nets along their decks or taking stores aboard. We see these vessels on the move daily past the end of our wharf.

In the most remote corner of the inner harbour are the breaker's yards with rotting, sagging jetties, skeletal remains of wooden ships scattered like forgotten war victims, untidy stacks of rusting steel plates, wire rope in sagging, sand-filled coils colonised by the ubiquitous dandelion and dock; and listing, abandoned and partially submerged craft of many types.

The water is dead, a dull grey smear of liquid, edged with thick black oil and strewn with surrealistic debris. A paint pot nudges a baseball cap with the logo 'Surf's Up!'. A plastic bag of garbage bobs in the oil beside surprisingly recognisable underwear and a dead fish surges very slowly in and out of an old barrel. There's an old ship's wheelhouse set up as a watchman's hut and several derelict vessels being used as houseboats (perhaps hovel boats would describe them more accurately). Incredibly rotten mooring lines loop between them or hang uselessly from steel bollards which are themselves barely secure on the crumbling wharf edge. A strangely fascinating place where the earth peacefully re-absorbs the complex sea going structures into which man poured so much energy, ingenuity and so many hard won materials.

Such 'rotten rows' exist in many ports and invariably have a life quite separate, quite remote from the rest of their cities or towns. The denizens of these maritime junkyards are Hemingway and Dickens characters. Tramps, down-and-outs, if you should meet them outside their dock gates, but inside they are 'Cap'n Mac' or 'Skipper Jim', men with wonderful stories to tell and sometimes a little distilled wisdom to impart, left in a forgotten bottle in their grog lockers. Here, just such a 'Cap'n Mac' in shiny-kneed trousers and torn shirt, is carefully sorting a stack of bronze portholes and deadlights on the deck of his fantastically decrepit barge. Treasure to be recycled, no doubt; to grace another generation's vessels and to return in due course to another 'Cap'n Mac's' hoard.

Old Montevideo is delightful. Crumbling and decrepit but delightful. There are courtyards glimpsed through big ornately carved wooden doors: balconies, shuttered windows at siesta time which open to frame family gatherings in the cool of the evening; and old tiled roofs of warm texture and colour. There are many little treed squares, each one with striking statuary and the shops are open fronted and inviting, often spilling their wares onto the street. Cafes and bars are scattered throughout the warren of narrow roads. It seems a pity that cars are allowed to pollute and crowd these thoroughfares designed for people and horses. There is probably little of the original town left, which would date from about 1730, but a few buildings bear early 19th century dates, and some of the cool courtyards will have witnessed the games of six or seven generations of children.

The new city, considerably further from the ship, seems to have two distinct styles. There are high-rise buildings; the same starchy characters you see strutting stiffly in Sydney or London, but there are big, fountained squares here too, with older, more ornate, less overbearing buildings which have a Spanish flavour. Artigas, the great patriot, who embodies the spirit of Uruguayan independence, presides magnificently on bronze horse back in one of these fine squares. His tomb lies below, guarded constantly by solemn, armed troops. Artigas actually failed to liberate the people from Spanish domination in his lifetime but fired and fuelled the determination which eventually resulted in nationhood. But Spain still dominates through language and style.

Around the squares are many pavement cafes where we enjoy the thick black coffee, the flamboyant menus, the quick waiter service, the unfamiliar tastes and the cheap, pleasant wine. Our lack of Spanish is not too disastrous. There is always someone about who can manage English or it is easy to second someone from another table. There is a friendly, helpful atmosphere on the footpath. There is fun to be had on the inside too. While enjoying an end-of-passage crew feast in a big restaurant, we can't help noticing that a nearby table houses another large group party; perhaps 15 ladies of all ages. Their common denominator eludes us. The guessing becomes a general, though furtive, topic of conversation. Computer operators, teachers, bank clerks, all the obvious possibilities are suggested but discarded. They are not outdoor types and the younger ones are not wearing fancy make-up or mod clothing.

'Retired prostitutes,' suggests one wag and, 'not retired' quickly follows. Perhaps it is a family reunion. We just can't pin it down. Finally I go across and explain our problem. They are delighted and break into laughter.

'You could have guessed all night without a chance of success', one explains in good English. 'We are archivists!'

'What? I had a vague idea that such people lived forever underground, wore bifocals, were bald and male!'

'No, no. They are all beautiful women as you can see', says one with an expansive gesture, causing more laughter.

'Well, what about us? Have a guess what we do. Three guesses!'

'Sailors', they laugh.

'Hell, is it that obvious?'

'Yes, you are tanned and weathered looking. We noticed as soon as you came in. You look like civilised pirates! How do you like Montevideo?'

'Great, and we'll drink a toast to the lovely lady archivists of this fine city'.

They accept the accolade happily and give us 'handsome sailors' and 'happy Christmas'. The incident is indicative of the easy, friendly atmosphere we find in Uruguay.

New Year's Eve in the port is wild. Firstly there is the joint party with 'Eye' which carries us to midnight when traditionally 16 bells are struck; eight from the oldest person on board to see the old year out, and eight from the youngest to usher in the new. Anne has just started proudly on hers when the port erupts with a deafening cacophany of ships' sirens and fireworks. Joel's eight bells are lost in the din. For 10 minutes the noise is tremendous and the last ship only runs out of compressed air 20 minutes into the new year. Hundreds of parachute flares drift over the harbour, while fireworks burst and cannon around the city. Then it's off to the 'Too Much', through streets alive with fire crackers, to work off all our festive season food on the dance floor. Mind you we will probably contract lung cancer from the thick smoky atmosphere! If anything the place is wilder than on our first visit and the wooden floor does actually give way in a couple of places. We tumble into a taxi about 0400 very happy in the knowledge that there will be no work onboard this day. The walk from the wharf gates is a tonic of wonderful fresh air and pale crescent moonlight after the awful turbid and ear-splitting cellar.

On January 2 we are scheduled to leave for Punta del Este, a man made harbour some 65 miles east of Montevideo. It is a large marina basically, with the town built on a sand spit. The Monte Carlo of Uruguay. There is some confusion about our departure. The weather deteriorates with the wind reaching gale force and Tiger and Tony disagree about whether to put to sea. We are steadily grinding the fenders to pieces lying alongside 'Eye' so we have to shift and in the end we decide that an overnight sail in rough conditions with a favourable wind is preferable to an uncomfortable night at anchor. A tug assists us off the berth and soon we are racing down the estuary under short canvas, scudding past the winking, heaving channel buoys and testing the helmsmanship of our new voyage crew and guests. The latter are two naval officers and the local ship chandler. They get a great sail. One of the new voyage crew, Charlotte, has sailed aboard previously, so there are only three greenhorns; Sarah, Nick and Ben, all Brits. It's a wild, wet night for their first sail.

We have an exciting time berthing in Punta del Este marina. The strong westerly of the night has given way to a lighter sou'wester with clear skies by early morning but it is piping up again as we approach the harbour and as we edge around the boulder breakwater the crosswind has reached near gale force again. The scene inside is frightening. A tremendous congestion of pleasure craft in marinas berths and on moorings leaves just a narrow lane for our passage and it seems scarcely possible that we can reach our allotted berth without colliding with or fouling something. Tony is masterful as usual, but this time there is yelling and cursing, especially aimed at the two marina launches which try to swing us the wrong way. As we make the 90 degree turn required to come alongside we miss the yacht moored to port by about three feet and the old engine shakes and shudders and belches black exhaust smoke in emergency full-astern mode as the quickly rising wind blows us down on a luxury launch at the end of the berth. By the time we are finally secure, with many extra mooring lines, Tony's head of steam has dropped below safety valve pressure, but a full gale is lashing spray high over the breakwater. There is definitely no room for another square rigger in here, so it's as well 'Eye' is still in Montevideo.

She reports a full gale there and does not finally make it to an anchorage behind a small island a mile from the marina, until the following day. She sends her people ashore by rubber dinghy and they look in amazement at our berth and its approaches.

Punta is a full-on town. At 0200 we sit at a sidewalk cafe and take it all in. The street is thronged. Buskers and shoe-shine boys work the tables, music spills from every shop, taxis weave through carefree strollers who greet each other with hugs and kisses, loud voices and expansive gestures. Beautiful women walk by with suave escorts and gangs of chattering, denim-clad teenagers swoop and swirl down the roadway. It's still all happening at 0300 and the restaurants and cafes are still serving meals. When do these people sleep? Come to think of it — when do we? Strangely there is no dance or disco in town. The nearest place is four miles along the beach and the beautiful Ximena, our guide, advises against it. The taxi fare is beyond us anyway.

At 1400 we are still taking it all in while we prepare the ship for an open day and the forthcoming sea passage. Big launches and yachts pass close by all day and on almost every deck are a species of female to gladden the heart and sear the eyeballs of any poor seaman. They are fantastic. Such slinky figures, bronzed flesh and beautiful complexions. The 'in' swimwear here is extremely tenuous, exposing wonderful brown buttocks, delicious smooth bellies, and leaving little of their tophamper to the imagination. Oh, la, la!

There are other memorable views. An extremely friendly and generous family offer a tour of the surrounding countryside. Five of us pile into the four-wheel-drive vehicle with Walter, Stella and son José for a six hour guided tour. Walter is an expert on the flora and fauna with Stella to translate, so we see and learn a great deal: vultures to hummingbirds, snakes to butterflies, old farmhouses to lighthouses and lakes to forests. This Maldonado district is very beautiful rolling country, much of it cleared to grassland for cattle, but there is wild dune country and forest too. There is a fine, big lake with waterfowl and stretches of beach for the public. Many of the roads we drive are unsurfaced but well maintained. The lasting impression is of a green, though summer-dry country, well stocked with wild and domesticated life, drowsing quietly under a hot sun, with too many abandoned farmsteads. We stop at one with plastered sun-bleached dwellings, stables and storage sheds around a well and the remains of a garden and orchard. The whole is shaded and sheltered by big old trees, now tangled with vines and figs run amok.

'Such farms are not now — how do you say — economic,' Stella explains. An old, sad story but there are some beneficiaries: the tangled garden is humming with bees and the swifts and pigeons nest in peace.

While in Montevideo we painted the topsides but now it is scrub and scour, polish and wash everywhere for a visit from Luis Alberto La Calle, the President of Uruguay. Diego and Andy have been busy again. It turns out to be a low key affair. He and a retinue of about eight simply walk down the jetty.

'Pearmissyon to com on bord capitan?'

He knows something of ship's etiquette. We are suitably impressed. Our officers are all in white uniform and the rest of the ship's company in clean blue 'Søren Larsen' shirts but there is no official inspection. Gifts are exchanged, short speeches made on the foredeck and they all tour the ship with Tony. The President is perhaps 55; dark, thick and greying hair, casual clothes, clear eyes and relaxed manner. Definitely not the textbook South American military martinet. In fact he is only the second civilian president Uruguay has fielded for several decades. The group only stays aboard for 20 minutes and we are left with a wonderful array of food and drink prepared especially but scarcely touched. No problem!

Sailing day is hilarious. The time set is 0600 and all hands are up and about by 0530 downing cups of tea and preparing for departure. But where is John? And has anyone seen Andy? Oh, oh. Better have a head count. Sure enough John, Andy, Nigel and Sandy (now there's a surprise!) are all absent. The Old Man is getting ratty. His conversation is terse. At 0555 they appear at the far end of the jetty, arm in arm, and very merry. At precisely 0558 they jump aboard full of bonhomie and grinning from ear to ear.

'Mornin' all'. That's Andy.

Me — 'Where the hell have you been?'

Tony — 'Stand by fore and aft'.

John has the early signs of leglessness and is loud.

'We won a million dollars my friensh; a million dollars. Broke the bank. Fantashtic!'

'A million bucks! You can buy the beers for the rest of the trip John!'

'Well no — I mean a million peshos; but hell, ish a lot of cash.' (U.S. $400)

The story will have to wait. Right now Tony is agitating to cast off and get clear of the tangle of yachts while the morning calm lasts. We manouvre around the knuckle of the jetty using the D.O.T.I. boat and motor seaward to join 'Eye', which is just setting sail. We have to have a coffee break before the last of our canvas is hoisted, to settle the reprobates and prevent them falling about — mainly with laughter as they recount their casino story.

Their run of luck hadn't come until 0400 when the place was about to close down, thus enabling them to avoid the usual gambler's indescretion of not knowing when to stop. A few drinks on the way back, to celebrate, had sent the alcohol levels zooming and even Sandy, who is basically teetotal, had risen to the occasion.

'I gave her a double whiskey,' said Andy, 'and before I could ask ask what she'd have with it, she'd downed it in one!' He demonstrates vividly. 'Bloody hell, I'd hate to be with her when she really gets going!'

Sandy's face is still a match for the rising sun!

The topsail is hoisted to 'Whiskey Johnny' today. It's slower than our usual 'Haul Away' shanty but more suitable to today's energy levels.

> *If whiskey were a river and I could swim,*
> *Whiskey, Johnny!*
> *I'd stand on the bank and fall right in,*
> *Whiskey for me Johnny Oh!*
> *Oh, whiskey's gone to Sandy's head,*
> *whiskey, Johnny!*
> *There's a glint in her eye but she feels half dead!*
> *Whiskey for me Johnny Oh!*

When we finally get all the canvas on her and close with 'Eye'

as we set our course eastward we give them a very ragged version
of 'Spanish Ladies':

> *Farewell and adieu to you my Spanish Ladies,*
> *Farewell and adieu to you ladies of Spain;*
> *For we've received orders for to sail for old England,*
> *We bid you adieu 'til we see you again.*
> *We-e-e-e'll rant and we'll roar like true British sailors,*
> *We'll rant and we'll roar across the wide sea,*
> *Until we strike soundings in the Channel of old England;*
> *From Ushant to Scilly is thirty-five leagues.*

But there are no Spanish Ladies to hear us. Ximena came to say
a fond farewell to Marti, but she's long gone. Life in Punta is at its
lowest ebb at 0700.

CHAPTER FOURTEEN
The Worst Harbour in the World

Now Tristan da Cunha's the next on the list,
But it's so bloody small that it might well be missed;
We'll stand off and on, for the gales they do blow,
She's a Colchester Packet, O Lord let her go!

LAND HO! Fine on the port bow!'

I win the tot of rum again! It's a bright breezy day and we are running fast towards Tristan da Cunha, one of the world's most isolated islands. There are actually a group of three islands and we have just sighted 'Inaccessible', which lies 20 miles west south-west of Tristan itself. We pass close alongside its southern side marvelling at its precipitous cliffs and mantle of soft green vegetation: tussock and scrub.

Islands have a special fascination for me. I was born on an island, spent most of my life on mobile islands and now have my home on an island off the New Zealand coast. Mind you the surrounding water is the only common denominator. The Isle of Man had 50,000 people, my island home has a population of three. The former is over 300 square miles in extent and the latter 0.3. Tristan da Cunha is about 30 square miles. Nevertheless the sea approach lends a certain fabulous and intriguing air to all islands and their inhabitants are always a little foreign and special.

This time we've been 17 days from Punta del Este with a wide swing to the southward to find favourable winds which brought fog and drizzle with them. A reasonably steady run though, and everyone has settled to the new watch system with only five or six in each watch.

We shall be visiting many islands on this Atlantic passage but surely none will be more fabulous and intriguing than Tristan da Cunha rising 6800 feet into the very middle of the South Atlantic; 1900 miles from Cape Horn and over 2000 from Montevideo. Its sea cliffs rear as much as 2000 feet straight from the sea for much of its circumference. A rugged, wild place, about 6 miles in diameter, and for millenia the haunt of thousands upon thousands of sea birds, seals and penguins. Human settlement spans less than 200 years. Discoverd by, and named for, a Portugese admiral in 1506, it was not until 1811 that an attempt was made at settlement, by an American, in a failed bid to develop a private kingdom. A British soldier, William Glass, was the founder of the present community. A British garrison had been stationed on Tristan in 1816 to deter the French from using the island as a base from which to assay the release of Napoleon, exiled on St Helena some 1300 miles to the north. When the garrison was withdrawn a year later Glass, his 15 year old wife, and two stone masons elected to remain.

William had married Maria before arriving at Tristan. She was then 13 and in due course had 16 children on the island just to get the ball rolling. Their great, great, great grandchildren now dig their potato patch. In 1975 there were still only seven surnames on Tristan; two British, one Dutch, two American and two Italian, all barring Glass deriving from shipwrecked mariners who stayed. The distaff side counts British, Irish, South African, Portugese and St Helenan amongst its number and the latter almost certainly contains negro blood. So although there has been much intermarriage of close relatives, the stock is so varied that few hereditary problems have arisen. The population varied between 50 and 150 for much of the settlement's history but has now risen to 300.

For those early settlers the subsistence life was enlivened by frequent visits from passing sailing ships with whom they bartered for flour, sugar, timber and kerosene with potatoes and meat. Sheep and cattle have been on the island since garrison days. Later, in the early 20th century, when power driven ships displaced sail, Tristan became extremely isolated with only a rare ship visit because the ships no longer needed to follow a route which kept them in favourable wind patterns. At that time the islanders suffered considerable privations and when potato crops were poor they almost starved. It was a tough lifestyle on an island subject to violent squally winds, almost constant surf on the beaches and

Approaching Tristan da Cunha

TALLSHIP SØREN LARSEN

high rainfall. There is snow on the upper part of the mountain in winter although at the village the temperature is never below 5°C.

The history of Glass's settlement is dominated by two dramatic events. In 1885, 15 men were lost when a boat failed to return from a passing ship. This removed three-quarters of the adult male population of that time and precipitated a major upheaval in the close-knit community. Then, in 1961, the 'extinct' volcanic cone became active again with an eruption at the very edge of the village at the base of the cliff wall. After weeks of fear and growing concern the villagers left their island and were eventually settled in England. In the event the volcanic activity subsided almost from the day they left and after two years of exile most of them returned, but their enforced sojourn in a modern society has forever changed their community spirit and their unique form of gentle anarchy which had served them for 150 years.

Our approach from the south west prevents us seeing the settlement on the northern coast until we are a scant mile away,

167

but the stupendous cliffs deeply slashed with shadowed ravines hold our gaze, as do the huts on the low green plateau lying at the northern extreme of our view. These turn out to be at the potato growing area. The old, bare, cinder-cone peak of the island lifts symmetrically into an unusually clear blue sky. As the village slides into view so do two ships. This we did not expect. Both are at anchor but our curiosity as to their names and why they are here abruptly vanishes when I find 'Søren's' wheel suddenly jammed!

'All hands there, all hands on deck. Stand by to brace. Hands to the mainsheet'. The deck is a scene of frantic activity. 'John, Marti, rig the reef tackles to the tiller. Nigel give a hand; quick as you can, now.' Grant is desperately unbolting the inspection plate from the steering gear while Tony and I discuss methods of using the sails to steer. Fortunately we are on a course which will take us clear of the north western headland and on into deep water again bound for Africa. So long as she doesn't take a sheer in towards the land.

'James, flake the throat and peak halyards and set taut the lee lift. We may have to hand the main if she runs inshore.' James and the others jump to the task. There is adrenalin running.

'Bloody teeth stripped'. Grant's eyes are wide with surprise.

'Just disconnect it; get the crown wheel out,' urges Tony, *'get it out!'* We are passing through the anchorage now and Tony's eyes are everywhere, weighing all the possibilities.

'Get some sail off. T'gallant and course.' I'm along the deck in an instant with an eager gang. Grant prises and heaves and picks out broken bronze gear teeth.

'There she goes. Try the tackle now.' With two men on each four-fold tackle the tiller can be inched across either way.

'Jim, clew up the tops'ls and heave the headsails down. Grant, engine!' With Marti, John, Elmo and Nigel heaving and straining on those steering tackles we round into the wind as the diesel thumps into life, the mainsheet is rounded hand over hand and the headsails 'screel' down their stays. Tony stands by the useless wheel conducting the tiller gang and conning us back towards the other ships. The rest of us square up the rope spaghetti on deck, the result of our hurried sail handling.

Within an hour we are safely anchored about half a mile offshore and a mile from the village. Greatly relieved, we now have time to check on those ships. Well, one ship — 'Arctis Carrier' we read — a small general cargo ship under the Danish flag. The other vessel is a speck on the eastern horizon having moved off, unnoticed, while we were preoccupied.

'Sod's f***ing law at work that was,' expostulates Grant as he pulls the steering mechanism to bits. 'Whole flamin' ocean we cross and the bastard jams just when it matters most!'

'Could have been worse.' Marti always looks on the bright side. 'Could have happened as we sailed through the narrows at Port Stanley.' That's a sobering thought. Grant quickly figures out how to make the gear work again while avoiding the damaged teeth and it is together again and tested before the local policeman arrives to check our papers.

The most remote island settlement on earth, but here we have a uniformed policeman: a British 'bobby', chequered cap and all, not to mention a young lady representing customs and immigration. British bureaucracy has spread its net far and wide indeed.

The paper work is soon completed and we don't seem to have any Tristan undesirables aboard so Conrad Glass, the policeman, offers to take a 'shore party' with a return trip before sunset. The 20-foot, half-decked motor boat is busy towing a strange looking barge out to 'Arctis Carrier' but soon comes leaping and swerving across the six-foot swells. 'Søren' is pitching and rolling too, so transferring to the launch is a matter of timing and considerable agility. Anne and Margaret decide not to attempt it and since Tony needs to visit the Administrator I will remain aboard too, with most of the crew.

From our exposed anchorage the island prospect is daunting. There's white water all along the rocky shore and a small grey beach, which seems as if it should be sheltered, has big surf running up it. The wrecked hull of a yacht lies as a warning on another surf-pounded beach to the westward. Through the binoculars I watch the heavily loaded boat head for the surf. It stops some distance from the rocks, disappearing in each trough and shooting up on each roller; waiting. Suddenly it's going at full speed, straight in, rushing down the face of a wave. It seems suicidal. Just as suddenly it's gone. There must be a little cove of some sort but I'm damned if I can see it. A few minutes later I can see the little coloured figures straggling up a steep path to the plateau on which the village is built and the boat appears again and heads off for the other ship, so it too has survived.

Both wind and sea increase during the afternoon and will render boarding from that launch very dangerous, so we heave up and move closer inshore, motoring diagonally across the swells to give some shelter on one side without too much rolling. We rig all the fenders we have and the whole crew stands by. Again timing is vital. As the launch surges violently up against the fenders there's a momentary pause before it falls sickeningly back into the trough and at each such pause it is 'NOW!', and crew arms wrench the unfortunate aboard. In the boat the trick is to be balanced, ready for the leap with the craft gyrating and cavorting all the while. It's

The worst harbour in the world on a good day! Our ships anchored off. AUTHOR

a damn good job Anne and Margaret didn't go ashore. With only minor damage to the boat and some loss of topside paint on 'Søren', we head eastward with the fading light to look for shelter in the lee of the island. 'Arctis Carrier' heaves up too and we use her local knowledge to find a precarious anchorage. The wind comes in swirling gusts off the cliffs and our cable rumbles across the rocky bottom so we maintain three-crew anchor watches in case quick action is needed. We are only about a cable off the rocks and some of the squalls are vicious.

Two days later we are still weatherbound, together with 'Arctis Carrier', 'Eye', which arrived late that first evening, and 'Hecla', the other vessel we glimpsed during our steering gear pantomine. She is a large South African fishing vessel whose owners have fishing rights around Tristan. Her skipper Eugene chats in a wonderfully deep, gravelly South African patois to Eddie the supercargo on the other ship. They obviously know each other well.

'Ya, Eddie, it should be fine har. Dis vesterly, he can blow a few days yet.'

'Eugene, you old bastard, be a bit more cheerful. We've got one hundred tons to land still and we've been here six bloody weeks already, man.'

'Ya, Eddie; it's a hell of a place. You should be sittin' home weeks gone.' Deep chuckles. 'Whars them fine li'l sailin' ships comin' from Eddie?'

'They're flyin' the Red Duster Eugene, but they both come from Australia round that Cape Horn. Goin' through to Europe.'

'Zat so, zat so? Fine lookin' vessels Eddie. Harn't seen yorts like dem fo' yars. Skipper must be some kind millionar.' Eddie breaks into Afrikaans so we don't know his thoughts on that. But Eugene's voice is well worth listening to, even in Afrikaans. So sonorous and such chuckling.

We are not idle at the anchorage. Each day we land with difficulty on the beautiful stony beaches and explore. On every rocky ledge and outcrop behind the beach there are Rockhopper penguins, sometimes in scuffling competitive groups, sometimes alone. They

171

are all young birds waiting to finish moulting their fluffy grey down before taking to the sea. The groups push and scramble around, squawking at our approach, but the solo birds are so tame that we can touch them. Queer little fellows with their red eyes and weird yellow ear tufts, like exaggerated stage makeup.

Further up the steep gullies nesting skuas are unhappy at our intrusion. The big fierce, brown and white flecked birds swoop and churn the air noisily with fanned pinion feathers, just above our heads. It's impossible not to duck. Higher still some intrepid climbers find Yellow Nosed Mollymawks by the thousand, also with nests, but not in the least belligerent. We have seen these birds wheeling high against the green cliff faces, drifting noiselessly and without wing movement under the cloud driving over the immense escarpments. On early morning anchor watch I've seen these graceful members of the albatross family take to the air swooping down from their cliff roosts so that the sky seems alive with them.

There are fur seals amongst the tumbled rocks at almost every headland but they don't stay to be admired.

For those remaining on board there is excellent fishing. With a single baited hook each, Squizzy and Tisha squealingly haul in over 20 fish in half an hour while Nigel and Andy return with 25 crayfish in the same time. Fishing such as you usually only read about.

We have time for ship visiting too both on 'Eye' and 'Arctis Carrier'. High on the bridge of the 3000-ton cargo carrier we see our own ships, our homes, from a new perspective. They are so tiny, so insubstantial against the massive bulk of the island which, paradoxically, is itself such a tiny rock in the vast ocean. In fact it is difficult to see 'Eye' at all with her dark hull and tan canvas. In Eddie's formica-clad cabin we drink cold South African lager and exchange stories. Eddie, our V.H.F.correspondent, is a jovial, plump host and good raconteur, who has been employed by the Danes to oversee the cargo handling because he once lived on the island. With 2000 tons of cement and reinforcing steel in her wide holds, destined for a planned extension to the sea defences of Tristan's harbour, the ship has lain at anchor for over six weeks, working perhaps three days out of a week if the weather gods are kind; seeking shelter and relief from the incessant rolling whenever they are not. The cargo first arrived months ago, onboard a Yugoslav ship, but her master was so horrified at the conditions and the islander's methods that he refused to allow discharge to proceed and scuttled back to Cape Town. The easy-going Danes with an immense tradition of seafaring are much more philosophical about the situation.

On our first afternoon off the village I watched the drama of discharging 'Arctis Carrier'. The island barge is actually two very large, net covered rubber dinghies joined and covered with a wooden grating, the whole measuring perhaps 30 by 15 feet, and towed by the same 20-foot launch that we used. Alongside the ship it is secured with very long lines leading fore and aft, and necessarily allowing sufficient scope for the moments when the barge is down in a trough, and therefore slack when it's on a crest. The ship's crane lowers a net full of cement bags (perhaps two tons) over the side, gingerly, to a level just clear of the upward surge of the barge. At the ship's rail stands the most vital man, arm upraised, awaiting the right moment. The ship, anchored, uses engine and rudder to get across the sea to make some lee. Even so the barge surges and plunges and jerks at its lines while its life-jacketed crew hang on grimly at both ends.

The arm knifes down as the barge comes up and if the crane operator reacts quickly enough the slingload lands somewhere on the grating deck, the man at the rail trips the hook and the crane whips the lethal lump of metal back aboard. If all does not go according to plan the load lands off the edge, or partly so, or on one end, necessitating a hurried dive overboard for two islanders. With luck and determination two or three netloads are transferred, the barge is released and the mile tow to the harbour commences. It is not a method of cargo handling for the squeamish. Nor will it be found in any text book.

Later, I witness the other half of the proceedings, on shore. The harbour is an incredible 150 feet by 120 feet with a 30-foot entrance. On a good day three out of every five swells break and surf through that gap. An experienced islander stands high on the end of the western breakwater, arm held high and eyes on the sea. Consummately skillful eyes, perfected over six generations of scanning this sea. When his arm drops, the launch — waiting some 100 yards out — opens the throttle and charges at the gap without so much as a glance astern. As soon as the entrance is gained the launch turns sharply to starboard, jerking the ungainly barge in behind the breakwater before casting it off and engaging full astern power to avoid charging down the concrete end wall. The barge, meanwhile, richochets around the little basin until it can be tethered. I've never seen anything like it. A small hydraulic crane gets the net loads ashore and tractor-pulled trailers get them to a storage shed.

Prior to the 1961 eruptions, these tough people handled everything with their own boats from a 'good' beach just eastward of the settlement where they could launch and retrieve on about 100 days a year. When they returned in 1963, it was to find their beach completely obliterated by a lava flow. This was a major disaster and forced the decision to build the boat harbour. It was started in 1965 but the breakwaters have been repeatedly damaged, even smashed down by storm swells, to be rebuilt, strengthened and extended each time. Now the main bulwark, the north breakwater is 25 feet wide and 5 feet above high water while on the seaward side 2000 tons (yes, 2000!) of Dolosses have been dumped. These anchor-shaped reinforced concrete fabrications weigh over three tons each and are made on shore and then dumped, higgledy-piggledy, where they interlock and form a massive honeycomb of concrete which absorbs a great deal of the wave energy. There has been immense labour involved in building and maintaining what must surely be the world's smallest and worst harbour. The overall result of this effort is about 60 days a year on which they can get to sea. The materials from 'Arctis Carrier' will be used to attempt a seaward extension of the main breakwater. It will be a huge undertaking for the little community and is far from guaranteed to succeed. The Tristanites are an heroic breed.

It is on the fourth day that I learn all this detail for it is then that the weather permits a return to the anchorage off the harbour and lets us get ashore. 'Eye' is with us so several launch trips are necessary to land about 40 people. Each time the boat waits for the hand signal then rushes forward as if to destruction before the sharp turn and quick stop act. There is remarkably little surge actually alongside the concrete wall although there is a four foot lift at the ship, and every third wave breaks across the harbour mouth.

All the able-bodied men are down at the harbour assisting with the cargo. They reply politely to questions in strangely accented English but never proffer more than a minimum answer and rarely ask questions. When they turn to speak to each other it's like double Dutch. I pick out a few words and they are English but perhaps English as spoken in 1850 with a strong Cornish accent. It is amazingly foreign sounding and quite unintelligible.

The village, Edinburgh, is delightful. Tiny concrete surfaced roads run here and there all bounded by close-cropped turf, which is a source of food for the house cows which wander freely; fine looking beasts. Sharon, a milk-loving New Zealander is overjoyed. Every household has an abundance. The small, low houses seem to snuggle down out of the wind behind hedges, fences or stone walls. There are concrete block dwellings but most are rough stone and even the more recently built have stone gable ends. The few original style cottages are very picturesque, their gardens crowded with a mixture of wild flowers and old fashioned garden varieties; small flowered roses and hollyhocks; grasses and big grey rocks. Their white-washed stone walls are topped with roofs of thick layered flax (New Zealand flax in fact!) and crowned with a sod ridge. All are simple in design and Margaret reports that the interior of the 'modern' cottage into which she was invited was cosy, comfortable and homely. She was offered English tea in china cups with real milk. which totally made her day and lent a magical air to her visit. Here was a real piece of England established in a foreign sea.

Indeed Tristan is just that. It is run by an administrator appointed by the British Government and responsible to the Governor of St

Helena. He is assisted by an Island Council of eleven (of whom at least one must be a woman). Prior to 1963 the islanders attended to all their own needs and consistently followed the principle laid down by William Glass in 1816, that everyone should be equal, so that there was never a 'headman' as such. Each family took care of its own subsistence, had its own boat, its chosen potato patch and each man bartered seperately with passing ships, although traditionally they rowed out in a communal village lifeboat.

Imagine then this remote, wind swept island with an incredibly hardy, self-motivated, ingenious and mildly anarchic community, feeding , clothing and governing themselves for 150 years. Now walk with me up the little road to the Post Office and read the public noticeboard:

VEHICLE LICENCES TO BE PAID ON 4TH FEBRUARY

PLEASE PRODUCE YOUR WARRANT OF FITNESS

Upon enquiry I learn that there are five miles of road (rough track in fact), 20 tractors, two cars and one old-folks bus amongst the 300 population. The bureaucrats have even got their grasping hands on Tristan da Cunha.

Behind the village the rock-strewn sheep pastures rise steeply into nearly vertical ravines and thickly scrub-covered cliffs which today disappear into mist and swirling cloud. Our walking group is dwarfed by huge boulders which must have crashed from the mighty walls of grey rock. We traverse eastward above the village, crossing deeply water worn gullies and the odd fence until we can climb the 1961 volcanic cone. It is all raw, jumbled lava; black and russet, often loose and very tough on footwear. The small, irregular crater still has warm spots up here 600 feet above sea level. Looking down on Edinburgh, immediately below, I can understand the fear the people must have felt as they watched this extrusion grow from the cliff base, belching and rumbling and throwing out rocks and hot ash. It could have very destroyed the village in one outburst. Still could I suppose.

From up here the layout of the tiny village can be clearly seen and I spot a row of white boats on a clear stretch of green turf near the big building with the Union Jack flying. Fifteen minutes later I am lying on that turf peering up at the constructional details of one of the five upturned Tristan-built craft.

They are all similar, though not identical; about 28 feet long and unique in having two layers of painted canvas in place of planking. There is only one type of tree worthy of the name on Tristan, which is suitable for some of the framing and knees but cannot produce planks. Traditionally the boats were manhandled in and out of the water on a fairly steep surf bound beach, so they could not afford to be heavy. Canvas was the answer to both difficulties. As well as using them for fishing, the men made several trips to Nightingale Island, about 20 miles to the south, each year for guano and birds' eggs, so they had to be good sea boats of ample capacity and easily rowed or sailed. Here, beside the administrative building, they are upturned and lashed down against the frequent gales while the men are busy at the harbour. Since the fishing company has supplied small motor boats for the islanders' fishing exploits now, I have the distinct feeling that these immaculately maintained, hand-built boats may never be used in earnest again. A great pity.

A South African-based company not only pays for a fishing concession around the islands but pays the islanders for any crayfish brought to the processing plant they have set up near the village, which employs local labour and supplies electricity to the whole village. Shades of the 'Company Store'. The firm's two big ships, which normally take their crays from around Nightingale and Inaccessible can, and do, take up to six passengers on their journeys to and from Cape Town. The Tristaners no longer hold their fate in their own hands.

By late afternoon eveyone is back aboard. While the diesel-powered windlass gets into its stride, gaskets are cast off and when the anchor comes home we set and back the lower topsail and headsails and swing offshore. John leads us in some mighty cheers for the islanders and for the crew of 'Arctis Carrier' as we settle, with 'Eye', to a north-easterly course for St Helena, 1300 miles away. In the early dusk it's good to hear a shanty again as the upper topsail sways aloft. It's James in the lead this time:

Oh, when I was a little boy
Me mother used to tell me,
Way, haul away, we'll haul away Joe!
That if I didn't kiss the girls
Me lips would grow all mouldy,
Way, haul away, we'll haul away Joe!

King Louis was the King of France
Before the revol-u-shion,
Way, haul away, we'll haul away Joe!
But then 'e got 'is 'ead cut off
What spoiled 'is consti-tu-shion,
Way, haul away, we'll away Joe!
Way, haul away , we'll haul away together, t'me!
Way, haul away, we'll haul away Joe!

Coincidentally the Dane is weighing anchor too. Her last bags of cement went ashore this afternoon. After seven weeks they must be very pleased. Three ships together at the anchorage, sometimes four, has been unique for Tristan, but tomorrow the islanders will once more have their little kingdom to themselves. No doubt there will be work out at the potato patches if it's a fine day. The cargo handling and work at the worst harbour in the world has kept them from the land too long.

Tristan da Cunha bids us farewell with a rare and fabulous display of lenticular cumulus cloud hovering like a huge spacecraft in the setting sun. It is the child of powerful winds swirling away from that high, lonely South Atlantic peak.

CHAPTER FIFTEEN

Napoleon's Isle

St Helena's a dot on the chart, so they say,
But we'll find it and anchor in old Jamestown Bay,
To the steps we will leap and to Ann's place we'll go,
She's a Colchester Packet, O Lord let her go!

THE MID-ATLANTIC RIDGE curves through the ocean like a great sea serpent with its head above water in Iceland at 64° north, its tail at Bouvet island at 55° south, and humps breaking the surface at the Azores, St Paul Rocks, Ascension Island, St Helena and Tristan da Cunha. Our voyage will track this mighty sweep so St Helena will be our next anchorage.

We see the island first from about 30 miles, black and crouching under a heavy woollen cloud cap. The usual excitement that accompanies a landfall runs through the ship as minds begin to dwell on shore delights: telephones, leg-stretching walks, even hairdressers and perhaps, in this case, English beer. It is interesting how the appearance of land seems to urge people out of the calm routine and mutually supportive habits of shipboard life and into much more aggressive and self-seeking behaviour.

St Helena has an interesting history most notably as the place of Napoleon Bonaparte's captivity after his defeat at the Battle of Waterloo although this is not, in fact, the most significant episode in the island's fortunes. Discovered in 1502 by Joao da Nova Castella, it is unusual in having had a single inhabitant for a big chunk of the 17th century. This man, Lopez, was returning to Portugal from India, in disgrace for having taken an Indian bride. When the ship anchored at the verdant island of St Helena, to take on fresh water, he asked to be left behind rather than face the humiliation and shame in Portugal. Lopez became the Atlantic's Crusoe. He turned to horticulture and in the equitable and moist climate his labour bore fruit: literally. Ships calling for water began to bring plants and seeds for the exile and the bays on the western side became wonderful orchards of tropical fruit and citrus. There were stands of native ebony trees too, and a rich flora, although the goats landed in 1502 were making inroads on the understorey.

Upon the death of Lopez, the British East India Company decided to make the island a victualling and watering stop for its fleet of merchant ships plying between England and the East via the Cape of Good Hope. A thriving settlement grew, with traders and craftsman to serve and repair the ships; entrepreneurs and prostitutes to entice and gratify the crews. Jamestown developed, in a steep-sided, heavily forested valley sheltered from the prevailing south east tradewinds and boasting the best anchorage. The Dutch and the Spanish coveted this productive island too, so the British fortified it strongly with guns high on the cliffs commanding the anchorage, and barrier walls across other beaches where landings might be effected. Hundreds of troops were required to man these fortifications.

The island began to suffer from the influx of people. Trees were cut to clear the land for farming, for firewood and construction. A lucrative trade developed in goat leather, which stopped the depredations of the creatures but at a dreadful cost. The skins had to be cured and tanned and to this end the bark of the ebony trees fell victim. The forest was wiped out and the coastal valleys reduced to barren volcanic rubble. Today those steep valley sides harbour nothing but a few cacti-like plants.

But we are not ashore on this rugged island yet. Landing is a small adventure. The island is subject to what are locally known as 'rollers'. These are very long, low swell waves which on approaching the coast build into surf waves of 6-15 feet, rendering the anchorages dangerous and landing difficult and hazardous. Depressions, passing irregularly across both north and south Atlantics at about latitude 50°S, generate these waves so they travel immense distances and occur at unpredictable intervals. It is vital to anchor outside the line where these rollers build into dangerous surf; which means half-a-mile offshore.

Nowadays, landing can be effected most of the time, at a set of steps cunningly built into the end of a stone and concrete wharf, just where a tiny cove has been scoured from the cliffs on the north side of the bay.

Above the steps, lengths of rope hang from a steel bar set into the concrete each side. When your boat gets within a couple of feet of the steps you leap for a rope and swing onshore. The locals perform nonchalantly of course, and the boatmen calmly bring their craft within inches of destruction at each approach. Our efforts with the rubber dinghy are lubberly by comparison and the surge sometimes carries it, plus its occupants, bodily up the steps. But the surge at these special steps is tiny compared to what is happening on the main beach some 200 yards away. There the rollers are powering up the beach to smash into plumes of spray against a massive curved sea wall, hurling boulders in the process. Landing on the open beach in earlier days must have been extremely difficult, and on many days quite impossible, I would think.

So now we are safely anchored and have made our leap ashore. A short walk past storage sheds and the Customs House set right into the overhanging — and awfully crumbly looking — cliff, brings us into the quaint old-fashioned town square, and between those awesome valley sides.

They slope at about 45 degrees, as evidenced by the 699 concrete steps which scale one side, with equal rise and tread. The original stone-built incline, which the steps have replaced, was used for hauling ordinance and stores to the Ladder Hill fort. It's an awful, gasping, leaden-legged endeavour to mount the steps — Jacob's Ladder — but you would have to be very phlegmatic not to want to have a go. The vista, when you can stop gasping for breath and summon the strength to turn around, is marvellous.

Jamestown lies packed in the valley bottom looking exactly as if the houses have lost their footing on the volcanic scree and gone slithering down into a chaotic jumble. Roofs cant at every angle with tiny lanes picking their way inbetween. 'Søren', 'Eye' and the few yachts and local craft are a scatter of toys on a deep blue carpet of sea fitted neatly into the angular, russet-walled bay. Tufts of tradewind cloud fade seaward down an endless sky while inland the barrenness is relieved by misty green peaks swathed and patchworked with trees. Close at hand is the old stone fort which

181

Jamestown, St Helena

commanded Jamestown Bay and which necessitated the construction of Jacob's Ladder. The soldiers would certainly be fit. I wonder if they descended like some children do as I stand watching. They spit on their hands, grasp the shiny metal handrails and launch themselves off the top step. Their feet barely tap each step as they whizz down, although they have to stop every so often to re-lubricate their palms. It takes them little more than a minute to become a pedestrian dot on the street below. I walk down the zig-zag vehicular road and take about 20 minutes — just a little longer than it took me to get up there via the steps. I am unreliably told that the record for the Jacob's Ladder climb is about six minutes. The holder must be a proponent of levitation.

On that road down I see my first St Helenan walls. Beautifully constructed cut stone walls about four feet high protecting the road edge, but when I peer over down the slope, the wall is 10 or 12 feet high on the outside. These amazing structures, scrawl up and around almost every island hillside. They were built by soldiers and prisoners who obviously had time on their hands. St Helena was garrisoned for 200 years and Boer War prisoners were interned here.

The local strain of humanity now is a rare vintage. African negroes brought here by the British as slaves and workers, British soldiers and traders, Boers, and crew from every kind of ship left progeny here, as did the scions of the British gentry who governed. A heady brew! Certainly they are a pleasant looking folk ranging from white through swarthy to pale brown, and very cordial and loquacious. Ann, the proprietress of the restaurant, reminds me of a sharp-witted, sharp-tongued, jovial West Indian huckster except for her pale skin. She banters throughout the crew dinner we arrange for both ships, which must have been a big night for her. There are few tourists since there is no airfield and the supply/passenger ship only calls every two months. There are a few visiting yachts, as there are everywhere now, but it is hard to imagine that Ann does a roaring trade.

Another enterprising local has a tour bus. What a vehicle! A 1926 Chevrolet charabanc. I suppose the dearth of tourists has something to do with its longevity. Certainly the terrain it covers is wearing for its ancient gear box and engine, but it never falters. Up hill and down dale it happily carries 15 of us, singing, waving, laughing and clicking off dozens of photographs. Its leather, innersprung bench seats complain and its fragile convertible canvas top, although present, is in tattered retirement folded around the rear end. The door and side panels are missing, but 'number 82' is resplendent in fresh British Racing Green and just the thing for a crew outing.

Inland, St Helena is beautiful, a verdant, moist, fruitful countryside scattered with small farms and tree plantations. It is a quiet, peaceful island interlaced with tidy little roads, where half the 5,000 population live in Jamestown, and other centres are tiny, one-store hamlets. There is no industry, no tourism, no commercial farming but, oddly, very little subsistence farming either. In this green fertile land we can only buy South African milk and eggs. Local production has been banned because of animal and bird diseases. What a crazy situation!

The British government pours in about £6 million every year to support this far flung dependency which used to be a thriving trading post and a major producer of flax for rope making. Synthetic fibres rendered flax redundant in the 1960's, since when the Phormium tenax (New Zealand Flax) has left its ordered ranks in fields and marched unchallenged over whole hillsides and now assaults the roads. There are gangs of government employees armed with machetes defending the 'highways'.

Our 'Chevy' tour takes us to Napoleon's residence of course. You cannot avoid the Emperor here although his sojourn on St Helena seems to have been rather dull in fact. Waterloo really seemed to take the wind from his sails. He did not burn midnight oil racking his brain with grand designs for recovering his earlier glory; no plots for his escape were hatched, no French fleet hazarded his recapture. Rather, he seems to have behaved like a dispirited squire of a country estate and slowly gone into decline, apparently abetted by arsenical poisoning from the wallpaper in his bedroom.

Longwood House and grounds now belong to the French government and are maintained as a museum. The gardens are attractive though rather wild and the interior of the two-storied, largely rebuilt, rambling dwelling is laid out much as it would have been when the great man died there.Only the main entrance rooms are splendid with tall, heavily draped windows, pillared doorways, fine big paintings and huge engravings in heavy frames and a bronze head of Napoleon, as death left him in 1821, lying impressively on a cool stone plinth. The rest is country farmhouse. Plain, rather sparsely furnished, with that too-silent, carefully arranged air that museums have. There are some interesting exhibits, like the two big world globes of his day, a collection of Napoleon crockery, another of medals and a kitchen laid out with the intriguing hardware of that era. but in the main it is not a happy or inspiring place.

From the British point of view St Helena was an ideal place in which to exile this 'jumped-up' European emperor but it must have cost them dearly. His oblivion was secured by a permanent and considerable garrison on the island, and others stationed on Ascension Island and Tristan da Cunha, with all the back up

'Longwood, Napoleon's house of exile, St Helena   AUTHOR

services required by this body of men stationed 4500 miles from London. Fortunately the island's fortifications needed only minor upgrading as 'John Company' had seen to all that 100 years earlier. Fortunate, too, that their captive only lived another six years.

Napoleon's tomb is solemn, even opressive. From the road we walked down a grassy track into a damp, green, heavily treed little valley to peer through mossy, cast iron railings at a big, plain slab of lichen-mottled stone. As if to make doubly sure the spirit of French dominance would have no chance to resurrect, the emperor was interred in no less than four coffins under this ton or two of stone. Now, in fact, his remains lie in Paris so this slab, these railings, mark only a place he chose for his tomb. It is a beautiful but obscure spot, buried in forest and seeing no far horizon, no wide vistas. Perhaps this reflects the state of his mind as he eked out his last few years on St Helena.

On down the tiny, twisty road we drive, singing to dispell the tomb's rather depressive mood, waving to the flax slashers, chattering to our jovial driver. A sharp turn into a shady side road brings us to the Governor's residence. A Georgian pile describes

185

it I suppose. Impressive in its bulk and four-square solidity but not pleasing, definitely not beautiful. Later, Tony and Tiger were graciously entertained at this hill residence and reported the interior much more charming than its outward face.

The grounds contain something impressive in bulk and solidity too, and of doubtful beauty: three very large, very old tortoises. One is reputed to be over 200 years old and was here with Bonaparte. This exile is from the Seychelles, and with more of a grasp on life. The totoises are incredible creatures. The hugely thick shell, perhaps three feet across, cover an immensely wrinkled, aged body which moves so ponderously that a turn of its reptilian beaked head, or the movement of one scaly and horny leg, seems to require a decision taken by a panel of judges. Awed, we wait minutes for this undying creature to move its own length through the grass. I suspect they have spent the 200 years checking the perimeter of their two acre compound for escape routes; they are probably on their third or fourth circuit by now.

The Chevy accomplishes the winding descent to Jamestown without problem and we adjourn to a local hostelry to slake our

Aboard the 1926 Chevy charabanc, St Helena AUTHOR

dusty and strained vocal chords on a sample of local brew. We declare it fit for a second glass. Upstairs we are shown a games room, a meeting room, built from ships' timbers and spars, some of the latter still in the round and complete with iron fittings. Everything is beautifully preserved and cared for.

The town is a strange combination of substantial English village and New Zealand clapboard and corrugated iron back-country town; of creeper-covered stone buildings housing government departments and verandahed wooden pubs where you would expect to find horses hitched to the rails. There is a small supermarket, 1970 style, and shops where window displays have not been changed for years. Jamestown is undoubtedly pleasant and the people welcoming, but these incredibly steep valley sides are disturbing, like a frame too heavy and ugly for its picture.

Back on board we find the day's standby crew bubbling with excitement. The day's work list lies forgotten, A huge whale shark has been in the anchorage and proved so docile and even friendly that half a dozen people have been in the water with it, even ridden on its back. Consensus has it at 35 feet long and photographs later confirm it. Physical contact with this massive fish has really set people alight and they talk and talk. James is so excited that he cannot remain in one place for more than a second or two. I suppose it is exciting to be bunted aside by the head of a whale shark with a cavernous maw some three feet wide. I would call it terrifying, but strangely no one was in the least terrified. There have been a pair of manta rays around the ship too, about 10 feet across, so its been a remarkable day for fish.

St Helena is the scene of a minor mutiny aboard 'Søren'. It's a one man affair but causes quite a stir nevertheless. It is a standing practice in port that permanent crew are split for time off. Half remain aboard at any time to continue with ship maintenance and for any emergency that may occur. At night a watchman is detailed who must stay awake and make regular rounds. If the ship is in an exposed anchorage there are a minimum of three crew aboard at night. Here each crew member has been allocated one full day and one half day off but Garry suddenly informs me that he is going ashore during his working day. He feels it is ridiculous to work at non-urgent maintenance when we are visiting places we will probably never see again. Now Garry is a very bright, clear-headed young man and must know that this attitude will cost him his job on board, so I suspect he has already decided to leave in Lisbon. His intelligence and ability are an asset to 'Søren', and although he rarely donates any of his time off watch to the ship, which the rest of the crew do in large measure, he is reliable, consistent and of happy disposition. However, in a ship's crew teamwork is paramount. Everyone has some problem reconciling personal interest with 'team requirements', and Western philosophy generally places emphasis on the rights of the individual. But the responsibility of the individual is an equally important corollary which the youthful crew on 'Søren' seem to understand well. Garry must also understand that his action will be unfair on the day's remaining workers and cause much bad feeling. But this does not deter him any more than my wishes or advice do. When he returns in the evening Tony immediately tackles him and makes it clear that he will not be required after the ship reaches Lisbon. The crew, with the exception of Joel who is Garry's cabin mate and personal friend, are very clear that Garry's action was unreasonable and indefensible. Garry has been crew on 'Søren' for several voyages prior to this 'Homeward Round the Horn' venture, so understood fully the ship's work and safety ethic.

For the remainder of the voyage Garry worked normally and was treated without distinction but I think his dander was up because he formed a stupid relationship on board which inevitably led to more trouble, and was again due to undervaluing team necessities and wellbeing. The other party was equally to blame of course. I spent hours of my watch below trying to sort out the problem.

We leave Napoleon's Isle on February 11 with a fine south-east tradewind and the topsail is hoisted with a suitable verse of our favourite halyard shanty:

> *King Louis was the king of France*
> *Before the revol-u-shyon,*
> *But then he had his head cut off*
> *Which spoiled his constit-u-shyon*

There is in fact a shanty called 'Boney' which outlines Napoleon's life and it can be used for halyards:

> *Boney was a warr-i-or,*
> *Way-aye-yah*
> *A warr-i-or, a terr-i-or,*
> *Johnny Franswor.*

The short 'i' sounds are always pronounced as 'eye':

> *He was sent to El-ba*
> *Way-aye-yah*
> *Wisht he'd never bin there,*
> *Johnny Franswor.*
> *He whacked the Proosians squarely*
> *He beat the English nearly;*
> *'Twas on the plains of Waterloo,*
> *He met the boy who put 'im through;*
> *Boney went a cruz-aye-in*
> *Aboard the Billy Ruf-fye-in;*
> *They sent him into exile,*
> *He died on St Helena's Isle.*

Bonaparte was taken to St Helena on a British naval vessel called the 'Bellerophon', which the illiterate tars of the day converted to 'Billy Ruffian'. Franswor is Francois, the seaman's nickname for any Frenchman.

But I didn't know 'Boney' at the time of our departure, so the French connection through the revolution had to suffice. Singing continues around the wheel in the evening as the island fades with the gentle arrival of the friendly stars. The 'Eye', in close company, slowly develops into a marvellous silhouette against the dying light.

In the Atlantic

IAN HUTCHINSON

CHAPTER SIXTEEN

Flying Fish Days

We'll sail with the Trades up to Ascension Isle,
We'll have a cold beer at the old Club Exile,
Green turtles we'll see, to Green Mountain we'll go,
She's a Colchester Packet, O Lord let her go!

ST HELENA, and Ascension Island 750 miles further along the serpent's back, are firmly in the south-east trade-wind belt all year round. The winds average about 15 knots and blow from between south-south-east and east for 18 days or more out of every 20, with fine warm weather the norm; so different from the Southern Ocean. Here the days are full of warmth and the sea is a gentle friend; no greys, mists or overcast skies, but rather a world of clear blues. The sky is scattered with candy-floss clouds and the sea with well-trained white horses; different creatures altogether from those wild, unruly stallions of the south. And here the sparkling sea is under-run by a lazy swell, happy to be spending its old age in warmer climes. Flying fish weather, sailors call it, for these are the latitudes where those curious fish abound.

Not long after leaving Tristan we saw the first ones; big at perhaps 15 inches long and skimming low and long, rising and falling with the swell, remoistening their wing membranes with a rapid shudder of the tail in a wave top and gliding on for a 100 yards and more. But here, at 15°S they are mostly much smaller and skitter away from our surging approach in gleaming showers. Often they tumble back after only a few yards in the air to reappear seconds later in another bird-like flock. The sea abounds with them. One of their predators, the dolphin fish, streaks along under the flying school knowing that their flying time is limited and a meal must surely come at the end of it. Fast, muscular fish these, with a prominent forehead and bright rainbow colours which go through amazing changes if you are lucky enough to hook one aboard. It's a shame to kill such scintillating beauty but they are excellent eating.

Elmo is our chief dispatcher. A fish on deck seems to bring out some primitive hunter instinct and his knife has the creature in steaks or fillets in quick time. Sharon, and many others, look on rather appalled, even frightened, at the butchery, but few ever refuse the good fresh food. No-one enjoys it more than Elmo though.

The 'trades' have been with us since about 28°S, almost a week before St Helena, and should carry us up over the equator. With the breeze abaft the beam almost continually, this is excellent and easy sailing allowing us to undertake a lot of maintenance on deck, some sail repairs and there's even time to laze in the sun a little. It's excellent weather for playing games with 'Eye' too. We have kept her in sight ever since leaving Tristan and although she is still dragging her weed-infested hull Tony and Tiger have determined to make this Atlantic leg a real sail in company. She's been carrying every stitch she can muster including a very effective topmast stuns'l, while we have been reducing sail as necessary. Often we sail in close company for hours; and I mean close. The distance we can throw a heaving line in fact, which is probably not more than 120 feet; less than a ship length.

On the day 'Søren' crosses her 1987 outward track to Australia, 'Eye' sends over a bottle of rum on a heaving line with which to celebrate. It is promptly despatched on the foredeck as an aperitif (with toasts to 'Eye' of course) to the special champagne in the evening. With the rum we especially congratulate the people who have circumnavigated: Tony, Andy, John, Tisha, Margaret and Anne. Anne responds and continues with a detailed and very moving reminisence of the loss overboard of Henrick Nielsen, the Mate of 'Anna Kristina', which was one of the outward fleet. It happened close to our present position. Anne recalls and recounts the incident so well. Never at a loss for a word, she has a flair for descriptive language. She's great. So our little celebration ends on a rather sombre note and everyonegoes to lunch subdued.

The evening party has the theme 'Naughty and Nautical' (Andy is the designer-in-chief of such themes) so there is a rare mixture of uniforms and bare flesh. Margaret (naughty!) who only ever drinks champagne, has a wonderful evening and turns in very

'Søren Larsen' and 'Eye of the Wind' sailing in company.   TALLSHIP SØREN LARSEN

happy after we've sung for her both 'Colchester Packet' and 'The Søren Larsen Song'. Anne (also naughty!) is in fine form too but perhaps John outstrips the naughty contingent in having the most flimsy wardrobe and he suffers at the hands of the girls, led by whacky Charlotte, who seem to want to outstrip him in turn. Tony has a very relaxed evening too with many an anecdote and many a song. His night orders look as if they were written by a stranger. Well...you don't complete a world circumnavigation in a square rigger every day.

The heaving line is used again on my birthday. This time I send a bottle to 'Eye' so that they can toast me, which they do immediately and noisily. Their singing is not up to our standard but 'Happy Birthday' yelled across 200 feet of tradewind is certainly unique. The whole birthday is in fact. I should be on the forenoon watch but I am forcefully torn from my bunk at 0730 by five 'Hawaiian maidens' (Sharon, Sandy, Gabrielle, Sarah and Tisha) suitably and alluringly attired, who bedeck me with plastic flowers (filched in Sydney during that flower festival.) and deposit me in a hammock slung on the main deck. There I have to stay, or else. Breakfast is brought to me; books, drinks and pillows are produced at a word and Tony announces I am out of action for 24 hours. What a day, and it's rounded off with a beautiful cake iced with a sextant, and with a big card cunningly designed by Gabrielle and signed by everyone. Not just signed either. Here is Squizzy's effort:

> *To the love of my life*
> *The most wonderful person in*
> *The whole wide world.*
> *Handsome, charming, witty...*
> *From the most wonderful cook in*
> *The whole wide world.*
> *Beautiful, desirable, irresistible...!*

Andy's is clever and typically misspelt:

> *To J C — the one who sailes*
> *Not walks on water!*
> *Have a great year.*

There is a rhymer amongst us too:

> *There was a young man named Jim*
> *Who was so painfully thin,*
> *So we fed him right up*
> *Put rum in his cup*
> *And now he fits into his skin!*

This from someone who undoubtedly thought they suffered a weight problem so she shall remain anonymous. Perhaps Joel's effort is the most pithy and intriguing:

> *To Jim (a sound geezer)*
> *Only live fish swim upstream.*

My favourite starts:

> *To the cuddliest Mate around!*

Any decent sort of bucko mate would surely have a fit at that. The card is correctly annotated:

21 18' S 4 52' W
6/8ths cloud, baro 1016
Wind ESE 2
Fine and clear

And the corner is torn with the note:

'Happy Birthday from Ratty'.

Thereby hangs a 'tail' worth telling.

Ratty, whose proper name was 'Chafe', arrived aboard one night in Montevideo. The night watchman gave chase but that *Rattus norvegicus* knew a good ship when he saw it and signed on for the passage. A sensitive little creature, he went around garnering a living very quietly, just leaving the odd calling card here and there and daintily munching a corner from a bag of dried peas or apricots. But character will out and 'Chafe' was forward and cheeky at heart. He defiled the Captain's cabin. The hunt was on in earnest. John was in charge but badly hampered by the fact that we carried neither trap nor poison. But ingenuity we did carry in quantity so wicked rat guillotines and smashers were built, publicly tested, modified and improved. Grant's trap chopped the rat-like test carrot mercilessly but failed to so much as snag a whisker of the awful miscreant. In Jamestown we were reduced to buying poison which quickly produced results. But, hang on, the result was a minute creature not corresponding to the original description or subsequent sightings. Oh, oh, — this was an infant. Big trouble! Lockers were ransacked, the food store turned out, Tony's cabin searched — nothing. More poison produced more infants.

Then at 0330 today 'the' rat is seen running from deck to deckhouse and under a stove. 'Batten down; arm yourselves; we have her!' All access and exit is barred and slowly the deckhouse is taken to pieces, lockers emptied, refrigerators removed, cookers unbolted and lifted, deep freeze skewed out from the bulkhead, crockery compartments cleared. All the while three or four brave souls stand with belaying pins at the ready and jean-legs tied with twine. After more than an hour the deckhouse door is flung wide and six sweating gladiators gulp fresh air...no rat.

'Should be renamed bloody Houdini'. Nigel vents his frustrations.

It takes another hour to reconstruct the galley.

Eventually traps catch two more and six are poisoned including, finally, the cunning parent who had obviously been specifically looking for a well-stocked maternity ward when she descended from the wharf in Montevideo. Perhaps she was a water rat and knew like 'Ratty', from 'Wind in the Willows', that :

'There's nothing — absolutely nothing — half so much worth doing as simply messing about in boats!'

The ship sleeps easy again and normal maritime affairs occupy our days.

Until Tony's birthday, that is, which is also Valentine's day. We close with 'Eye' again and they serenade Tony at some length as we swoop along together at over six knots. On this occasion we do not resort to water balloons but with so much sailing in close company we are getting good practice and Gary, in particular, is getting pretty accurate. The 'Eye' has taken to asking for quarter on the pretext that they have wet varnish or paint on deck. Mostly true unfortunately. Today we leave them in peace as we have other revelries to attend to.

Tony's gift from the crew causes great amusement. Even Margaret's sense of humour is tickled past the point where she can maintain a stiff upper lip. Let me explain.

Once a week Tony and I make a thorough inspection of the ship, checking everything from deck leaks to galley stores and cabin hygiene. On one occasion, in the foc'sle, on James's bunk, we find a *Penthouse* magazine. After scanning it quickly (but thoroughly.) James is called to task with tongue in cheek. He's a bit embarrassed but claims it's all to do with his art; figure drawing, anatomy and all that. There is much amusement at his expense, especially from the other foc'sle occupants. Tony threatens to confiscate the magazine but James destroys it instead. He cuts up all the pictures into odd segments; a breast, face, arm, crotch and so on and packs them loosely into a large gin bottle, making a sort of voyeur's kaleidescope. When Tony is presented with this as a wrapped gift with a speech from James in a serious vein he assumes it's a bottle of spirits and unwraps it to check. Strange;

Close engagement: a catapult lined up on 'Eye of the Wind'   IAN HUTCHINSON

what the hell is it? He holds it up and shakes it...the perfect reaction. He can't resist turning and shaking again and again until it dawns on him what it is. Meanwhile our mirth is painful and James's is an agony.

James has scarcely featured in the narrative as yet, but he is an important crew member. He's the Australian joker in our deck. A young man torn with conflicting desires and emotions; troubled with a lack of time to properly pursue his talents; graphic art, music and sailorising. There has to be time for the female of the species too. The net result of these conflicts is a chameleon; wild colonial boy, circus clown, balladier, budding Picasso and Lothario separately and in amazing combinations. Perhaps it is the intensity of the facets in his character that is unusual. Certainly they all have outlets onboard.

Although there are several crew with instruments; guitar, clarinet and mouth-organ, James is undoubtedly the ship's musician. He happily plays his guitar, and sings, whenever opportunity affords and he is always eager to involve the rest of us. His watchmates get serenaded, or chivvied into singing shanties or rounds on quiet evenings and his flamboyant renderings of 'pop' songs like 'Gloria' (G-L-O-R-I-A, GLOR...RIA) complete with melodramatic body language and violent guitar twanging are popular party numbers.

On this Atlantic leg he spends wonderful hours with Nick who is a professional guitarist, songwriter and singer. They juggle old songs into new forms, scribble down new ideas, work up duets and frequently perform for an audience.

Similarly Gabrielle has bolstered his artistic talents. Their art is not similar but more of James's precious hours off watch are spent pouring over projects, discussing techniques, learning and teaching. The two develop a close relationship based on their mutual concern for artistic and philosophical aspects of life, and I'm sure they both gain from it. James left art school in Sydney to make this unique voyage and did so with many misgivings and after much heart searching, both of which return to plague him but I'm sure he will come to see the voyage as an invaluable source of inspiration. His sketch books are full of strange views of, and from, the ship. The rest of the crew, Tony included, are often irritated to see James, sketchbook in hand, while the rest of us are hoisting sail or scrubbing decks, but I'm inclined to let him draw unless I feel the extra pair of hands is vital. His efforts have sometimes resulted in cards, posters and tee-shirt designs which are very much a part of the ship's advertising so James's art has a very practical side to it also.

His clownish acts are mostly turned on at parties, especially theme parties. He will ransack the ship for materials to make suitable attire for a dashing (and usually late) entry as a madhatter or French cyclist (including bicycle) or a yelling, cutlass-swinging pirate complete with blackened face, torn trousers and so on. Heaps of effort, heaps of ideas, heaps of extroversion. There are others with equally clever 'get-ups' (particularly Tony) but they rarely act their parts with the vigour and élan of James. On second thoughts perhaps James only surpasses in vigour. I can recall John rigging himself up as the 'Cheshire Cat' so effectively that he had me open-mouthed. He actually purred. Cath, Darryl and Nigel as angels were pretty amazing too.

James   PHOTO: IAN HUTCHINSON

James finds outlets for his 'colonial boy' aspirations through his penchant for the poems of Banjo Paterson and the writings of Norman Lindsay. His recitation of Paterson's 'The Man from Ironbark' is enthralling. The rough Australian accent is second nature to him, his expressive eyes roll and flash under a wide brimmed, flat-topped Australian bush hat and his large nose and shadowed chin add to the gruff, unsophisticated rendition:

> *It was a man from Ironbark as struck the Sydney town,*
> *He wandered over street and park, he wandered up and down.*
> *He loitered here, he loitered there, 'til he was like to drop,*
> *Until at last, in sheer despair he sought a barber's shop.*
> *" 'ere! Shave my beard and whiskers off, I'll be a man of mark,*
> *I'll go and do the Sydney toff up home in Ironbark."*

Then with an abrupt change of tone and a furtive look James tackles the barber's part:

> *The barber man was small and flash, as barbers mostly are,*
> *He wore a strike-your-fancy sash, he smoked a huge cigar.*
> *He was a humourist of note and keen at repartee,*
> *He laid the odds and kept a "tote", whatever that may be,*
> *And when he saw our friend arrive, he whispered "Here's a lark!*
> *Just watch me catch him all alive, this man from Ironbark."*

The barber's little joke goes wrong of course and James wades into the telling of the debacle in the same manner as the Ironbark character wades into the barber and his shop. I recommend you to the full poem but I recommend you find James to read it to you. His watch is often regaled with chapters of Lindsay's 'The Magic Pudding' too, and again James brings it to life with voices for each character.

Another notable facet of James's character is his inability to clothe himself satisfactorily. His watch mates lay odds on how many times in a watch he will add or subtract layers. It's frequently three or four.

At work he is meticulous. If you want a 'sailorising' job done properly and thoroughly James is your man but you musn't be in a hurry. If you need a lecture on sail handling James will tackle it in exemplary manner, but again give him plenty of time. A good keen man is our James and an asset to the ship.

Our games with 'Eye' develop considerably and even include swapping voyage crew for the day. Both ships heave to within a quarter mile. The windward one lowers her rubber dinghy which runs down with passengers while the ship drops down to leeward so that the dinghy has another downwind run to get home with the exchanged crew. Then it's brace the yards and ease the main sheet, and away we go with the 'trades' again. Other days we find that by sailing into the disturbed air under 'Eye's' lee quarter, we can hang there almost as if connected to her. We can only get past if we drop away about a quarter mile. Once past we can slowly forge ahead and cross her bows, then lower the t'gallant and drop back on her weather side until we are astern again. Sometimes we go through this manoeuvre near sunset so that both ships get a wonderful variety of photographic opportunities. 'Eye's' tan sails glow in the low reddening sun. It's great fun sailing in such close company. Sometimes, at night, we let 'Eye' sail almost out of sight ahead, then pile on canvas at daybreak to see how quickly we can catch her.

One morning watch we are closing on her from her weather quarter with a view to rounding under her stern. It's a fine clear day, moderate swell and about 15 knots of breeze. We get to within 200 yards and begin to brace as we come to the wind. Suddenly there's a shudder as if we've run into some small object. No — nothing to be seen, and we certainly haven't stopped or slowed down. Odd. A few minutes pass before the lookout comes aft:

'Er... there's a piece of chain hanging from the bowsprit.'

Not a very nautical description but clear nevertheless.

'Helm up — starboard — bear away', I yell at the helmsman, as I run forward. Sure enough the big chain bobstay is hanging from its fitting at the bowsprit end. Potentially, the bobstay carrying away is disastrous, because the whole fore and aft staying system for the masts depends upon this chain.

'Let's get most of the sail off her. Call all hands', I instruct as I dash back to the helm. 'Steady now — steer just so — keep the wind well astern'. The pressure of the wind from aft will help relieve tension in the forestays. The headsails are run down quickly. We get almost all sail off so that we can work over the bow. It's the big shackle joining the chain to the hull-fitting down at the waterline that has parted.

Nigel goes below to find a replacement in the bosun's store while we slack up all the outer head stays and unwind the big bottle screw under the bowsprit that tensions the bobstay. Another gang rigs ropes to haul the chain down to the hull-fitting and to take out the catenery. Action man John strips for the leading role while we hang a bosun's chair for him at water level. Fortunately it is not too cold because he gets a ducking each time the ship dips to the swell. With some juggling and gargled orders he gets the new shackle connected and we begin to set things taught again. All told it is a hectic hour or more and we are very lucky it happened in such quiet conditions. In wild weather we must surely have lost some of the rig. Inspection of the broken shackle shows that it had been cracked half through for some time. Tony and I shudder to think for how long. Suppose it had parted in the force 10 conditions before the Horn?

The bowsprit chain   IAN HUTCHINSON

We've kept 'Eye' informed of our manoeuvres and by now they are seven or eight miles ahead and it takes most of the day to catch her. A day of scribbling for Anne who writes up the mishap and repair in fine detail; a day of 'what ifs' for Tony and myself. We are both rather quiet.

Our good spirits soon return however, and the afternoon finds us clicking our fingers to Nick's daily guitar session. He practices at least an hour every day. Often James and he, sometimes Ben too, will play for hours. Folksie blues mainly, if it has to have a name, but they do shanties, traditional songs and some pop too. Nick's fingers on the frets are mesmeric and often I lose the song just totally absorbed visually.

He has another talent too; impersonation. Not so much specific individuals, but types and especially accents. It seems to be a natural talent or perhaps, like the guitar, it is so well practised as to have become second nature. It's hilarious to hear highly enunciated 'Indian' English roll of his tongue, or broad Yorkshire, Highland Scots or 'Dinkum' Australian. No accent seems beyond his tortured vocal chords. It's even funnier to watch the production of these wonderful sounds because Nick's rather colourless, stubbly face leaps into violent contortions which presumably help in the production of the sound effects. He is a wonderful entertainer and good on deck and aloft too.

Sarah, his wife, looks and sounds like the archetypal willowy 'dumb blonde' but she's actually a practising doctor and as bright as they come. Her voice and appearance are so persuasive though that I often react condescendingly even though I know she can propound her views on everything from medicine to education in a very clear-headed manner and has tackled navigation very successfully and quickly. Blonde — yes; dumb — no.

The discussion on education is a marathon running from dinner time to after midnight — well after. Elmo and I end up beseiged in a corner of the deckhouse defending our view that education has done as much harm as good. With its heavy reliance on the written word, logical thinking and the comparting of life into subjects, we argue education has done us a disservice by compromising, even destroying, our innate ability to see life as a whole and to act in a responsible way towards each other and our environment. Education has given us technology and a view of life which allows it to trample us to death. Education has divided the world so that the educated oppress the uneducated as if they are inferior beings. The opposition brings all manner of armaments to bear.

Grant: 'We'd all be bloody Abos mate, runnin' round eatin' witchety grubs!'

Gary: 'We'd be a pretty dumb lot without education I reckon. Surely it's the thing which has civilised the human race. We've done lots of things badly but surely that's our misuse of education, not education itself. As for separating people — how would we even learn other people's languages without education?'

Elmo booms in: 'Well little kids can learn languages before they can read or write.'

Gary: 'Yeh — well — maybe — but that's pretty basic stuff; a long way from politics or aerospace.'

Sarah: 'I reckon — I mean — it seems to me — that without education our brains would be hardly used. The intuitive part, the motor mechanisms, the ability to observe — they would be better developed but all the analytical ability, the huge potential for calculating and reasoning would be unused. Surely we should use all the brain's facilities.'

My turn: 'Trouble is, education has developed only the calculating side and taught us to be very suspicious of the other side. If it's not logical — throw it out. You guys have so much trouble learning where everything goes on the pin rails because you want to analyse it and force it to make sense to form a logical pattern. In fact your brain has the ability to handle the pin rail very adequately if its educational shackles are removed. You would then follow the ropes, discover their function and find why they are in that particular order; then you'd have it.'

Nick: 'Nah — nah. Just 'cos yer can read music doesn't mean the ability to play it is removed.'

Me: 'But maybe reduced. An artist friend of mine reckons the worst thing an artist can do is go to art school. Just think how good you'ld be on the guitar, man, if you were even less educated than you are!'

Nick: (pulling an imbecilic face) 'How do I get de-educated? Stay aboard here long enough I suppose!'

Sharon, who has only been listening for 10 minutes, puts in her practical pennyworth: 'You guys are nutty. We've got education, like it or not. All we can do is change the direction or content. It's all educated bloody talk to try to figure out whether we should have been educated or not. Get sensible. Anyway, you don't need a PhD to figure out it's time to turn in. G'night. See yer Elmo.'

'Ok, Li'l Darlin'. Sweet dreams. Now where were we?'

So it goes on with members of the watch occasionally sticking an oar in as they pass through on rounds or bustle in to make Milo (in which we also indulge but without pause). We get onto the pros and cons of compulsory education.

Squizzy: (making her point in heavily 'put on' Cockney) 'Wewl, if oi 'adn'a bin foeced t' gar t' schoow oi wouldin' a bin able t' speak proper would oi? Then yew lo' wouldon'a 'ad th' hadvantage o' my hopinions. Which his...(waiting for the laughter to subside)... which is: that education is vital. Once it got underway anyone without it was at a real disadvantage.'

It's another Cockney that brings all argument to an end.

Ben: 'Bleedin' education's driven yer all araand th' bend if yer arsk me. Need yer 'eads seein' to, sittin' 'ere at two in the flamin' mornin'.'

There are no converts of course, even after hours of argument, but perhaps we have all absorbed a point or two unthought of previously. It's good to air our intellects anyway; they are battened down most of the time with the tarpaulins of routine and attention to practical matters.

Another session, but at a sensible hour of the day, is devoted to metrics. This time there is a more evenly split camp. Gary, who is an aviator and builder, leads the metric team and surprisingly, Grant, the professional engineer is most vocal in defending the imperial system of measurment with myself as his second. We maintain that traditional systems grow from human needs and the

In the tropics, Elmo and Li'l Darlin' in the foc'sle.

A STUDY BY JAMES PARBERRY

'natural' units thus have a real connection with our bodies and surroundings. Metrics are easier, and particularly well adapted to electronic calculations but not necessarily 'better' for all that. Where's the fun in visiting foreign countries if you don't have to deal with odd currencies; dollars, pounds or ringgits. How boring to have no inches, acres or miles with their antique antecedents in 'ynce', 'oecer', 'mil' which have 'real' meanings; 'twelfth', 'field' and a 'thousand paces'. The metric proponents are all for speed, slickness and simplification and against 'illogical' measurements. I think they win the debate if only because their argument is more logical.

The fair wind brings us gently to Ascension Island, in late February, where we anchor in Clarence Bay off Georgetown, the capital and only centre of any size. Ascension is about the same size as Tristan da Cunha and also volcanic in origin, but that's where the similarity ends. Here there are over 50 miles of surfaced road, a two mile long runway, and over 1,000 inhabitants none of whom can call the place home. It is literally a pile of volcanic rubble and ash, absolutely barren except for the top few hundred feet of its highest peak, Green Mountain, where growth approximates a Phillipine jungle. Ascension is a communications centre. The stark landscape is rendered even more sterile and moonlike by the plethora of radio antennae, masts and domes which meet the eye at every turn. The BBC. are here; the USAF, NASA, RAF, GCHQ, Cable and Wireless; just about anyone in the West interested in transmitting or receiving world-wide or space communications. The runway is an emergency landing strip for the American Space Shuttle (never yet used I believe) as well as a refuelling stop for flights from Britain to the Falklands and from America to God knows where. A large tanker is permanently anchored off Georgetown to supply the airfield and refuel the large electric-generating plants, and as an emergency store should there be another Falklands naval battle. It was at Ascension that the British fleet assembled before their push to evict the Argentinians from those islands. The navy have nicknamed Ascension 'The Stone Frigate', although that dates from 1815 when the first garrison was stationed here by the navy, as a deterrent to any French attempt to rescue Napoleon on St Helena island.

Some 350 technicians and administrators tend the complex communications gadgetry, supported by about 700 St Helenan workers, all receiving the bulk of their life support from Britain or the U. S. A.

Green Mountain farm, up at 2700 feet in the rain bearing cloud, is fascinating. Grinding in low gear up the tortuous approach track, built originally for donkey transport, it seems the change from inhospitable volcanic debris with sparse dry scrub, to lush greenery, takes place in a climb of 100 feet. This impression is heightened by the view when you step out at the old stone farmhouse and stand at the battlemented wall. You seem to be in a new land; a cool, green cloudland floating above a scorched country which could only be the haunt of dragons; Tolkien's Frodo peering down on the awful Mordor.

The buildings, dated 1863, are surely the inspiration of a man of the English Cotswolds or from Buckinghamshire. A fine stone farm gateway, a bell and clock tower, mullioned windows, stables, pigsties, workers cottages and a big rambling farmhouse with flagstoned kitchen; all this set around a traditional farmyard which is now a fertile vegetable garden. Imported fruit, timber and ornamental trees are everywhere but the tropic air, or dragon's breath perhaps, have intruded so that everything has sprouted, climbed, straggled and burgeoned until the original inspiration and plan is swamped, almost buried, by a wild profusion of greenery. The remaining farm is obviously a shadow of its earlier self although it still supplies a few vegetables to Georgetown and the bizarrely named 'Two Boat Village' in the centre of the island. I have the impression that more energy is required now, to battle the encroaching jungle, than is recoverable from the productive land that remains. It is a wonderful place to wander amongst the trees, through cool rock archways or even down a dark miry tunnel joining farm buildings and grazing land. Such a relief from the dust, glare and oppressive dry heat among those cinder cones and the uncanny steel webs arranged to catch the silent messages pulsing over the Atlantic.

Another place in which to cool and refresh is the Exile Club overlooking Georgetown harbour. It is in the old British Army barracks from the expansive days of the 19th century so it has the grand spaciousness, open rafters and wide verandahs of that era. The beer is deliciously cool; the village crouches beyond the balcony, under the glare of the shadowless sun, and oddly empty. There are parking lots, kids' playground, swimming pool, shops, but no people. Siesta time seems to extend over most of the day. I wave to little groups from our ships who stride purposefully, and far too quickly, up the hill from the landing into town. They almost all end up on the verandah beside me, baffled by the silent town and oppressed by the heat. There is a Post Office and mail from England is delivered every week by the Falkland Island shuttle. There is another set of special stamps issued here in our honour so when the Post Office does open it sees a roaring trade.

The fecundity of Green Mountain is matched at sea level by the Green turtles which for millenia have used Ascension as a nursery. Each full moon between December and March, these large creatures arrive by the thousands from the wide reaches of the tropical Atlantic and appear miraculously out of the boiling surf to labouriously climb the sandy beaches and dig pits in the dry dunes, in which to deposit their eggs. It is awesome and heartwarming to sit in the moonlight and watch these 400-pound reptiles arrive from a 1000-mile unerring journey and bury their dozens of white eggs before lumbering back to their element and another year of unconcerned wandering. Only a few young turtles ever make it safely to the water when the hot sand hatches the eggs but at least, as adults, they are no longer in danger of appearing as turtle soup.

Ascension is barely 500 miles from the equator so both ships are 'up to the line' in less than four days still carrying light trade winds. The shellbacks (those of us who have been across before) make sure that Neptune does not miss our passing into his northern domain.

Anne makes a very regal and pompous King while Tony is a dreadfully salacious Queen complete with wig and balloon boobs which need constant attention. Four burly policemen, Elmo, John, Ian and Andy literally drag the unfortunates from their hiding places and they are thoroughly plastered with a mixture of flour, water and cochineal while those that fight hardest end up with strange haircuts. When they finally admit their sins and swear allegiance to Neptune they can join the police force in looking for the next victim. Nigel is hardest to locate. He is in the bilge tightly wedged among spare engine room oil drums under one of the heads where he sweats like a pig and crosses his fingers, every time he hears the telltale plish and trickle, that no-one will miss the bowl. I think he is glad to be discovered eventually. Gabrielle, Sandy and Sarah suffer the same ignominies as the men and are handled only a little less roughly. As prosecutor, in wig and gown, I escape most ot the melee until Sarah realises that I am not even wet, whereupon she promptly empties a jug of cochineal brew over my head.

'Contempt of court!', I roar, but to no avail. The Queen has had a boob pricked by this time and is squealing piteously while Neptune resolutely calls for the next victim. Finally it's a swim for all hands and a huge wash down party before we proceed to tackle the northern hemisphere, and we bolster our resolve with a good tot from the skipper. 'Eye' has her celebration lying about half a mile away but unfortunately Ross, the bosun, ends up with fourteen stitches in his scalp after diving overboard — straight into the bottom of their dinghy.

There is a final episode to our ceremony. Nigel, Grant, Marti and Garry decide to remove the evidence of their newly acquired status as shellbacks by having haircuts. Nigel and Grant end up shorn-headed while the other two settle for 'Mohican' styles. The lines of a shanty immediately spring to mind when they gather at the wheel for a photograph.

> *Twas on the quarterdeck where first I saw 'em,*
> *Such an ugly bunch I'd nivver seen before;*
> *There was a bum an' a stiff from every quarter,*
> *An' it made me poor ol' heart feel sick an' sore.*

Two hundred miles on we suddenly run out of the trades. Rain squalls drive in from every quarter. It's the doldrums.

CHAPTER SEVENTEEN
Portuguese Prospects

Its over the line to the bright Western Isles,
A starboard tack passage of three thousand miles;
The girls will be waitin' for Søren to show,
She's a Colchester Packet, O Lord let her go!

THE ROAD TO THE Western Isles (as seamen used to call the Azores) is a long one for us and mainly uphill. Some judicious motoring gets us clear of the squalls and calms of the doldrums but the trade winds in the northern hemisphere are out of the north-east quadrant so our northerly course to the islands will see us hard on the wind. Good 'flying fish' weather for the most part, but the days of sailing large are gone for a while. Now it's the fore tack close aboard and the helmsman's eye on the weather leech of the t'gallant rather than on the compass, and our foredeck is wet with spray as we drive our way up the hill.

Abreast the bulge of Africa the Sahara sand fills the air and dulls our vision: a pale ochre haze over 1000 miles of ocean. Imagine how much land is blown to sea by this gentle breeze off the land. Millions of tons every year?

I was once in a sand storm in the Red Sea and when the wind dropped there happened to be a solar eclipse. The combination produced a most singular violet gloom, almost as dark as night but eerie with it. A ship, passing half a mile off, was a ghost trailing its faint lights through a weird nether world. Had a sailing ship appeared I would have instantly believed in the 'Flying Dutchman'.

The haze clears slowly as we sail northwards over the next three or four days until, imperceptibly, the normal trade wind weather returns with its occasional showers and now a faintly detectable whiff of the cooler north. The sunbathers begin to search out sheltered spots rather than the open deck; shirts appear that have been at the bottom of the kitbag for months and James hurries with the final coats of paint on the 'Dudley Docker', which he

211

has been renovating on the run from Tristan. By 27°N we lose the steady breeze and the watches are full of sail handling and bracing to make the most of the more fickle breezes. Still we creep north and west until we are about 400 miles south-west of the islands where we pick up a southerly and can turn our bows to our destination with a fair wind.

Tony decides to make for Horta on the island of Faial, the westernmost of the main group making up this Portugese archipelago. The intention is to visit at least one other port before heading for Lisbon where he has organised for 'Søren' to be drydocked on or about April 1. He is more agitated these days. Drydocks are expensive, timing critical, arrangements complex. He works on lists of jobs to be tackled during our three weeks in Lisbon and his temper gets a little frayed. Perhaps we are all a bit scratchy after six months aboard together. Andy is to fly ahead from the Azores to tie up final dry-docking arrangements.

'Eye' is almost a week astern now, but since she is to follow us into the drydock her steadily decreasing speed is not a major problem. Except for John! Sylvia, one of the cooks on 'Eye' has taken a leap year opportunity and proposed to John. He is delighted. Now it's a case of absence makes the heart grow fonder. The odd radio call is all that they can manage and we never give him privacy for them of course. 'John and Sylvia' jokes are all the rage. The two became enamoured in Montevideo but I think the bells began to ring when Sylvia came aboard for a day during one of our mid-ocean crew swaps. Sylvia is a lovely, petite, soft-eyed Peruvian lady and John is a fine, handsome American whose more detailed attributes are set out in chapter three.

St Patrick's day arrives; green as the best turf and hilarious as the best of Irishmen. Cath, of the Cape Horn leg, has sent us an Irish flag and a packet of Irish shamrock from which we have raised one minute seedling over which everyone duly wishes. Breakfast, a -la-Andy-and-Ian, is horrendous with green everything: milk, butter, toast, bread and the ultimate horror — eggs! By the end of the day we are completely paranoid about the colour but wiser to the tune of dozens of Irish jokes. I shall resist the urge to pass them on but I will tell you John's story, which has a wonderful

Irish flavour, and is true.

He boarded an Aer Lingus flight from somewhere in southern England to Dublin and suffered the usual information ritual from the solo hostess as the engines warmed up. She finished the safety demonstration:

'Now to be sure an' it'll be a foine floight. Just relax now wit' niver a worry.' With that she walked to the door and disembarked.

What about the two Irishmen flying home from France in a four-engined plane? Oh, no — I promised to resist the impulse.

We get through our side-splitting day safely enough and no leprechauns or other wee folk invade or molest us. Perhaps you need to imbibe some genuine porter or Irish whiskey to meet up with them. We think a lot about our Irish Cath, and wish for her soft lilting voice and bright personality, but the tiny shamrock is not up to that much magic.

On another occasion Gabrielle turns on a bit of artistic magic though, using silhouette. One by one, she sits us in the library out against the ship's side with our heads up against a white panel (the front panel of an electric storage heater in fact) At a distance of aboout 10 feet she arranges a single electric light bulb and switches off all other lights. The result is a sharp silhouette of each head, around which she quickly draws in pencil. The next person is positioned a few inches along the panel and alternate profiles are eventually painted black. The result is stunning. Everyone fits onto three heater fronts which now form an intriguing and eye-catching record of the Atlantic leg crew. (What an amazing set of noses!) There may be nothing particularly dextrous about drawing silhouettes, perhaps, but they definitely create a little minor magic, nevertheless.

Gabrielle has an inner well of artistic spirit. When she draws from its waters it brightens her eye and firms her tread as well as guiding her pencil. Then she is a warm, gay person, busy and gregarious, keen to sing and haul and polish brass. But sometimes the well seems too deep, the rope too short, and a melancholy wraps her as she thirsts. Then she is quiet and withdrawn. Unfortunately the drawn water is sometimes spilled by clumsy folk who do not realise its properties and value. Sadly I have to number myself in that stumbling gang and one or two others kick the bucket rather violently. Like Margaret, Gabrielle has seafaring in her blood from a forbear who was master of the well-known and handsome wool-clipper 'Cromdale', which I wrote of earlier when discussing icebergs. This voyage is partly a search for a tangible link to that sterling seaman.

Ben, on the other hand, has no family seafarer in whose wake to sail and has never set foot on a ship before. But he did go to school for a while, with Joel, and his arrival on 'Søren's' deck in Montevideo is in large part due to that connection. At first Ben was a non-swimmer out of his depth, but now, as a dayworker, his feet are back on firm sand. He's a painter by trade so he has been put in charge of the paint locker and has Joel as his apprentice learning the finer points of handling paints, oils, varnishes, brushes and cleaning agents. Gradually Ben has grown less taciturn and his cockney humour has risen to the surface together with a talent for the guitar. By the time we sight the Azores he is enjoying himself, though I can't say he has the making of a sailor.

The 7700 foot volcanic cone on the island of Pico is our landfall and Margaret is prompted to be the first to see it (she is on lookout at the time) and thus win the traditional tot of rum — which she dislikes — so she gives it to me. The sharp peak sails above the clouds about 30 miles away so it is several hours later before we glimpse the lower land, strewn with buildings. At close quarters there are some surprises. Tiny fields, surrounded by dense hedges, give the hillsides a very geometrical air and the town of Horta looks like a film set for a Mediterranean epic: sun-washed colours, churches and a harbour transported from Italy or Greece.

Tony's choice of Horta is a happy one for it proves to be a most interesting town on a very beautiful island. The harbour is man made in the sense that a substantial stone and concrete breakwater encloses a bay which has natural protection only from the western quadrants. Inside this massive defense wall there is a commercial and fishing port at one end and a large marina for small craft at the other, behind yet another breakwater. As is fitting for our status we are berthed in the middle, at the custom's wharf, which

Horta Harbour   AUTHOR

happens to be very handy to town. Arrival formalities are quickly completed and the voyage crew are scouring the local shops within an hour of us berthing. It's the first time they have been able to walk ashore directly from the deck, since leaving Punta del Este over two months ago.

The wide esplanade, which runs the length of town, has narrow streets angling away up the slopes, their shops and houses crowding flush onto the narrow cobbled pavements. These have beautiful geometrical and animal designs in black let into the white cobbles; (they are setts actually since they are angular and flat topped rather than rounded). They are people streets but unfortunately and rudely taken over by large numbers of vehicles which lunge and thrust and park hard up against the buildings, forcing the pedestrians to take to the lethal road. Most shops seem locally oriented; tourism is muted.

Yachting is not. Hundreds of European and American sailors make their way here every summer and Horta's marina breakwater is world renowned for its pavement artistry. Each yacht leaves its mark in the form of a painting on the inside face of the breakwater

215

wall. It's quite a gallery and has overflowed onto· the walking surfaces. While admiring some striking designs left by Norwegian yachts I find myself standing on the mermaids and dolphins of a Frenchman's dreams and the portraits of a crew of four Danish girls. Some paintings are simply representations of the yacht, others of the crew, some are cartoons and the odd one is impressionistic; even surrealistic in one instance I saw. New Zealand is well represented including several vessels I know personally and in due course James adds a 'Søren' exhibit. In fact he is given a 'day off' to tackle it. The expectation is for a splendid full-sail representation of our brigantine blazoned in bright colours for everyone to trip over (it is on a large flag stone). You may imagine our amazement and Tony's dismay, when we return in the evening to find a grey/green sombre picture of huge waves with a tiny scudding sailing ship barely scraping into the picture in one corner. James is not weighed down with praise.

Meanwhile we have discovered 'Cafe Sport' set on a rise overlooking the old harbour and serving everything from beer to coffee, food to postcards, bus tours to bicycles and taxis. Peter, the proprietor accepts any kind of traveller's cheque, bank cards or cash (except Uruguayan pesos). The place is a sailor's delight. You can yarn on a bar stool, lounge in a sidewalk chair, or join the babble at the crowded inside tables, and you can order any drink under the sun, in almost any language. It's frequented by locals as well as yachtsmen and 'sailors'. The decor is anything-goes-nautical, from flags to models and brass lamps, pictures to tee-shirts and fishing buoys. You can spend an hour among the crowded bric-a-brac without even buying a drink if you like. In my first hour I met a woman author, three girls off a Dutch yacht (one of whom knows a friend of mine in Holland!) an Englishman I had last seen in New Zealand, Peter the owner, and an American lady looking for a man — any man! I have also been dragged to a table hosting eight 'Søren' crew and been invited to another at which two crew factions from a little topsail schooner are getting ready to fight out their differences. Quite a place this Cafe Sport. The final surprise lies upstairs accessed through a tiny corner door behind Peter's desk and only after some silver has crossed his palm.

A daughter guides us up a long flight of stairs and opens the door on a magnificent museum of scrimshaw.

Amongst scrimshanders Peter's collection is world-renowned. Certainly the display is both beautiful and inspiring with items ranging from a carved whale jaw bone, through the more usual decorated sperm whale teeth of the very finest workmanship, to whole ship models of ivory and trinkets of every description: letter openers, pastry cutters and amazingly intricate wool winders with expanding latticed arms. This museum alone is worth the visit to Horta.

But there is more. Peter arranges a car for an island tour, which takes us through green pastoral country dotted with white farmsteads and clustered valley villages; through woodlands and hamlets where old ladies and girls sit in windows fronting the road talking to passersby and where sombre men in small-brimmed trilbies talk business on the corners. On past lovely hedges of azaleas and rhododendrons and others of massed hydrangeas. This island (Faial) is famous for the latter which in the height of summer transform the landscape from green to blue. At the furthest west point we come to a desolate area of roofless cottages and grey sand and cinders. This is the devastation caused by the spectacular birth of a volcano in 1957. An ash and cinder island arose out of the steaming sea just half a mile off the extreme western end of Faial and grew, fitfully, to over 1000 feet in height and sveral square miles in extent. The local population was removed and just as well because several times the vent was breached by the sea giving rise to explosions of nuclear magnitude. Rocks and mud were hurled 2000 feet into the air and ash falls buried whole villages. The 100-foot Ponta dos Capelinhos lighthouse nearby was buried to half its height. Fortunately the whole process was witnessed by a vulcanologist and his photographic record is neatly and spectacularly displayed in a one-room museum by the roadside. The actual event must have been truly awesome.

The centre of Faial is dominated by an extinct volcano some 4500 feet high with a huge, luxuriantly vegetated crater almost a mile across and over 1200 feet deep. This is the upthrusting giant whose eruption many millenia ago formed the island.

On the return journey in late afternoon, we stop beside a lovely, 20-foot high statue of the Virgin in white marble on a hill overlooking the whole of Horta, and there, across the three-mile channel, the dark symmetrical cone of Pico pierces the cloud, touched by the setting sun. A dramatic moment to end a delightful day.

Pico from the heights above Horta, Azores. AUTHOR

I cannot leave Horta without returning to whaling. From the earliest days of oceanic whaling, in the 18th century, Azorean men were sought after as the best crew for the extremely hazardous and arduous task. The men from Horta were most favoured of all. Here a shore based industry thrived too, in the south-west facing bay across a narrow isthmus from Horta. From this Porto Pim the men rowed and sailed into the open Atlantic for the chase and towed the massive creatures home an unbelievable 5, 10 or 15 miles afterwards. No wonder they were considered the world's best oarsmen. Their boats developed into the most beautiful whaleboats ever; 30-feet long, slim, strong and swift. Whaling ceased about ten years ago so these lovely craft are no more (although I was told that there are still two in existence I could not locate them) but if the foot-long model I saw was a true representation of the real thing, then such boats would have been arguably the very finest open work boats ever built, anywhere.

Ponta Delgada, the other port we visit, on Sao Miguel Island, is almost 200 mile to the eastward. It is a much larger port, but again formed by a huge breakwater and backed by green, enticing hills. This is a bigger island too; some 40 miles by 10, but actively volcanic in common with all the spinal protuberances of our 'Atlantic serpent'. There are several crater lakes in the mountains and many thermal springs, some commercially captured, others in beautiful natural forest settings where we splash about happily with local families. Here, as in Faial, the country villages are almost medieaval in appearance and this impression is heightened by the numerous donkeys and horses. We meet old and young alike plodding by in wooden-wheeled donkey carts, on horseback, or simply walking from village to village. In the evening a horseman comes clattering at full gallop down the main street of Furnas with large milk churns slung either side, the rider nonchalantly riding side-saddle. A stirring sight but to the locals it is obviously unremarkable. Perhaps it is a unique method of butter churning. I also saw a milking system where the cows wandered to the roadside fence of their field to await their turn at a portable milking machine towed behind the farmer's little tractor. I guess in that way they can own a few cows without owning any farm buildings.

The Azoreans are physically, singularly colourless people of sallow complexion with dark, mysterious eyes; not flashing or smouldering like the Spanish, but intriguing rather. The Portugese settled the Western Isles in the 15th century and have been in unbroken control ever since. There were no indigenous people and the only non-Portugese in those early days were some Flemish folk who colonised a small part of Faial and whose separate culture still flourishes in their town: Flamengos. Throughout the countryside the older folk invariably wear dark clothing, oddly formal and unflattering. The girls, in somewhat brighter dress, all have wonderfully thick black or dark brown hair, usually worn long. The boys seem to have adopted the universal jeans.

If volcanic activity has shaped the landscape then religion has shaped the people. Everywhere there are churches and shrines, religious statuary and other marks of Christianity. The houses often have beautiful ceramic plaques above their doors in dedication to a saint. The fishing boats are similarly marked and named for a saint too. At Ribeira Grande on the northern coast of Sao Miguel the whole town is out of doors, bands are playing and the ornate Baroque church is prodigiously and spendidly decorated with flowers; all to celebrate the return of the town's young men who have been away at priest's school. Social life revolves around such religious festivals throughout the Azores. They are frequent, colourful and often date back centuries. Each one requires special clothing, food, music and rituals.

Another dominating factor in their island lives is the sea, of course. Like the mid-Pacific Hawaiian islanders, the Azorean men were sought after as excellent and reliable seamen, particularly on ships engaged in whaling or fishing. Boat handling in the Azores is learned in a vast playground — there's a 1,000 mile fetch in any direction — where good natural harbours are scarce. The result is strong, sturdy boats and men. On the harbour beaches the stout, well maintained fishing craft are still cared for by men who know their boats are more important than their houses. At Vila Franca do Campo (what wonderful names to the tongue) I find an eye-catching fleet of these sturdy craft, all hauled out on a stone ramp, bows to the land, in a tiny cove protected by the inevitable stone

Neat and tiny harbour at Vila Franca do Campo   AUTHOR

breakwater. Their equipment is neatly stowed, paint bright in and
out, names boldly painted on each bow: 'Sao Joao', 'Oriana-
Margarida', 'Sacadura'. Along an old stone wall above the harbour
a group of fishermen lean, looking seaward over their domain
with quiet Sunday eyes, seeing the sea, the breakers on the
entrance reef, and the sky as no one else can possibly see them.
Weathered faces and knarled hands, men grown to the sea. They
talk quietly among themselves and I long to understand. I would
love to return to the bright Western Isles with more time to study
their boats, to sit in Cafe Sport and to see the hydrangeas in bloom.
But a good west wind beckons, offering a fine sail to Lisbon.

> *To Lisboa town we will sail fast and free,*
> *We'll dock the old Søren and go on a spree;*
> *The port wine we'll sample, the tales they will flow;*
> *She's a Colchester Packet, O Lord let her go!*

Getting away from Punta Delgada proves somewhat difficult
however. Upon arrival we dropped an anchor to assist with
swinging the ship in the rather tight corner allotted to us between
the very root of the breakwater and a stone pier, and now when

we heave it up a bight of large chain comes with it plus some lengths of old snaky wire. The chain is very ancient but firmly secure at both ends somewhere so we have to pass a heavy rope around it, make fast both ends, drop the anchor clear, motor forward a little and heave up again while letting go the rope. Well, that's the theory, but the trouble is that in this instance the anchor comes up the second time foul of another big chain, so we have to go through the whole process again. Third time lucky. Not quite, as the anchor is foul with wire this time. Fortunately they are short pieces and easy to clear as we motor slowly seaward nearly half an hour later than intended.

We leave the Azores with a new hand in the form of a small, odd and turbulent character called Gonzalo, who is a journalist, son of a retired admiral of the Portugese navy and descendant of the famous 15th-century navigator Vasco da Gama. In return for a passage to Lisbon, 'Gonzo' will make sure we get publicity and he will liase for us with Portugese authorities, drydock officials and the like. In fact he proves to be almost a liability. Onboard he is unpredictable and drinks too much (although not much). Ashore, although immediately recognised by customs, police, mayors, editors, taxi drivers, bar tenders and various unsavoury characters, they all duck for cover at the first opportunity. We never do find the secret of his ability to make people melt away, but I suspect it is because no-one knows what the hell 'Gonzo' might do next.

In Lisbon he almost succeeds in killing Andy in a wild, drunken, city car escapade where their vehicle is finally abandoned in the middle of a city roundabout. The police take the keys but no charges are laid. It makes a great story but must have been hair-raising in reality.

The wind holds fair for the whole 900 mile run to Lisbon and we career into the River Tagus with a living gale to find a lousy sea in the tide-swept estuary and more shipping than we've seen in five months. The wide estuary is home to a very large and busy port capable of handling any ship afloat and offering the largest drydock in the world: which could accommodate a one million ton vessel – if there was such a thing.

Tony berths us competently and with his usual skill, in our awkward, allotted corner of the drydock company's area. We end up secured across the gate to a dock with a stone wall a few feet ahead and a big merchant ship overhanging our stern. Never mind, we're here and we've completed the last leg of our 'Homeward Round the Horn' journey, and what's more we've met the deadline for the drydock with two days to spare thanks to the brave west wind. Soon we assemble to thank and farewell our voyage crew. We try to lighten the moment by making fun of the time they've had onboard, but it is a sad day nevertheless, especially for the ones who have fallen in love with 'Søren' (or one of the crew). Even the redoubtable Margaret and Anne are leaving, although only for a couple of weeks. They'll be back before sailing day.

Anne and Margaret, the two circumnavigators   AUTHOR

Tony hands out voyage certificates: 8970 miles for those who joined in Montevideo; 17,772 for our long-haulers — Sandy, Gabrielle and Ian. Garry is leaving too, of course, and Grant has decided that a certain lady in New Zealand will benefit greatly from his presence in the role of bridegroom! Kitbags and boxes are manhandled onto the grimy dockside; the final hugs and handshakes; the last scramble over the bulwark; the final arm raised in salute.

The long haul from Australia to Europe is over. The ship has done us proud but now, for a while, the music of wind and sea will be usurped by the clamour and cacophony of dockyard and city.

CHAPTER EIGHTEEN

Lisbon

In Lisbon drydock we will scrub and we'll clean,
But by night in the pubs and the clubs we'll be seen,
The music'll be great and the girls won't say no.
She's a Colchester Packet, O Lord let her go!

LISBON IS FANTATASTIC, full of life, picturesque, and steeped in history. It's full of people places too; restaurants, bars, night clubs, discos, markets, cafes, art galleries, churches, small shops, parks and pedestrian squares full of lovely statuary. The traffic is diabolical, especially on the highway into town from the ship, but at least there are trams so you can avoid some of the mayhem. In the old part of the city these swaying wooden carriages creep up incredible slopes and around impossible corners tortoising the lower orders of humanity, including us, to a hundred destinations while the better-off bunny hop around the maze of narrow streets in their cars pretending to be hares. Why do cities allow their smaller streets and alleys to be clogged with vehicular traffic?

From the battlemented walls of the beautiful Castelo de Sao Jorge I look down on a sea of fairytale roofs; orange, red and buff, juggling and sliding into complex angles and corners, the tiles marching in unruly platoons across acre upon acre of city landscape. The crumbling castle walls surround cool green gardens with peacocks and lovely statues, old trees and ancient buildings. There is even a dark, mossy, willow-hung moat. Throughout the city there are fine buildings, inspiring statues, archways and ornate fountains. There are buildings lavishly faced with pictorial ceramic tiles and exceptional examples of the stone-mason's art at every turn. Even the warrens of the Alfama district have an architectural charm (which undoubtedly hides horrendous plumbing problems.) with glimpses of towers, domes and the wide river here and there between the clutter of angled walls and rippled tiles.

Amongst all this stalks a fascinating history, where Moors strut the winding cobbled alleys, crusaders swarm ashore on their way to the Holy Land and Phoenicians sell fabulous eastern wares at the river side. Vasco da Gama plots his daring voyages; Roman Visigoths and barbarians stride the hills. I haven't felt so good about a seaport for years. There is a feast here for the eye and soul of almost anyone.

For the ear too, there is music. Jazz; live, late night jazz — what a tonic. We wedge ourselves into a corner of the 'Hot Clube' cellar and let a mellow saxophone and trilling flute wash over us, or we dance at the 'Ritz' to Dixieland with a soaring, racing, liquid clarinet. Wonderful. There is other music too at the 'Kremlin', a wild disco cavern on the dock road where we sip outrageously expensive drinks and fling ourselves around amid the smoke and scintillating lights until our shirts stick to our backs. When our ears are beaten into submission we elbow our way out through leather jackets and spiky-haired girls, past the burly doormen and into the seething lane full of young folk, cars, motorbikes, hot-dog stalls and (no doubt) marijuana pushers. Along the dock road (Avenue of the 24th July as the city fathers have pompously and typically named it) a couple of blocks we thread into a tiny lane. It is cluttered with scaffolding, doors are chained, grimy windows peer onto blank walls, the cobbles shine from a million human feet and in dark corners there is refuse and urine, but this lane holds a treasure: the 'S.S.Club'.

When the doorman has eyed us through his peephole we are permitted to enter the tiny one-room bar (the front room of a house in fact) decked out in black and chrome with an amazingly well-stocked bar at one side and a corner fitted with sophisticated sound equipment. There are two bar girls, a waiter and a doorman running this place which can scarcely hold 20 people. The 'dance floor' is a crush for three couples. Some nights we are the only customers. How can such an establishment make ends meet? There are dozens, perhaps hundreds of such bars in Lisbon.

Two nights a week, after eleven, a rather gaunt, seductively attractive young woman sings here and it is she we come for (well, Marti has a fancy for one of the bar girls too.). Accompanied by a very clever and equally gaunt guitarist her incredibly rich, soulful

A happy crew arriving at Lisbon AUTHOR PHOTO

voice washes over us. It matters little that many of her songs are in rolling Portugese. The expression. the body language, the swelling and whispering notes are captivating and the guitarist weaves magic around her. We usually leave around three in the morning. The bar girls work from ten until the custom fades, six days a week; the money thus earned pays for their university courses. Amazing.

Mind you, we are leading much the same sort of life; working flat out all day in the dry dock, sleeping from seven to ten, when we gather in the deckhouse to decide on the night's adventure. We usually manage a couple of hours back in our bunks before the 0630 call for breakfast. It's a hard life but great fun and an occasional full night onboard seems to ensure full recovery. Marti snoozes for 10 minutes every coffee or meal break and is unstoppable. Tisha and Squizzy take every second night off, Joel staggers through many days in a haze, James is a breakfast Zombie, Andy's snoring becomes more and more abandoned and he dashes to morning appointments with yard managers or ship chandlers shrugging into a jacket, or buttoning his shirt as he runs down the wharf. His acumen and bonhomie never suffer though — only his cabin mate.

John, Nigel, Charlotte, Sandy, Ian and Nick all join our forays ashore from time to time but they are much more sensible about conserving their energies. Elmo and Sharon are saving money and energy for a trip inland.

Fortunately 'Søren's' underwater hull needs little attention other than the planned clean and repaint. The surveyor is happy with her condition too so we only have to work more than nine hours on a couple of days. The biggest single job is to scrape, sand and repaint the topsides and the biggest problem is the weather. For our first three days in Lisbon the rain just buckets down and Tony and I are getting worried. By the time the water blaster has cleaned the hull and we have the anchors and cables ranged in the dock bottom the weather clears and our remaining five days in dock are fine and clear. Our efforts are considerably boosted by Sandy, Charlotte, Ian and Nick who have offered to remain onboard and help. They are working like slaves, but without the whips. Charlotte and Sandy, in particular, are persistent and thorough at any task thrown at them.

We have also acquired a large and colouful helper in the form of 'Pinky' who has travelled from England to meet us. She is well known to Tony, Andy, John and Charlotte from the voyage out to Australia in 1987 and she is a legend to the rest of us. Pinky is large and ebullient and not given to doing things by halves. She is exceedingly generous and helpful, but you have to enjoy being bulldozed and railed at to appreciate her fully. Tony and I are both non-starters and I find her loud, theatrical manner disconcerting in the confines of the ship. However, she stays for about a week, living ashore; supplies us with quantities of chocolate, wine and local produce, and undertakes many useful tasks including endless galley duties. For me she performs a minor miracle for which I have been waiting for months: she manages to adjust the waistband of my favourite trousers which no other seamstress has dared to tackle because the said trousers are so devilishly constructed. At the end of a week Pinky offers a typically forthright ultimatum:

'Either you have me stay onboard or I take the afternoon train north'.

You can't make ultimatums to Tony so Pinky disappears leaving a large gap and an uncanny silence. A forthright and fun-loving lady and I wish I had been less negative towards her warm-hearted, albeit Bohemian ribaldry. By day my head was too busy with a hundred drydock tasks to admit the attention she needed and by night I was too busy trying to absorb Lisbon.

We line the dockside to give 'Eye' a cheer as she slides into a berth near our drydock. It's good to yarn with old friends again and John is reunited with his loved one at last (we don't see any more of him on our nights out). Chris, the mate, seems embroiled in several difficult relationships onboard which are promptly exacerbated by the arrival of a girl friend from England. Lisbon is no peaceful haven for him.

'Eye' takes our place in the dock and half our crew are dispatched on a week's leave, while Tony flies to England for a break and to complete some business in London. The rest of us carry on the maintenance work and send down the main topmast which has had three feet broken off by a careless drydock crane operator.

It's a time consuming task we could well do without, even though the dockyard is footing the bill and making the repair. They complicate matters by a stupid saw cut which means an eight foot new pole instead of four. There is some good fortune though in the arrival of Kim, an ex-mate of 'Søren' who buckles to onboard in return for a bunk. He has been touring in Europe and figured we might need an extra pair of hands.

'Søren' is now back alongside the dock wall amongst Bulgarian deep-sea trawlers and laid up merchant ships. Our days are full of chipping rust and painting, rigging work and varnish, sandpaper and grease pots. The cooks strip and paint the galley, cabins are overhauled and the heads renovated. There are a dozen small tasks every day too, and we have to think about restocking for the forthcoming Atlantic crossing with up to 40 souls onboard.

The 'time-offers' return with stories of a very friendly and picturesque Portugal, beautiful villages, wonderful wine, unusual river craft and excellent weather. They are quickly back in harness while their hard-worked shipmates take off for their attempt on the defences of Portugal. I'm to have time off when the ship is in Cadiz next month but I do down tools for a day now to visit the old town of Sintra which is some 20 miles inland. I am assured that the sea is normally visible from the heights above the town so I shouldn't feel too insecure.

Back on board it is time to move to the big Alcantara dock where the ships will assemble for the commencement of the 'Grand Regatta Columbus' conceived to commemorate the 500th anniversary of the discovery of the New World. The whole world's tall ships have been invited to sail in company on a circuit of the North Atlantic beginning in Cadiz and calling at the Canary Islands, Puert Rico, New York, Boston and finally Liverpool. There are two feeder fleets: one from Genoa and ours from Lisbon. There will be four days of festivities before we sail. Some big square riggers are berthed at riverside wharves and the rest of us in this dock. The ships' crews are invited to take part in a plethora of activities ranging from church services to soccer matches and open days.

We are the first ship to move into the dock so we get the 'best' berth across the blind end immediately adjacent to the main festivities venue; which means we are blasted with amplified music and announcements all day and much of the night.

We are inundated with sightseers too and covered with a layer of fine dust, kicked, scuffed and blown, off the cobbled dockside. But we mostly enjoy the four days of 'razzamatazz' and fun. There is a section of wharf mocked up as a 15th century Portugese village complete with goats, sheep, donkeys and people. There's traditional food, an ancient but efficient bread oven, a blacksmith at work and everyone in period costume. Nearby a stage is host to everything from heavy rock to poetry reading, shanty singing to classical choral music, and a special play about the great Columbus, while in a big marquee there is a display of the explorer's activities. Commercial folk are in evidence too with stalls displaying and selling everything from ice cream, beer and food to sophisticated marine equipment.

Sunrise, Alcantara Dock, Lisbon   AUTHOR

  The dock becomes a wonderful sight with the bigger ships
ranged right down one side and yachts and smaller traditional
vessels at a specially constructed marina near us. The lovely 'Anna
Kristina' from Norway arrives, with many good friends aboard.
She's a venerable ship, well over a hundred years old with a rig
peculiar to Scandinavia. 'Eye' takes a berth close by, looking very
trim and smart after her drydock spruce up, and the replica 16th
century caravel 'Boa Esperanza' is attracting a lot of attention just
ahead of us. People flock to the open days when they can visit
onboard, talk to the crews and buy souvenirs: cards, shirts and
books. Open days are something of a headache. Several thousand
landlubbers have to be escorted on and off the gangway safely,
as many queries have to be answered, children watched like hawks
lest they come to grief clambering where they shouldn't, and the
sales team for the day have their work cut out juggling escudos,
U.S. dollars, Sterling and Deutschmarks and trying to maintain
orderly stocks of shirts while a dozen folk at a time try on this
size and that. Not that open days are unusual. Ships like 'Søren'

231

have them wherever they go both to stimulate interest in adventure sailing and as a source of revenue. Crew always anticipate them with misgivings nevertheless. Volunteer voyage crew are very helpful and frequently excellent salespersons. They can also use the opportunity to display their newly won and precious nautical knowledge to the naive and credulous landlubbers.

Our night revelries ashore come to an end partly because of all the activity in the dock area including many ship parties, and partly because on our last visit to the tiny bar the singer is absent — sick — so we are a bit dispirited. It's time to leave; to get to sea. Ports rot both ships and men according to an old adage, so let's be off.

In the impressive harbour authority building with its absolutely stunning murals of Portugese maritime history, the ship masters congregate to be issued with details of the highly organised parade of sail which will see the 60 ships, led by the Portugese barque 'Sagres', sail in flotilla down the Tagus to a start line off Cape Raso. Everything is planned to five minutes accuracy. In fact this all comes unstuck at dawn on departure day when the tugs fail to turn up to swing the big ships in the dock. When everyone is over half an hour late 'Simon Bolivar', from Venezuela, develops engine problems so we are delayed again. We leave over an hour late and almost come to grief when a Polish ketch called 'Ark' tries to overtake in the dock and gets her masthead foul of our course yardarm. Quick action at our braces averts damage, but he is lucky not to spring his topmast. It's the second tangle we've had with them. They came alongside us briefly when we were at the shipyard and managed to foul our yardarm then too. The last we see of them as we pass out of Alcantara dock is with their propellor fouled around a group of mooring buoys. Much haste — less speed indeed.

In the river there is a shambles. The flotilla system has gone overboard. Anarchy reigns. Fortunately the Tagus is wide and deep so no one gets into difficulties although at one stage we have the big 'Kruzenshtern's' bowsprit almost over our stern! We motor-sail down past the impressive statue of 'Christ the King' blessing Lisbon with outstretched arms from a hill on the opposite shore, then under the thundering suspension bridge and close by the beautiful, white stone monument on the water's edge dedicated to the Discoverers. It is the sweeping prow of a ship lined with beautifully executed figures of Magellan, Vasco da Gama, Columbus and their like. The carvings of the great seafarers welcomed us to Lisbon a few weeks ago. They would have recognised a kinship in our sea-worn ship, and her weathered crew. Now, as we sail in the wake of their most illustrious member, they seem to salute and bid us 'fair winds'.

Lisbon, beautiful, memorable Lisbon, lies astern.

To sea again.

Monument to the Discoverers, Lisbon   AUTHOR

233

S.T.V. SØREN LARSEN
S.T.V. EYE OF THE WIND

S.T.V. SØREN LARSEN   S.T.V. EYE OF THE WIND

BOUND FOR EUROPE, GREAT BRITAIN & THE UNITED STATES
— BY THE —

INCLUDING COLOMBUS '92 CELEBRATIONS

CAPE HORN

PORTS OF CALL

Sydney, Auckland, Port Stanley, Montevideo, Tristan da Cunha,
St Helena, Ascension, Acores, Lisbon, Cadiz, Canary Islands, Puerto Rico,
New York, Boston, Liverpool, Isle of Man, Scotland, Denmark,
Germany, London, Portsmouth, Bristol.

The voyage poster for 'Homeward Round the Horn'   TALLSHIP 'SØREN LARSEN'

CHAPTER NINETEEN

'Leave Her Johnny'

We'll make for the Bar on the flood and then swing
Into Old Canning Dock where we'll have our last fling,
We'll sing and we'll dance and put on the last stow.
She's a Colchester Packet, O Lord let her go.'

TO SEA AGAIN, but our original joint-venture — 'Homeward Round the Horn' — suffers a four-month delay after Lisbon. 'Eye of the Wind' and 'Søren Larsen' join the 'Grand Regatta Columbus', an 8700-mile, four-month circuit of the North Atlantic to commemorate the five-hundredth anniversary of Columbus's fateful voyage of discovery. The circuit, made as part of a fleet of almost thirty square riggers and over fifty other traditional vessels, demands another book as full of characters and places, calms and gales, fun and interest as the tale recounted here. There is the added excitement of racing too and the spectacular parades of sail staged by Puerto Rico, New York and Boston.

The last leg is a race from Boston to a finish line off the Conningbeg Lightship on the south east corner of Ireland and from there it is but a day's run up the Irish Sea to Liverpool, the final mark in 'Søren's' circumnavigation and the completion of 'Homeward Round the Horn'.

That last night is one of good brisk sailing in a freshening breeze which drives us over the adverse tide and brings us to the river entrance in the early morning. Since I last worked up the winding Mersey in 1963, the Bar Lightship, a homing beacon to a million seafarers over a hundred years of commerce, has been replaced in the interest of economy, and at the blind urging of technology, by a 'Lanby', (Large Automatic Navigational Buoy) — a poor creature for the comfort of a sailor who respects the solid, bright red, conspicuous lightships with their powerful revolving lights and hardy crews. Gone too is the big, black-hulled seagoing pilot vessel which cruised near the lightship, its pilots available on demand. Now the pilot journeys from a shore base by fast launch and requires at least twelve hours notice.

The new flood hurries us through the stumbling short seas with their unruly crests, past the clanging lightfloats and buoys fretting at their monstrous chain moorings. These mark the ten-mile-long winding, approach channel with its unique revetements: underwater walls which confine the flow of the river so that it carries its thick silt out into the open sea. This channel always has a certain grimness to it, a slight dread. Perhaps it is due to the swirling tides which do not set fair in the reaches, or the prevailing westerlies piling on the hard sand so close to leeward, or maybe it's the unnerving 30-foot range of tide which is, at once, the making and the scourge of Liverpool. This huge change in sea level every six hours turns a shallow sand-encumbered bay into a major port, accessible to the largest ships for several hours each day. The vast quantities of water involved in this cyclical rise and fall cause tidal flows of up to five knots, rendering pilotage and shiphandling difficult and sometimes dangerous.

What sort of unsung heroes were the men who sailed their ships into such a treacherous river bedevilled with swift cross tides, shifting shoals and primitive navigation aids? The successful shipmasters and pilots then were surely steely-nerved men of superlative seamanship and their crews must have demonstrated an enviable facility and skill in sail handling when working such a river. They were real seamen, rough perhaps, but men as totally immersed in their craft, their vocation, as their ships in the wind and the sea. Those men were critical to winning a flourishing port from a very inhospitable shore and if they marked the importance of their ports by reference to them in song, then Liverpool ranks highly.

Stan Hughill, whose requiem I was to attend here, rated Liverpool as the greatest sailing ship port of all. There are dozens of Liverpool verses scattered amongst the work songs and forebitters and a few shanties especially dedicated to the port. Our 'Colchester Packet' is based on an earlier 'Liverpool Packet'. Then there is 'Liverpool Judies', with its unusual and haunting melody:

> *From Liverpool to 'Frisco a 'rovin' I went*
> *For to stay in that country, well it was me intent,*
> *But drinkin' strong whiskey, like other damn fools*
> *Soon had me transported back to Liverpool;*
> *Chorus: And it's ro-o-ll, yes, roll bullies roll!*
> *Those Liverpool Judies have got us in tow.*

The chorus rolls and rants stirringly until the last verse finds the ship back here:

> *And now we've arrived in the old Canning dock,*
> *And all those flash Judies around us do flock,*
> *We've a gallon of whiskey an' a five pound advance,*
> *So I think that it's time ye got up for a dance;*
> *And it's ro-o-ll, yes, roll bullies roll!*
> *Those Liverpool Judies have got us in tow.*

'Paddy Lay Back', which we've sung regularly, is often called the 'Liverpool Song', although it contains no direct reference to the port in any version I've heard. 'Maggie May', a bawdy ballad still heard in pubs, was originally a shanty and the verses include references to many Liverpool streets. One version of the well known 'Blow the Man Down' certainly begins in Paradise Street (not far from our allotted berth), and alludes to sailing out over the Liverpool Bar. 'Paddy West', an infamous Liverpool boarding house keeper, has his own forebitter, and a favourite homeward bound capstan shanty: 'Goodbye Fare-ye-well' has Liverpool as the port for which the singer is longing, and its Salthouse Dock and Limestreet as the venues where they will find girls and grog. But perhaps 'The Leavin' of Liverpool' is the forebitter whose chorus turns the heart of Liverpudlians more than any other:

> *So-o, fare ye well, my own true love,*
> *When I return united we will be;*
> *It's not the leavin' of Liverpool that grieves me,*
> *But my darlin' when I think of thee.'*

Liverpool became Britain's second largest port with an impounded dock system stretching over six miles along the waterfront and, together with the sister port in Berkenhead on the opposite shore, offering over 30 miles of quay space. When I shouldered that first kitbag in 1950 the docks were already antiquated and badly damaged following the bombings of World War II. Nevertheless there were hundreds of ships busy at any one time, and near high water on any day there would be a dozen vessels locking in or out of the dock systems.

The river was a scene of frantic activity for a couple of hours, with tugs bustling about, passenger liners turning ponderously and signalling with wonderful deep-throated 'Western Ocean' steam whistles; cargo liners and trampships of a dozen companies rounding up to stem the flood, pilot flags cracking in the breeze while their crews made preparations for locking in. The Isle of Man ferries, miniature liners, would be hurrying between these ocean-going ships, their passengers lining the upper decks to watch the river's activity. Two or three big grey dredgers would be ploughing bluntly seaward on their unending dreary round of clearing silt from the ship channels. Coasters, trailing ragged smoke pennants, would be assembling outside the small docks while others, early escapees from the yawning locks, would be churning seaward at the river's edge to avoid both the strength of the flood tide and the bigger ships manoeuvering in mid stream. Launches, fussing about a score of maritime tasks, and an odd yacht bucking the steep chop would flit across the scene. The soupy brown, flotsam-loaded river formed the canvas for this lively seascape, while the strident blasts of ship's whistles melded with the cry of gulls in a stirring accompaniment.

Imagine the scene earlier, in the late 19th century, with 20 or 30 sailing vessels busy at the top of the tide. Smart clippers, yards precisely square, brightwork gleaming, anchors hove short with a tug fussing forward on a short towline to get them to the big sea locks. Outward bounders, still grimy and unkempt after weeks in port, towing out of the locks with the mate yelling at the newly boarded crew to get her squared up and shipshape. Sturdy brigs and trim topsail schooners shortening sail and rounding up off the smaller docks, anchors rattling down. A Packet ship is New York bound, decks full of passengers. A shanty comes faintly on the breeze from the foc'sle where the crew heave her anchor aboard link by link, and a smart boat pulls under her gangway delivering her top-hatted captain aboard with his clearance papers. Small sailing craft are busy with river traffic and perhaps a fleet of smacks will be running in with heavy, ochred sails, taut and urgent over hulls deep laden with fish. Everywhere sails and movement on the brown silty river and on both sides behind the lock gates and river walls, a myriad of masts and spars framing the scene.

Liverpool is about to relive a little of this maritime heritage. As we pass into the river proper and round up above the famous Pier Head with its trio of landmark buildings, the docklands are abristle with the masts and spars of the Columbus Fleet. It will be the largest gathering of traditional sailing ships here for over 70 years.

The dock gate creaks open for us as we put the last harbour stow on our sails and edge towards the harbour wall against the last of the tide. In time honoured fashion we hurl a heaving line to the dock head and warp ourselves through the curving mouth of the dock into the Canning half-tide basin which lies just where the very first primitive docks were dug. There are crowds to welcome us in; linesmen, relatives, shiplovers and the simply curious. The same sort of crowd would have been there a hundred, even two hundred years ago. A dock with the memories of a thousand such arrivals. Our lines are soon secure. I shake Tony's hand. The voyage is over. All hands gather midships to sing the traditional last shanty — 'Leave Her Johnny':

> *Oh the voyage was long and the seas ran high,*
> *Leave her Johnny, leave her,*
> *An' our bunks an' our gear was niver dry,*
> *Oh, it's time for us to leave her;*

The chorus echoes off the old stone walls between each verse:

> *Leave her Johnny, leave her,*
> *Oh-o, leave her Johnny, le-eave her,*
> *For the voyage is done an' the winds don't blow,*
> *So it's time for us to leave her;*

> *Oh the food was bad but the cook was worse,*
> *Leave her Johnny, leave her,*

The mate had his way with a kick an' a curse,
Oh, it's time for us to leave her.

The last verse, after the skipper, bosun, and even the engineer have been vilified, brings down the curtain on the voyage:

Oh I thought I heard the Old Man say,
Leave her Johnny, leave her,
It's time for you to get yer pay,
Oh, it's time for us to leave her.

'Eye of the Wind' berths immediately ahead of us next morning and we duly celebrate the successful completion of our long voyage 'Homeward Round the Horn'. It's a happy affair and I hope those Canning Dock ghosts appreciate the stories and songs of the new Cape Horners. They go on far into the night.

Our voyage across the wide Pacific and up through the Atlantics has not been hard, not measured by the standards of an old shellback. But we have stood our watches in calm and gale, rain and sleet, sun and thunderstorms. We have hauled the braces with cold Southern Ocean water in our armpits. We have fisted canvas on dark wet nights and we have suffered the galley awash. We have been tried and tempered a little and our good ship likewise. She has stood the rackings and twistings of 40-foot quartering seas, the strains of storm filled canvas and the scorching timber-killing heat of the tropic seas.

Now it's time for me to leave and carry my kitbag along that dock road again where, for me (and you) this all began. But this time:

We've crossed two great oceans,
we've doubled the Horn.

As for 'Søren Larsen', well:

'She's a Colchester Packet, O Lord let her go!'

T-shirt design; Søren Larsen at Night   ILLUSTRATION: JAMES PARBERRY

Postscript

'Soren Larsen' did not end her voyaging in Liverpool. She has since returned to the Pacific and will continue to offer voyages under square rig to all ages and nationalities. Her home base is in Auckland, New Zealand.

Contact 'Square Sail Pacific' to become part of her sailing adventures; telephone and fax.: (+64) (09) 411 8484.

See you there!

Meanwhile, 'fair winds' as sailors say in parting.

Nautical Glossary

This is not an exhaustive nautical glossary but rather an explanation of terms used in this book, including a few which are not nautical.

ABACK Wind blowing on the wrong side of sail.

ABAFT THE BEAM A direction behind a line at 90 degrees to the vessel's course.

ABEAM At 90 degrees to the vessel's course or nearly so.

ALMANAC Nautical calendar of celestial events.

ALTITUDE Angle of an object, e.g. sun, above the horizon.

AREA RAILINGS Protective rails around sunken road access to some old city houses.

ARTICLES Official document of agreement between captain and crew.

BACK 1. To back the sails is to trim them so that the wind blows on the forward (wrong) side of them. 2. Wind backs when it changes direction anti-clockwise.

BACKROPE Wire or rope stretched between yardarm and centre of yard to which crew can clip safety harnesses.

BACKSTAYS Permanent wire rigging supporting masts and preventing forward movement of them.

BAGGYWRINKLE Anti-chafe device made from old rope and wound around wire rope to protect sails.

BARQUE Sailing vessel with three or more masts and all square-rigged except the aftermast.

BARQUENTINE Sailing vessel with three or more masts, only the foremast of which is square rigged.

BEAM 1. Width of a vessel. 2. Constructional cross members supporting a deck and connecting the sides of a vessel.

BEAM ENDS A vessel is on her beam ends when she is lying on, or almost on her side.

BEAR OFF, BEAR AWAY Turn a vessel away from the wind.

BELAYING PINS Short hardwood, or steel, bars fitted into pin and fife rail for securing ropes.

BERTH 1. A bunk; a specific area designated to a person onboard a ship. 2. A vessel's allotted space alongside a wharf, pier etc. 3. To berth a vessel is to manoeuvre alongside a wharf etc.

BILGE Space between hull and lowest deck. Any water entering a vessel can be pumped from this space by a BILGE PUMP.

BINNACLE Box or container supporting and protecting the steering compass and usually fitted with gimballed supports.

BITTS Pairs of solid wood or steel upright deck fittings for securing ropes or wires.

BLOCK Wooden or metal devices containing one or more pulley wheels.

BLOCK AND TACKLE Two blocks with a rope threaded through their pulleys. the resulting device can be used to obtain mechanical advantage when pulling, hoisting etc.

BOBSTAY Chain connecting outer end of bowsprit to the stem near the waterline.

BOLLARD Post on deck or onshore, to which mooring lines are secured.

BOOM Spar stretching lower edge of a fore and aft sail.

BOSUN Shortened form of 'boatswain'. He is the leading or chief seaman.

BOTTLESCREW threaded metal device for tensioning standing rigging.

BOWERY Old red light area of Lower Manhattan.

BOWSPRIT Spar projecting forward of a vessel's hull.

BOX THE COMPASS Swinging through 360 degrees or more.

BRIG Sailing vessel with 2 masts both having a full set of square sails.

BRIGANTINE Sailing vessel with 2 masts, foremast square rigged, main mast fore and aft rigged (see HERMAPHRODITE BRIG).

BRIGHTWORK Varnished timber.

BRING UP To securely anchor or stop.

BROACH To swing uncontrollably across wind and sea.

BULWARK Solid built up rail at vessel's side above deck level.

BUNT Whole central part of a square sail.

BUNTLINE Lines, controlled from the deck, which gather the bunt of a sail up to the yard above.

CABLE 1. Old seagoing measurement — 1/10 mile, approx. 600 feet. 2. Anchor chain.

CAP Top of any section of a mast e.g. topmast cap.

CAPSTAY Wire standing rigging leading from mast cap to ship's side aft of the mast.

CAPSTAN Revolving drum with vertical axis for hauling on ropes, anchor chain etc. and originally operated by bars radiating horizontally from the drum at chest height above the deck.

CATHEAD Sturdy timber projection on either bow used for bringing the anchor aboard.

CHAINS OR CHAINPLATES Metal fittings bolted through a vessel's side to which the lower ends of standing rigging are secured.

CHANNELS Horizontal timber or steel plates outside the hull over which the chain plates are fitted. They increase the spread of the lower rigging.

CHOCKS Blocks of wood shaped to fit the underwater shape of a boat secured on deck.

CLEW Lower corners of a square sail or the aftermost lower corner of a fore and aft sail.

CLEWLINE Line used in raising the lower corner of a square sail to the yard above.

CLEW UP 1. To raise the lower corners of a square sail 2. General order to give up, or dispense with, a lower topsail or course sail.

CLOCK CALM Absolutely windless.

COME UP Order to release the tension on a rope so that it can be secured.

COMMANDING BREEZE Any wind from abaft the beam.

COMPASS ERROR Difference between true goegraphic north and north as indicated by a magnetic compass.

COUNTER The type of stern which extends beyond the rudder, an overhanging stern.

COURSE 1. The direction in which a ship is heading 2. The lowest square sail on a mast which carries a full set of square sails (the foremast on Søren).

CRINGLE Eyelet in a sail such as at its corners.

CROSSTREES Transverse fixed spars fitted across masts to spread the upper shrouds.

DAVITS Arms supporting a ship's boat by

which it may be swung clear of the ship for lowering or hoisting.

DEVIATION Effect of a vessel on a magnetic compass, caused by iron and steel fittings, hull, engine etc.

DISPLACEMENT Actual total weight of a vessel and everything contained therein.

DOCK Protected area of water for berthing ships, sometimes entirely enclosed and maintained at a fixed water level.

DOCKHEAD Entrance to a dock.

DOLPHIN STRIKER Vertical spar, under the bowsprit-end, to spread the stays holding the jibboom down.

D.O.T.I. BOAT Mandatory 'Department of Trade and Industry' inflatable dinghy carried for rescue purposes.

DOWN HELM Steer vessel towards the wind.

DOUBLE To pass a headland.

DOUBLING The overlapping portions of a mast.

DRAFT Depth of a vessel below water line.

DRYDOCK Specially constructed dock which can be sealed off and pumped dry to facilitate repair work on vessels.

EAST INDIAMAN Old type of commercial sailing ship of a type developed in the 17th century.

EBB The flow of a falling tide.

EMBAYED Caught in a bay with the wind blowing onshore so that a sailing vessel will have great difficulty in sailing out.

ENSIGN National maritime flag usually flown right aft or from the gaff on the aftermost mast.

FALL The hauling part of a block and tackle.

FALLS The block and tackle system used to lower or hoist a ship's boat.

FATHOM 6 feet or 1.83 metres.

FENDER Object used to separate — and protect — a ship from a wharf, ship from ship etc. Usually made from timber, cane, rubber etc.

FID Pointed, hardwood, narrow cone-shaped stick used in splicing rope.

FIDDLER'S GREEN Sailor's heaven or Elysium.

FIFERAIL Strong wooden rail around a mast about waist height above the weather deck arranged for securing items of running rigging.

FLOATING DOCK Submersible strucure onto which a vessel can be floated and lifted clear of the sea surface by pumping water out from numerous tanks in the structure.

FLOOD Flow of rising tide.

FOC'SLE Short for 'forecastle' 1. Raised deck right forward in some ships 2. Sailor's quarters which were traditionally under the raised foreward deck.

FOOTROPES Rope or wire running from yardarm to centre of yard under each yard, for crew to stand on while handling square sails.

FORE AND AFT SAILS Those sails which naturally lie along the longitudinal axis of a vessel when the wind is from ahead.

FORECOURSE Lowest squaresail on the foremast — often called simply 'the course' on 'Søren'.

FORESAIL Another name for the forecourse.

FORETACK Foremost lower corner of the forecourse.

FORESTAY Heavy wire stay leading from the head of the fore lower mast to the forwardmost part of the hull.

FULLRIGGER Full-rigged ship. Square

rigger with three or more masts all with square.sails. Traditionally called simply 'a ship'.

FUNNELATOR Funnel shaped sling with strong elastic hand held lines attached, and used to project water balloons!

FURL To gather up and secure a sail with lashings (see GASKET).

GAFF Spar which extends the upper edge of a four sided fore and aft sail.

GALE Wind between 35 and 50 knots.

GAM Verbal communication between ships stopped in close proximity at sea. Often conducted by transferring personnel by ship's boat.

GANGWAY An

GASKET 1. To secure a sail with lashings 2. Rope lashing for securing a sail when it is not in use.

GIMBALLED Pivotted so as to remain horizontal despite movement of vessel.

GIRT Bound restrictively. A rope across a sail restricting its natural belly is said to be girt across the sail.

GREYBEARD Mountainous breaking seas particularly in the Southern Ocean.

GROG Mixture of rum and water, but more generally used to mean any spirits.

GROUND SWELL Very low ocean swell which becomes apparent in shallow water where it becomes shorter and steeper.

GROWLER Final remnant of a decayed iceberg, usually barely visible above the sea surface.

GUNWALE Upper edge around a small boat.

GYPSY Specially notched barrel of a capstan or windlass which fits the links of an anchor chain.

HALF DECK Deckhouse where apprentice officers lived. Traditionally situated between crew's quarters forward and officer's quarters aft.

HALF TIDE DOCK Dock of impounded water which normally has gates left open from time when tide is half risen to time when it has half fallen.

HALYARD OR HAULYARD Rope, wire or chain for hoisting a sail, yard or flag.

HAND 1. A general term for a sailor or deckhand. 2. To dispense with a sail, to lower it or clew and bunt it up.

HATCH An opening in the weather deck for access, but which can be securely closed against ingress of water.

HAUL HER WIND Steer closer to the wind.

HEADS Toilet arrangement on a vessel; traditionally right forward.

HEADSAIL Any triangular sail set forward of the foremast, i.e. forestaysail and jibs.

HEAVE TO Reduce sail and trim some so that they work against the others thus stopping or almost stopping the vessel.

HEAVING LINE Long, small diameter rope with some form of weight at one end to aid in throwing the rope. Often used as a means of passing a larger rope to shore.

HELM The rudder control mechanism.

HERMAPHRODITE BRIG Originally a two-masted sailing vessel square rigged on the foremast and fore and aft rigged on the main. Now used to describe a brigantine with square topsails added to her mainmast.

HOOKER Sailor's slang for any vessel, usually used derogatively.

HOVE TO Past tense of 'heave to'.

HULL The body of a vessel excluding all superstructure, mast, rigging etc.

HULL DOWN A ship whose sails or superstructure can be seen above the horizon but not the hull.

HURRICANE Wind of more than 65 knots.

JACKSTAY Metal rod fastened to, but an inch or two clear above a square sail yard to which sails are secured and which can act as hanholds.

JIB Triangular fore and aft sails set on the jibstays which are secured to the jibboom.

JIB-BOOM Extension to the bowsprit.

JOHN COMPANY Nickname for British East India Company.

JUDIES Liverpool slang for girls, especially prostitutes.

KEELHAUL Ancient punishment where a man was hauled by ropes underneath the ship. Usually resulted in death!

KNOT 1. Speed of 1 nautical mile per hour [5 knots = 6 statute (land) miles-per-hour approx]. 2. Any method of tying ropes together other than splicing.

KNUCKLE Corner of a wharf, jetty or pier used as a pivot for swinging a vessel before she moves into or out of a berth.

LAY TO A method of combating storm conditions when sail is reduced to a bare minimum and the vessel lies between 60 and 100 degrees to the wind.

LAY TOPSAILS TO THE MAST Trim square sails aback to stop a square rigger.

LEAD BLOCK Pulley whose only purpose is to change direction of strain on rope. It offers no mechanical advantage.

LEAGUE Old measurement = 3 nautical miles.

LEE 1. Side away from the wind. 2. In shelter — in the lee of.

LEE SHORE Shore to leeward of a vessel and thus a dangerous shore because the wind blows onto it.

LEECH Vertical sides of a square sail, or aftermost edge of a fore and aft sail.

LIFTS Wires from masts to yardarms, to support yards when sail is not set. Also wires or ropes from mainmast to mainboom end.

LOCK Basin, with gates at each end, between a dock of impounded water and a river, in which water level can be raised or lowered to facilitate the passage of the vessel between dock and river.

LOGBOOK The official logbook is that in which legally notifiable events are recorded such as births, deaths and misdemeanours! The deck logbook, or mate's logbook is for recording events of navigational significance, weather, sail changes etc.

LOOM 1. Visible effect above the horizon of a light source below the horizon. 2. Handle of an oar.

LOWER TOPSAIL Second squaresail up from the deck on any mast, next above the course.

LUFF Forward edge of a fore and aft sail. 2. To steer towards the wind until the sails begin to shake and lose drive.

MAINMAST Generally the tallest mast. On both 'Søren' and 'Eye' it is the aftermost mast. On a barque or fullrigged ship it is the second mast from forward.

MAINSAIL 1. Large fore and aft sail on mainmast of brigantine or schooner. 2. Course on mainmast of barque or full rigged ship.

MAINSHEET Rope, wire or block and tackle controlling clew of mainsail.

MARTINGALE Another name for the dolphin striker.

MERCHANT SHIP Vessel employed in carrying cargo or passengers commercially.

MIZZEN On a barque or full rigged ship the third mast from forward.

NAUTICAL MILE One sixtieth of a degree of latitude (accepted as 6080 feet).

PAINTER Rope attaced to stem of small boat for towing or securing it.

PALM Leather device fitting around the hand to facilitate the forcing of a needle through canvas when sailmaking etc.

PARISH RIGGED Poorly equipped.

PASS THE STOPPER Order given to use a smaller rope to temporarily take the strain of a larger one while the latter is secured.

PASSAGE Journey port to port.

PAWL Small pivoted arm arranged to engage notches in the circumference of a capstan or windlass barrel, to prevent it turning the wrong way.

PEAK Upper, aftermost corner of a four sided fore and aft sail.

PINTLE Metal spike fitting for attaching a rudder to a vessel's hull.

PINRAIL Strong horizontal rail along the inside of a vessel's bulwarks into which belaying pins are fitted for securing ropes of running rigging.

PITCH 1. Tarry substance used to seal seams in hull or deck planks. 2. Longitudinal see-saw like movement of a vessel in waves.

PITCH OF THE HORN Refers to the termination of South America at Cape Horn.

POOP Aftermost raised deck.

PREVENTER Line or tackle arranged to steady a boom or other spar against unwanted movement.

PURSER Crew member in charge of cash, ship's official papers and clerical work.

QUARTER The sides of the vessel near the stern.

RADAR Radio Detection and Ranging. Electronic instrument which displays, on screen, the surroundings of a vessel in bird's eye view including other vessels.

REACH 1. A comparatively straight section of a river or ship channel. 2. To sail with the wind more or less at right angles to the ship's fore and aft axis.

RED DUSTER British red ensign, which is the national maritime flag.

REEF 1. To reef is to temporarily reduce the size of a sail. 2. The section of a sail taken out of use when a sail is reefed!

REEF POINTS Small ropes sewn to a sail on each side and used to secure the out-of-use bundle of sail when a sail has been reefed.

REEF TACKLE Tackle used to haul the clew of the sail down and out to the boom end when reefing.

ROARING FORTIES Belt of prevailing strong westerly winds which blow between about 40° and 55° South.

ROYAL Square sail above the t'gallant.

RUNNING Sailing with the wind from behind.

RUNNING RIGGING Ropes, wires or chains which are adjusted when setting, furling or trimming sails.

SAILING LARGE Sailing with the wind from over the quarter.

SALOON General purpose area below decks fitted out for meals and/or recreation.

SCHOONER There are many variations of the schooner rig, but usually a vessel with 2 masts (or more), fore and aft rigged, of which the foremast is the shortest. A topsail schooner has square topsails on the foremast.

SCEND The vertical surge of the sea

SCUPPER Pipes or openings at the vessel's sides for water to escape from deck to sea.

SERVE Wrap small line around a larger rope or wire as a protection.

SEXTANT Optical navigational instrument for measuring angles.

SHACKLE An anchor cable is made up out of measured sections of chain, each section being called a shackle and measuring 15 fathoms (90 feet).

SHEER 1. The line of the upper edge of a vessel's hull. 2. To swing offcourse.

SHEET Rope, wire or chain controlling the clews of a sail.

SHELLBACK Old seafarer. More specifically a sailor who has crossed the equator and been initiated by King Neptune.

SHIP 1. Any large vessel. 2. A full-rigged ship.

SHIPPING OFFICE Place where seamen sign on and off their ships before a government official.

SHIPWRIGHT A person whose trade is wooden shipbuiding and repair.

SHROUD Fixed rigging supporting masts sideways.

SKIDS Strong horizontal framework supported on pillars above the upper deck upon which a vessel's boats are stowed.

SKYSAIL Small squaresail set above the roayls in some lofty square riggers.

SLACKWATER The period near high and low water when the tidal flow ceases.

SNUGGED DOWN Sailing under reduced sail area because of bad weather.

SOUNDINGS 1. Depth of water. 2. 'In soundings' means in a depth that can be ascertained with a sounding lead.

SOUNDING LEAD Lead weight attached to a long, marked rope for finding the depth of water.

SOU'WESTER Traditional waterproof hat with a wider brim at the back for shedding water.

SPAR Any wooden or metal pole used to support and stretch a sail to the wind

SPIKE A metal tapered rod used for splicing wire.

SPINDRIFT Foam blown along and above the sea surface by strong winds.

SPLICE Intertwine the strands of a rope or wire to effect a join or make a permanent loop.

SPLICE THE MAINBRACE To issue a tot of grog or rum to all hands usually after some special event or after a spell of hard physical labour.

SQUARE RIGGER Any sailing vessel relying mainly on square sails for propulsion.

SQUARE SAILS Sails of more or less rectangular shape hung from spars disposed across the masts and pivoted at their centres.

STANDING RIGGING Fixed rigging which supports mast, bowsprit and jibboom.

STAY Fixed wire supporting a mast forward or backward.

STAYSAIL A sail hoisted with its foreward edge sliding up a stay.

STEM Foremost structural member of the hull, being a continuation of the keel forward and upward.

STERN Aftermost part of a vessel.

STERNBOARD Sailing backwards.

STOCKHOLM TAR Special pine tar used as a preservative, especially to protect wire from rusting.

STOPPER A short length of comparatively small diameter rope with one end secured to the vessel's structure and the other end hitched to a larger rope under strain. While the stopper takes the strain temporarily the larger rope can be made secure.

STORM Wind of between 50 and 65 knots.

STRETCHER Wooden bar across the bottom of a rowing boat against which a rower can brace his feet.

STUNS'L Abbreviation of 'studding sail'. A sail set outboard of any square sail.

SWATCH A small channel between sand banks, joining larger channels.

TACK 1. Forward lower corner of and fore and aft sail or course. 2. To alter course to bring the wind from one side of the vessel to the other across the bow.

TACKLE (Pronounced tay-cul) any arrangement of two pulley blocks and line arranged to give a mechanical advantage.

TALL SHIP Journalistic term for a square rigger!

TILLER Bar fitted to the top of a rudder post for turning the rudder.

'THE LINE' The equator.

THROAT Upper forward corner of any four sided fore and aft sail.

T'GALLANT Topgallant — the sail next above the topsails.

TOPMAST Second section of a mast from which the topsails are hung.

TOPSAILS Sails immediately above the course.

TOPSIDES The part of the hull outboard above the waterline.

TRANSOM Type of stern finishing square across the ship with no overhanging portion.

TRICK Period of assignment to the duty of steering a vessel.

UP HELM Order to steer away from the wind.

VARIATION Effect of the earth's magnetic field on a compass needle.

VEER 1. Slack away, especially anchor cable. 2. Wind veers when it changes in a clockwise direction to the observer.

V.H.F. Very High Frequency radio for short range communication.

VOYAGE The complete journey of a vessel from departure from the first port to arrival at the last.

WARP 1. To move a vessel by means of ropes led on shore. 2. A large rope used in securing a vessel to the shore.

WATER BREAKER Small water cask.

WEAR To turn a square rigger so as to bring the wind from one side to the other across the stern (past tense 'wore').

WEATHERSIDE Side upon which the wind is blowing.

WEATHERFAX Electronic equipment which receives and prints weathermaps transmitted from shore stations.

WEATHERSTEP On board ship, doors to the open deck are hung with their bottom edge well above deck level, the solid piece below preventing the ingress of water. This solid piece is the weatherstep.

WINDJAMMER Square rigger. Originally a derogatory term used by steamship crews.

WINDLASS Mechanical arrangement for heaving up anchor with a drum revolving on a horizontal axis.

YARD 1. Old measurement of three feet (or .914 metre). 2. Horizontal spar from which a square sail is hung.

YARDARM Extreme outer portion of a yard.

YAW To swing from side to side of the proper course.

ZENITH The point directly overhead of an observer.

Sailing Rigs

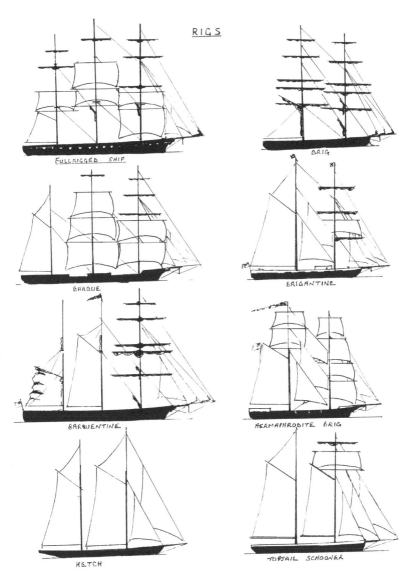

RIGS

FULLRIGGED SHIP

BRIG

BARQUE

BRIGANTINE

BARQUENTINE

HERMAPHRODITE BRIG

KETCH

TOPSAIL SCHOONER

SKETCHES BY THE AUTHOR

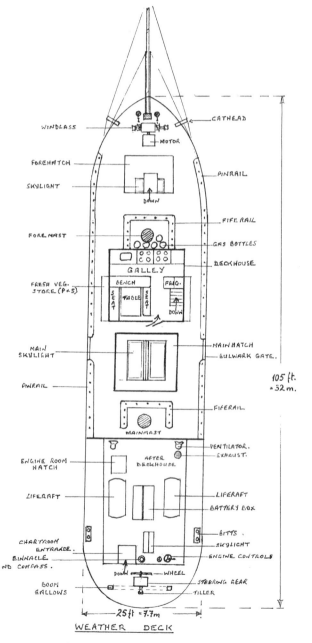

Søren

Deck

WINDLASS

CATHEAD

MOTOR

FOREHATCH

PINRAIL

SKYLIGHT

DOWN

FIFE RAIL

FORE MAST

GAS BOTTLES

DECKHOUSE

GALLEY

FRESH VEG.
STORE (P&S)

BENCH

FRIG.

SEAT

TABLE

SEAT

DOWN

MAIN
SKYLIGHT

MAIN HATCH

BULWARK GATE.

PINRAIL

105 ft.
= 32 m.

FIFERAIL

MAINMAST

VENTILATOR.

EXHAUST.

ENGINE ROOM
HATCH

AFTER
DECKHOUSE

LIFERAFT

LIFERAFT

BATTERY BOX

BITTS .

CHARTROOM
ENTRANCE.

SKYLIGHT

BINNACLE
ND COMPASS.

ENGINE CONTROLS

DOWN

WHEEL

BOOM
GALLOWS

STEERING GEAR

TILLER

25 ft = 7.7m

WEATHER   DECK

SKETCHES BY

Larsen

Plans

LOWER DECK

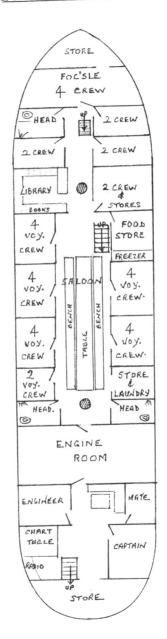

THE AUTHOR

Søren Larsen Sail Plan

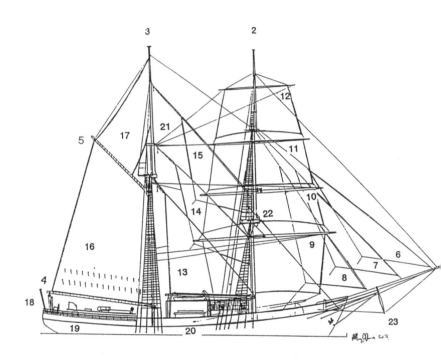

1. Jib-boom/bowsprit	13. Main staysail
2. Foremast	14. Middle staysail
3. Main mast	15. Upper staysail
4. Main boom & reef points	16. Mainsail
5. Main gaff	17 Gaff topsail
6. Outer jib	18. Gallows
7. Inner jib	19. Poop deck
8. Fore topmast staysail	20. Main deck
9. Course sail	21. Braces
10. Lower topsail	22. Foretop
11. Upper topsail	23. Dolphin striker
12. Topgallant	

Voyage of the Søren Larsen

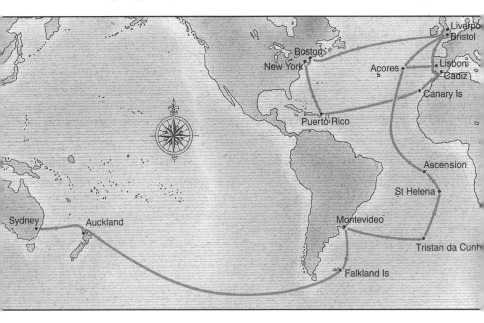

ABSTRACT OF THE VOYAGE OF SØREN LARSEN

Departed Sydney October 5, 1991 — Arrived Liverpool August 11, 1992
Total distance 25,910 nautical miles, in 201 sailing days.

Sydney to Auckland 1350 miles, 9 days; Auckland to Port Stanley 6390 miles, 46 days; Port Stanley to Montevideo 1060 miles, 7 days; Montevideo to Tristan da Cunha 2200 miles, 19 days; Tristan to St Helena 1300 miles, 9 days; St Helena to Acension 750 miles, 6 days; Acension to Horta 3200 miles, 24 days; Horta to Lisbon 900 miles, 6 days; Lisbon to Cadiz 230 miles, 3 days; Cadiz to Tenerife 760 miles, 5 days; Tenerife to San Juan 2900 miles, 22 days; San Juan to Virgin Islands and return 200 miles, 2 days; San Juan to New York 1620 miles, 15 days; New York to Boston 250 miles, 3 days; Boston to Liverpool 2800 miles, 25 days.

About the Author

JIM COTTIER spends several months each year, at sea, as mate or master of various square-rigged sailing ships. He 'found his niche in life' about age 8 when he learned to row and sail near his birthplace of Ramsey, Isle of Man. His subsequent career at sea spans 47 years, more than 700,000 miles of the world's oceans and a wide variety of vessels.

Going to sea at 15, as an apprentice deck officer with the Blue Funnel Line, Jim Cottier obtained his Master Foreign-Going certificate in 1960, before moving to New Zealand in 1965. He came ashore to look after two young daughters following the untimely death of his wife but kept in touch with the sea by teaching celestial navigation, living on an old houseboat and making occasional yacht deliveries. In 1972, 1973 and 1985 he ventured to Moruroa with the fleet of yachts protesting at French nuclear testing in the Pacific. He also skippered a Greenpeace vessel to Antarctica in 1987-88.

By 1980, when Jim Cottier was ready to resume a full seagoing career, the sailing of square-rigged ships was enjoying a renaissance. On such ships he found a chance to foster the traditional seamanship and navigation skills which are his chief love; and the chance to work with men and women who go to sea for the love of it.

When not aboard a square rigger he sails locally, acts as caretaker on a tiny island in the Bay of Islands where he teaches navigation to yachtsmen, builds traditional small boats, 'tries to write' and thoroughly enjoys sharing life with his seafaring wife, Terri.